THE OSIRIS PAPERS

Reflections on the Life and Writings of Dr. Frances Cress Welsing

THE OSIRIS PAPERS

Reflections on the Life and Writings of Dr. Frances Cress Welsing

Raymond Winbush
Denise Wright

Black Classic Press
Baltimore

The Osiris Papers:
Reflections of the Life and Writings of Dr Frances Cress Welsing

Published 2020 by Black Classic Press

Library of Congress Control Number: 2019948255
Print book ISBN: 978-157478-162-5
e-Book ISBN: 978-157478-163-2

Printed by BCP Digital Printed (www.bcpdigital.com)
an affiliate of Black Classic Press, Inc.
For a virtual tour of our publishing and printing facility, visit:
https://www.c-span.org/video/?441322-2/tour-black-classic-press

Cover design by Michael Anthony Brown

Purchase Black Classic Press books from your favorite book seller or online at www.blackclassicbooks.com.

For inquiries or to request a list of title, write:
Black Classic Press
PO Box 13414
Baltimore, MD 21203

Acknowledgments

The spiritual "knowing" endowed to us by the Creator has only strengthened our resolve to outlive the blanket of oppression. There are so many stories not told that have transitioned to the Heavens by the way of our Ancestors. May this collection of writings pave the way for the unspoken words of those who came before us, to be heard. In this vein, the acknowledgment of my Ancestors, maternal and paternal grandparents and particularly to my parents (Mom-n-Da) who have inspired the words of enlightenment and liberation. Also to my surrogate brothers: T, Antonio, Donnie, Darren, Danny, Wayne, Dr. C and others on their feedback and direction, I dedicate this collection of work.

D. Wright

I dedicate this to my children, Omari, Sharifa Faraji, and Beverly; my grandchildren, Samarria, Jordan, Jason, Aubrielle, and Taylor; my nephew Nick, his wife Jazmine, and their daughter, Phoenix; and my friend Nadia Hyppolite, who made so many helpful suggestions during the editing of this book. May all of Us continue to teach about one of the greatest teachers the Afrikan world has ever known.

R. Winbush

This book has been a labor of love for our esteemed Ancestor, Dr. Frances Cress Welsing. She inspired all of those who contributed chapters and touched my life deeply. The editors and authors continue to be inspired by her. The editors owe deep gratitude to Black Classic Press under the leadership of Paul Coates, who continues to make knowledge of Afrikan people available to a wide audience.

Raymond A. Winbush & Denise L. Wright, Editors

Table of Contents

Preface

Raymond A. Winbush

"There are too many things to feel about this woman."

—Paul D. describing Sethe in Toni Morrison's *Beloved*

The Osiris Papers: Reflections on the Life and Writings of Dr. Frances Cress Welsing is intended to be the first of many treatises written to examine the life, theories, and contributions of Dr. Frances Cress Welsing. Some of these writings are hagiographic, while others are critical, but all will expand our understanding of one of the greatest African thinkers of the past 100 years.

For this volume, we assembled a group of scholars, social activists, and entertainers each of whom we asked to write on one of the Nine Areas of White Supremacy outlined by Neely Fuller in his monumental work *The United Independent Compensatory Code/System/Concept: A Compensatory Counter-Racist Code*. You will read how Mr. Fuller directly influenced the theories of Dr. Welsing. While Mr. Fuller asked "*What* is racism/white supremacy?," Dr. Welsing asked "*Why* is there racism/white supremacy?" There is an important difference between these two queries, and each will be answered in various ways throughout this volume by writers who either: 1) knew Dr. Welsing personally; 2) worked with her on various projects; or 3) are deeply familiar with her writings.

Dr. Welsing's first work, *The Cress Theory of Color-Confrontation and Racism (White Supremacy)* in 1970, was followed by her seminal book, *The Isis Papers: The Keys to the Colors* in 1991. *The Isis Papers* consists of 25 essays written by Dr. Welsing over a period of 18 years between 1970 and 1988 and includes her foundational essay on color-confrontation. She supplies the dates for all but one of the essays. Thirteen of the essays were written during the 1970s, 11 were written during the 1980s, and one entitled, "Black Child Parents: The New Factor in Black

Genocide" is undated. Each chapter elaborates on Welsing's major thesis and riffs on her definition of racism/white supremacy:

> Racism (white supremacy) is the local and global power system and dynamic, structured and maintained by persons who classify themselves as white, whether consciously or subconsciously determined, which consists of patterns of perception, logic, symbol formation, thought, speech, action and emotional response, as conducted simultaneously in all areas of people activity (economics, education, entertainment, labor, law, politics, religion, sex and war); for the ultimate purpose of white genetic survival and to prevent white genetic annihilation on planet earth–a planet upon which the vast majority of people are classified as non-white (Black, Brown, Red and Yellow) by white skinned people, and all of the nonwhite people are genetically dominant (in terms of skin coloration) compared to the genetic recessive white skin people.

Certain chapters of *The Isis Papers* have become classic and have found their way into popular culture in movies and music. Chapter 10, entitled "Ball Games as Symbols: The War of the Balls," was featured prominently in the 1992 film *Boomerang* with comedians Eddie Murphy and Martin Lawrence. Released just a year after *The Isis Papers* was published, there is an extensive scene in which Murphy and Lawrence debate the influence of racism in a game of 8-ball pool, using the same metaphor of a pool table found in Dr. Welsing's book. In 2001, ten years after her book was published, the opening sequence of John Singleton's coming-of-age film *Baby Boy* references Welsing in describing the challenges Black men face as they grow up in a white supremacist society. Finally, the seminal hip-hop group Public Enemy dedicated their important album, *Fear of a Black Planet*, to Dr. Frances Cress Welsing. *Wikipedia* notes that "The record's criticism of institutional racism, white supremacy, and the power elite was partly inspired by Dr. Frances Cress Welsing's views on color." The album was released in 1990, just before the publication of *The Isis Papers,* and similar to *Boomerang*, it was firmly anchored in the theoretical framework of Dr. Welsing's work.

Welsing's acclaim in both the academy and Black popular culture is due to the absence of an existing unified theory about *why* racism/

white supremacy exists as a global phenomenon. Social scientists have offered weak explanations for the existence of racism ranging from perceived economic threats on the part of non-white people to tipping points reached when non-whites "invade" the spaces and places of people classified as white. None of these "explanations" account for the universal violence and discrimination that white people have directed toward non-white people. Other than Frances Welsing, the few writers attempting to explain the global sameness of white behavior toward non-white people include Michael Bradley in his book, *The Iceman Inheritance: Prehistoric Sources of Western Man's Racism, Sexism and Aggression*, Vulindlela I. Wobogo's *The Prehistoric European Origin of Racism*, and Marimba Ani's *Yurugu: An African-Centered Critique of European Thought and Behavior*. These books argue that the harsh climate of Europe combined with white people's racial minority status created an aggressive culture that saw nature as harsh, and non-white people who comprised the majority of the human population as a threat to their existence. Similar to Dr. Welsing's works, these books were denounced as "racist" and "racially divisive" because they posited a unified theory of why Europeans are predatory, rapacious, and violent. Yet, despite white and some non-white scientists denouncing these four works as racist, their widespread readership among Black people continues to grow.

I believe these works are popular because they, like the Cress Theory of Color Confrontation, provide an explanation of what happens to non-white people throughout the world. The *sameness of white supremacy* around the globe is something that few non-Black scientists write about. The ill-treatment of Black people by police in France is identical to that experienced by Black people in Ferguson. Harshly disciplined Black students in London schools find their counterparts in Los Angeles schools, and racist depictions of Black people in Japan are derived from their exposure to white supremacist literature and stereotypes throughout European culture. Welsing's explanation for this global consistency of white supremacy is found in one of the most important chapters in *The Isis Papers*, entitled "Unified Field Theory Psychiatry," penned in

1980. She begins the chapter by discussing western psychiatry's failure to derive a *unified theory* of psychopathology, *e.g.*, explaining the global presence of schizophrenia in all cultures.

The notion of a unified field theory is derived from Albert Einstein's attempt to explain *everything* that occurs in the known universe with one hypothesis. In other words, how is time related to space and how are both related to gravity, the death of stars, and the creation of galaxies? Welsing argues that both Western psychiatry and quantum physicists fail "to see the interconnections that exist between many seemingly isolated, disconnected behavior-energy phenomena in Western culture." In other words, scientists are reluctant to connect seemingly unrelated phenomena to one common source. They prefer instead to create elaborate "subfields" of science which become so complex that the core of the subfield, initially connected to a similar phenomenon, moves to the periphery of an analysis and becomes disconnected from nearby observations. In studying global racism/white supremacy, Welsing argues that its presence in education has links to entertainment, law, politics, and other areas of people activity. For example, the reluctance to hire Black screenwriters in Hollywood is connected both to labor and entertainment. By using stereotypical images on the screen, *e.g.*, "Uncle Toms" and "noble savages," white screenwriters reinforce negative images of non-white people which indoctrinate young non-white children into believing that these are actual behaviors widely displayed by Black people. Thus, the fields of labor, law, and entertainment are interconnected to racism/white supremacy, even though we may initially see them as separate behaviors.

The Osiris Papers is also intended to be a companion volume to Dr. Welsing's only book, *The Isis Papers: The Keys to the Colors*. The title was chosen for two reasons: 1) Osiris was the brother/husband of Isis and 2) he was the Egyptian judge of the dead. These were Greek names for *Ast* and *Wsjr* (often translated "Aset" and "Asar" or "Auset" and "Ausar") because of the absence of vowels in the Egyptian language. Welsing's explanation for title for her book follows:

> Finally, the time has come for unveiling the true nature of white supremacy.

> For this reason, I have entitled this work, *The Isis (YSSIS) Papers: The Keys.* Isis was the sister/wife of the most important Egyptian god, Osiris ('Lord of the perfect Black') and the mother of Horus...The subtitle of this work, The Keys to the Colors, came from a statement made to me by a patient in a Washington, D.C. public mental health clinic in the late 1960s. The patient was a tall, thin, middle-aged Black-skinned man who, in a somewhat confused manner, talked earnestly to me about the problems he had experienced in his life. He said, 'Doctor, if we could just find the keys to the colors!' And he repeated it slowly. It was a statement I never have been able to forget. This work is a portion of my response.

The Osiris Papers is divided into chapters that cover the Nine Areas of White Supremacy (Economics, Education, Entertainment, Labor, Law, Politics, Religion, Sex, and War) initially outlined by Neely Fuller and elaborated upon by Dr. Welsing. Each contributor is either educated in or has vast experience in the area in which they write. They provide us with their own unique take on Dr. Welsing, her theory of color-confrontation, and the influence she had on their lives.

The book opens with a praise song to Frances Welsing written by psychologist Wade Nobles. It is an appropriate foreword to our dear Ancestor who once encouraged us to envision The Creator as being "blacker than a trillion midnights."

Dr. Conrad Worrill, who knew Dr. Welsing from childhood, shares an intimate glimpse into her upbringing in Chicago, where the Cress family made intergenerational contributions to the health and well-being of the American African community.

Patrick Delices examines how racism/white supremacy pervades all economic theories emerging from the white world. His historical analysis applies Welsing's ideas on how economic theory is constructed to support the system of white supremacy.

Educator Yaa Asantewaa Nzingha gathers personal testimonies from students, parents, and educators about how racism/white supremacy infects the education system in terms of hiring teachers, constructing and teaching curricula.

Harry Allen's interview with Chuck D, and Anthony Browder's

chapter on entertainment are particularly valuable. They provide a comprehensive view of how Dr. Welsing's theory on color-confrontation has influenced entertainment. Her theory also provides an excellent lens for understanding how racism works in the so-called "entertainment industry."

Historian Dr. José Pimienta-Bey describes how the labor of non-white people has always been dangerous and underpaid, but highly valued by people classified as white. The exploitive nature of labor within the system of white supremacy is directly connected to economics and shows how a "unified theory of racism" is applicable to these two areas.

Attorney Pilar Penn gives a personal view of her journey to become a lawyer, which was permeated with racism/white supremacy at the educational and professional levels. Penn's argument, that an understanding of "critical race theory" is the best way to understand "the law," is informed by Welsing's theory of color-confrontation.

Political scientist Dr. Ife Williams argues that politics have historically been used to create genocidal conditions to eliminate non-white people. Titling her chapter "We Charge Genocide!," a reference to the 1951 petition to the United Nations by W. E. B. Du Bois, Paul Robeson, and other African activists, Dr. Williams sets the stage for linking politics in the system of white supremacy with genocide.

Dr. Jeremiah Wright examines Dr. Welsing's arguments about white supremacy and racism, and expands her ideas about early Christianity and how it was corrupted by European racism. He raises questions about Welsing's omission of discussions about African religions which could have broadened some of her assertions about religion.

One of the most controversial aspects of Dr. Welsing's writings is her ideas about sexuality. Much of what Welsing cites about sexuality in the system of white supremacy is anchored in psychoanalytic theory, and her assertions about LGBTQ people have raised the ire of people who identify as such. Dr. Denise Wright discusses and contextualizes Welsing's views on this subject. Dr. Marimba Ani's monumental work, *Praise Song for Dr. Frances Cress Welsing: Our Race Champion!*, reflects Dr. Welsing's premise that people classified as white are at war with non-white people on a global level. She writes about the myriad ways in which this war is executed and how non-white people must see it as such.

Dr. Jeff Menzise's epilogue reflects on why Welsing's writings remain influential. He relates her writings to the ancient teachings of Egypt and explains why understanding the Isis/Osiris legend is important to assessing how racism/white supremacy continues its toxic influence on the planet.

Laini Mataka's closing poem affirms how despite Dr. Welsing's Transition, her warrior spirit will live on if we continue to challenge the insidious nature and manifestations of white supremacy in all that we do. Our battle to replace white supremacy with justice should be waged daily and not monthly or yearly. Her spirit will live on if we develop this habit.

Many people, including activists, health practitioners, and Black scholars, have said the best way to keep Dr. Welsing and her African-centered thinking present is study her work, write about her, and speak about her. This book is a first step in that direction.

Raymond A. Winbush, Ph.D.
Denise Wright, Ph.D.

FOREWORD

The Impact of Frances Cress Welsing: A Praise Song

Wade W. Nobles, Ph.D.

Ifágbẹmi Sàngódáre, Nana Kwaku Berko, I, Bejana, Onebunne

When viewed through African eyes and read with an African mind, this book on the work of Dr. Frances Cress Welsing should be considered a praise song. One of the most widely used African literary forms, a praise song is a series of flatteries applied to gods, men, animals, and plants, that capture the essence of the object being praised. Each chapter is its own accolade. Among some Bantu-speaking peoples, the praise song is an important form of oral history and a pre-visioning of one's destiny. The Sotho of Lesotho composed traditional praises of chiefs and warriors, and very young men would be allowed to create praises of themselves if they had performed feats of great courage. The Sotho, in some instances, required boys undergoing initiation to compose "praises" for themselves that set forth the ideals of action that they would live up to. Frances' life and work is her praise song to herself and to all of us. Ezekiel Mphahlele translated the praise song for the great Zulu chieftain Shaka as follows:

> He is Shaka the unshakeable,
> Thunderer-while-sitting, son of Menzi.
> He is the bird that preys on other birds,
> The battle-axe that excels over other battle-axes.
> He is the long-strided pursuer, son of Ndaba,
> Who pursued the sun and the moon.
> He is the great hubbub like the rocks of Nkandla
> Where elephants take shelter
> When the heavens frown…

Considered by Maulana Ron Karenga to represent the radical school of Black Psychology, Frances and Dr. Bobby Wright Jr., used their expertise in Western psychiatry and psychology to examine critically the behavioral dysfunction of the advocates of white supremacy. Accordingly, I want to ground my brief discussion of the impact of Dr. Frances Cress Welsing as a praise song.

To only sound-bite Frances' genius is almost insulting. Starting in the late 1980s, her scholarly contributions have been reflected in a series of annual melanin conferences led by Dr. Richard King. These meetings provided inspiration for the works of D. Phillip McGee, Carol Barnes, Neferkare Stewart, Edward Bruce Bynum and a host of Black psycho-biologists and neuroscientists.

The Cress Theory of Color-Confrontation and Racism argues that "White Supremacy is a mental illness." Specifically, it is a neurotic drive for superiority and domination that white people as a group suffer from. This neurotic disorder is due to their sense of "genetic inadequacy" and the "inability to produce color." This assertion was extremely impactful similar to the assertion by the Honorable Elijah Muhammad that white people were blue-eyed devils. Welsing's theory shook up the intellectual world of complacency that allowed white control over the minds of Black people to go unchallenged.

While some will say that her greatest contribution is found in the Cress Theory of Color Confrontation and Racism and others her Unified Field Theory Psychiatry, I think to honor Frances is to always let her speak for herself. She states in *The Isis Papers*, "White people are the genetically defective descendants of albino mutants." She went on to explain that certain inherent and behavioral differences between Black and white people were due to a melanin deficiency in white people. And she offered us a functional definition of racism as:

> ...the local and global power system and dynamic, structure, maintained by persons who classify themselves as white, whether consciously or subconsciously determined; which consists of patterns of perception, logic, symbol formation, thought, speech, action, and emotional response, as conducted, simultaneously in all areas of peo-

> ple activity (economics, education, entertainment, labor, law, politics, religion, sex, and war); for the ultimate purpose of white genetic survival and to prevent white genetic annihilation on planet Earth.

Frances' unbounded genius allowed her to reflect on the work of the world-renowned physicist, Albert Einstein, who coined the term *unified field theory* to capture his attempt to prove that electromagnetism and gravity were different manifestations of a single fundamental field. In so doing, he noted that, "within every event exists conditions that prevent another event from ever existing." Dr. Welsing's refinement became known as the "Unified Field Theory Psychiatry," where she applied field theory to the broader societal framework encompassing biology, psychology, and physics. Dr. Welsing used Unified Field Theory to further advance the concept of "behavior-energy" and its relationship to underlying racial conflict. In exemplifying the idea that "within every event exists conditions that prevent another event from ever existing," Dr. Welsing identified situations as social controls to exclude persons based on race, color, sexual orientation or wealth that were, in fact, racially-based aggressions that prevented other events from happening.

She developed this theory further to assert that the "behavior-energy" behind racial conflicts is also present in sexism and, more recently, homosexuality. In this regard, she explained that sexism is a natural stance to take for a male who feels inadequate to defend himself without using physical violence, and further notes that the generally poor treatment of Black women was due to the "behavior-energy" exerted by people in power whose aim was to disenfranchise Black women and thereby prevent or stagnate generations of Black people. She also suggested that by disenfranchising Black women, Black men feel no need to remain with their spouses once the pair produces children (the rise of single parent families being a kind of "behavior-energy" side effect or collateral damage).

Dr. Welsing references homosexuality with firsthand documents from the plantation overseers who blindfolded the so-called "bulls" and would force an insubordinate male slave to be raped. She suggests, as such, that the origins of Black male homosexuality stems from within white supremacists' "behavior-energy" during the colonial-enslavement era and should be understood as an event that prevents another event from ever existing. She concludes, in part, that homosexuality in Black men may not be by choice, but is a subconscious barrier placed on Black people by a white supremacist framework that serves to prevent the Black population from being sustainable. Whilst Dr. Welsing has received praise for the validation of her theory with regards to a sexist societal framework, acceptance regarding the application of the Unified Field Theory with regards to homosexuality within the Black community has not been equally forthcoming.

In her Unified Field Theory Psychiatry, she proposed a broader framework, encompassing biology, psychology, and physics, as prerequisites to understanding the etiology of a unified field of energy phenomena, specifically the "behavior-energy" underlying racial conflict. As a bold, unafraid African theorist, Frances relocated the idea of racial discrimination and sexuality as the consequence of "behavior-energy" that could only be understood through the unified fields of biology, psychology, and physics. Her thoughts and ideas, especially her unified field of behavioral energy theory, require and deserve the greatest of attention, study, research, critique, and application. The complete implications of her insight are yet to be fully understood. Her scholarship, in my opinion, helped to consecrate Black psychology's separation from the toxic psychopathic core of western thought.

The great word-Goddess, Maya Angelou, who preceded Frances in transitioning said, "Listen to yourself and in that quietude you might hear the voice of God."[1] She also said, "And when great souls die, after a period, peace blooms, slowly and always irregularly. Spaces fill with a kind of soothing electric vibration. Our senses, restored, never to be the same, whisper to us. They existed. They existed. We can be. Be and be better. For they existed."[2]

In this moment of quietude that Frances' transition requires, listen to her, as a mighty Black woman, whisper to our souls. Read her thoughts and ideas that can bring forth our electric vibration. Because Frances Cress Welsing lived, our sense of who we are can never be the same.

Whisper: *Dr. Frances Cress Welsing, as a great mighty Black woman, existed.* Or, rather than whisper, maybe we should shout out loud.

Frances was my longtime friend and sister in struggle. To speak of her transitioning to be among the Dwellers of Heaven is unexpected and very difficult. Like Queen Tiye, Hatshepsut, Queen Nzinga, Harriet Tubman, Cecile Fatiman, Sojourner Truth, Ida B. Wells-Barnett, and Barbara Jordan, she was a fiery warrior, a supreme intellect, a beautiful woman, a gentle soul, a defender of the race, and a lover of Blackness. She was our Queen Mother.

Dr. Frances Cress Welsing, existed. This great and powerful soul will exist forever. Her work and her life is deserving of praise.

A Praise Song for Frances Cress Welsing

Frances Cress Welsing, through the sacred womb of her mother, Ida Mae Griffin, seeded by the heavenly sperm of her father, Henry N. Cress, seeded the seeds in our souls.

She, Frances Cress Welsing, exists with the power of lightning.

Frances is the one whose first major contribution, *The Cress Theory of Color-Confrontation and Racism (White Supremacy)*, awakened and frightened us.

Frances, our great Mistress of the Mind, honored us in the documentary, *500 Years Later.*

She, Frances Cress Welsing, was the double axe, who met and defeated in debate the Nobel Prize-winning physicist and proponent of eugenics, Dr. William Shockley.

Dr. Welsing's Magnum Opus, *The Isis Papers*, was her eternal, everlasting gift.

Frances, the Warrior Woman, showed us what Black elegance and excellence looked like in *Hidden Colors: The Untold History of People of Aboriginal, Moor, and African Descent.*

Frances is the one who, without fear, demonstrated that the quality of whiteness is a genetic inadequacy.

Dr. Frances Cress Welsing received with high honor the Fannie Lou Hamer Community Award.

She, the slayer of ignorance, boldly taught the world that the state of

> color is the norm for human beings and [its] absence is abnormal.
>
> Frances' mother and father, without a doubt, sent the spirits of Asa G. Hilliard, Bobby Wright, Nzinga Coppock-Warfield, and Harriett Pipes McAdoo to escort her into the afterlife.
>
> She, the Wisdom Whisperer, now exists in the realm of the invisible.
>
> Dr. Frances Cress Welsing is the quiet thunder.
>
> Frances is the one who grasped the ungraspable.
>
> Dr. Frances Cress Welsing will exist forever amongst the Dwellers of Heaven.
>
> She, like Orunmila's daughter, exists in the unbroken circle of our minds.
>
> Dr. Frances Cress Welsing exists.

Above all, Dr. Frances Cress Welsing's life and works must be placed in the active resource arsenal for the liberation of the African mind and the restoration of the true equilibrium of humanity. I give thanks that I knew her and sat in her presence. May we all give praise that Dr. Frances Cress Welsing lived, walked, and loved amongst us.

Endnotes

1 Angelou, Maya (@DrMayaAngelou). 2014. "Listen to yourself and in that quietude you might hear the voice of God. Twitter, May 23, 2014, 11:23 AM.

2 Angelou, Maya. "When Great Trees Fall." Smithsonian National Museum of African Art, n.d., https://africa.si.edu/2014/05/when-great-trees-fall%E2%80%A8%E2%80%A8-by-maya-angelou/ (accessed November 5, 2019).

INTRODUCTION

Frances Cress Welsing and the Chicago Connection

Dr. Conrad Worrill

Introduction

The tradition of the African Diaspora is to remember, uphold, and commemorate those Ancestors who influenced the lives of millions through sacrifice and unselfishness. In the African tradition, it is the duty of the living to communicate and celebrate the lives of those African people and organizations that struggle for the greatest number of African people, regardless of conditions or circumstances. This tradition advocates the belief that those Africans and organizations working in the interest of African people must be recognized and remembered for their contributions to us. This is the case of Dr. Frances Cress Welsing.

Dr. Welsing is a Black heroine who contributed greatly to the Black Movement in America and the worldwide African Liberation Movement. Dr. Welsing was a fearless and dedicated advocate for the African principle, "the greatest good for the greatest number of Africans." Dr. Welsing made her transition believing in this principle which, unfortunately, is absent in the lives of many Black leaders in America today.

Frances was a dedicated psychiatrist, African-centered activist, author, and researcher who had tremendous impact worldwide. In this regard, Dr. Welsing explained in her public lectures that, "Black people have to get in their mind frame that Black means dignity and being serious, that people respect each other and that the strength of Black people is valuing ourselves, respecting ourselves, and having dignity."[1] She elaborated by repeatedly pointing out, "We must get over fear; learn and understand what is happening; begin thinking deep; start getting quiet so you can think; begin analyzing and planning; learn the meaning and practice of deep self-respect, and engage in the ultimate organizing of all the appropriate behaviors necessary to neutralize the great injustice of the white supremacy power system."[2]

My Personal Relationship with Dr. Welsing

My personal relationship with Dr. Welsing began when the Worrill family arrived in Chicago from Pasadena, California, on the Super Chief train on August 17, 1950. My father, Walter Worrill, came to Chicago to become the Executive Director of the Wabash YMCA. Little did I know that, as a little boy of nine years old, my father's job would allow me to meet the Cress sisters, who were members of the same Y and participated in girls' and women's activities. The importance of this chance meeting and subsequent friendship would not fully resonate with me until long after.

Years later, I was in the offices of Othello Ellis, executive director of the Abraham Lincoln Center at 39th and Cottage Grove. My father had hired Mr. Ellis earlier in his career as the program director of the Y. Mr. Ellis became an iconic figure in the Black community of Chicago, distinguishing himself by wearing a flower in his lapel every day. He was like a second father to me in terms of administering youth programs for young men at the Wabash Y. Later in life, as I was pursuing my own career as an educator, I would occasionally visit with him at his office so he could stroke my ego and tell me that I was doing all right. One day I went just to kick it with him for a moment or two. He said, "Oh Conrad, I have something to show you." He pulled a brochure from his desk promoting Camp Arthur in Dowagiac, Michigan, which was the camp owned by the Y that I had attended for several summers. On the cover of the brochure were Frances Cress Welsing, her sisters Lorne and Barbara, with me standing in front of them. Seeing the picture completely blew my mind. I didn't remember it and I didn't realize at the time that these young ladies were the Cress sisters, although, by now I had heard of Frances Cress Welsing through her "Cress Theory." I knew of her sister Lorne, who was an established member in the Student Nonviolent Coordinating Committee (SNCC), and I knew her sister Barbara through her work in the Harold Washington Mayoral Campaign. I knew them all, but I didn't remember that we went to the Wabash YMCA together as young people.

Black Belt, Bronzeville, Low End, and the Cress Family History

Frances Cress Welsing was born on March 18, 1935, in Chicago, Illinois, into a family that had produced two doctors: her father, the late Henry N. Cress, was a medical doctor as was her grandfather. Frances was the second of three girls. Her older sister, Lorne, was born March 31, 1934, and her younger sister, Barbara, was born in 1938. Frances lived with her siblings and parents at their family home at 3149 South Ellis Avenue. The Cress family fought vigorously against the gentrification threatening to dismantle the Black community in that area, and theirs was the last house standing before they were forced to move to a new home at 6111 South Woodlawn in 1953. Oscar Brown Sr. and Frances' mother, Ida Mae Cress, were co-chairs of the committee to stop gentrification and Black removal. The New York Life Insurance Company had purchased the land and collaborated with the City of Chicago using "eminent domain" tactics so they could develop the Lake Meadows housing complex that still exists today.

This particular area of Chicago has been given many names. It has been referenced historically as the "Black Belt." However, in St. Clair Drake's classic book *Black Metropolis: A Study of Negro Life in a Northern City,* the term "Bronzeville" emerged. In *Black Metropolis,* Drake notes that in 1930, the *Chicago Bee African American Newspaper* held a contest to elect a mayor of Bronzeville. A few years later, the newspaperman who had come up with the naming contest idea left the *Chicago Bee* and went to the *Chicago Defender* newspaper and continued this endearing term. This term grew through the popularity of the *Defender* and became institutionalized.

In *Black Metropolis,* Drake and co-author Horace Cayton explained:

> Each year a Board of Directors composed of outstanding citizens of the Black Belt takes charge of the mock-election. Ballots are cast at corner stores and in barbershops and poolrooms. The "Mayor," usually a businessman, is inaugurated with a colorful ceremony and a

> ball. Throughout this tenure he is expected to serve as a symbol of the community's aspirations. He visits churches, files protests with the Mayor of the city, and acts as official greeter of visitors to Bronzeville. Tens of thousands of people participate in the annual election of the "Mayor."[3]

Bronzeville, on the south side of Chicago, was an area seven miles long and one and a half miles wide, stretching from 22nd Street to 63rd Street between Wentworth and Cottage Grove. Even though the description Bronzeville has become a more prominent description of this area, Black people living in the area gave it another name — "The Low End"—a description that resonates today in the oral history of Bronzeville. Anything north of 63rd Street to 22nd Street was called the Low End as well as the Black Belt. Frances Cress grew up in the community that was often referred to in the 1940s as the Black capital of America, a major center of Black culture and nationalist sentiment.

Jean Baptiste Point DuSable is credited as the eighteenth-century founder of what is known today as Chicago. However, history often excludes the indigenous presence of the Native Americans with whom DuSable engaged in his major trading and business enterprises. Since the 1860s, there has been a population of African Americans migrating into the northern states and specifically to Chicago. At the turn of the late nineteenth century, with the escalation of lynchings throughout the South and the lack of economic resources, Black people were lured to the North and started the trek of what is called the Great Migration. By 1900, there were 30,000 Black people in Chicago; by 1935, there were 235,000 who had migrated there.[4] Chicago's Black Belt-Bronzeville-Low End became one of the major epicenters for Black life in the United States, post-reconstruction, in a northern city. Frances Cress was reared in the heart of this epicenter.

The impact of this legendary community of Black consciousness, Black pride, and Black institutional development on Frances and her family was critical. Her father, Henry N. Cress, and his father, Henry Clay Cress, practiced medicine in this burgeoning community of Black people. Frances' grandfather came to Chicago in 1887 and, according to Frances' sister, Lorne Cress, worked alongside the legendary Ida B. Wells in the anti-lynching movement and joined her in many campaigns fighting for civil and human rights for Black people. Lorne said that her grandmother described her grandfather as spending more time fighting for the issues impacting the Black community than he did practicing medicine.[5] The people in the neighborhood described him as a "Race Man."

Frances' maternal great-grandfather, Charles Augustus Griffin, came to Chicago from Canada in 1862 to join the Union Army. Following the Civil War, Mr. Griffin established several businesses. Steven A. Griffin, his son, inherited his father's inclinations for business and was inspired to open the historic Griffin Funeral Home in Bronzeville. Steven's son, Ernest Griffin, took over the business after his father's death. After Ernest made his transition, his wife and daughters continued to run the Griffin Funeral Home until it closed in 2007 at its location on 32nd and King Drive. Thus, Welsing came from three generations that managed to build businesses serving Blacks while remaining strong activists in their communities.

Frances' mother, Ida Mae Griffin Cress was an elementary school teacher who spent 41 years working in the Chicago Public Schools until her retirement in 1971. She had spent most of her years teaching kindergarten and primary grades at Drake Elementary School in Bronzeville. She graduated from Chicago's Normal Teachers College and the University of Chicago. She was a contemporary of Dr. Margaret Burroughs and helped her organize the DuSable Museum and the Southside Community Arts Center. Mrs. Cress was noted for starting a number of community programs, including the "Keep Chicago Clean" campaign, in which she distributed buttons and promoted a poster contest aimed at elementary school students. She was also noted for setting up a scholarship fund for Black medical students.

I had the delightful experience of interacting with Ida Mae Griffin Cress in the late 1980s. One day, I received a letter from her. The letter described some of the work she was engaged in and asked me to contact her so she could consult with me on the organizing work we were engaged in Chicago. It did not register with me that she was Frances' mother so I ignored the letter. Several weeks later, I received another letter from her, making the same request and including her telephone number urging me to contact her. Finally, I called Mrs. Cress and she said, "Conrad Worrill, I knew your mother and father. Further, I am Dr. Frances Cress Welsing's mother and I have been doing a lot of organizing work in the Black community before you were born. And further, you are not the only one who graduated from Hyde Park High School. I graduated from Hyde Park High School in 1923." I was obviously stunned by the spirit of the conversation with Frances' mother. This was during the time when Harold Washington had been elected the first Black Mayor of Chicago.

At Hyde Park High School (where I graduated from in 1959) we were involved in a program called "Black History Come Alive" in February during Black History Month that brought alumnus from the school to spend the day interacting with the current students. I suggested to the committee, led by the Assistant Principal Linda Murray, that we invite Frances' mother Ida Mae Griffin Cress (who at that time was at least in her early 80s) to be a special guest at the next "Black History Come Alive" program around 1989. She was delighted at the invitation to be the keynote speaker for the program. We made arrangements to have her picked up and driven to the school. Mrs. Griffin had over a thousand young people in the auditorium of the Hyde Park High School mesmerized. There is no question that Frances was greatly impacted by her mother, who made her transition in 1998 at the age of ninety-two.

In my interview with Lorne Cress, I asked how her sister ended up attending Antioch College in Ohio. She explained that it was her mother who did the research for Frances to attend Antioch and, in order for Frances to be accepted, she had to write an essay on why she wanted to attend the college. Even though Lorne was eleven months older, Mrs. Cress raised them as if they were twins. Frances skipped a grade in elementary school, so she and Lorne ended up graduating from Wendell Phillips High School together. Lorne was also slated to attend Antioch, but she rebelled and refused to write the essay. She eventually found her niche in the Civil Rights Movement and became a member of SNCC.

Undoubtedly, Frances was shaped by this community where notable Blacks had a presence, including heavyweight champion boxer, Joe Louis; world-renowned Gospel singer Mahalia Jackson; Congressman William Dawson; *Chicago Defender* editor, John Sengstacke; Johnson Publishing Company founder, John H. Johnson; and Nation of Islam leader, the Honorable Elijah Muhammad. The entire trajectory of Frances' development occurred in an iconic and legendary community of Black people.

In Her Own Words

Dr. Frances Cress Welsing was the banquet speaker at the 28th Ancient Kemetic Studies Conference of the Association for the Study of Classical African Civilizations (ASCAC), March 19, 2011, at Howard University, Washington, D.C. In her keynote address, affirming and verifying the impact her family and community had on her development, she gave the following testimony:

> I'm especially dedicating my remarks to some of my ancestors because of the help and guidance, even from afar, that they have given me. My paternal grandfather, Dr. Henry Noah Cress, a Chicago physician who died in 1909; my paternal grandmother who raised me, us, with my parents, she repeated to us over and over again when we were children that your grandfather was a race man—meaning that he prioritized the wellbeing of Black people. In later years, my father (his son), Dr. Henry Miller Cress, would show me notes that his father had written, one of which said, "How dare a person think he is superior because of the color of his skin, his white skin."
>
> Now, I never met my grandfather. He died in 1909; I was born in 1935. It astounded me that I would one day be writing about racism/white supremacy. Also, my father, Dr. Henry Miller Cress, a Chicago physician, who when I first discussed with him my paper, The Cress Theory of Color Confrontation and Racism/White Supremacy, (we were sitting at our dining room table), he said, "Now you have to find out what is in the melanin." He was the first Black physician to make this statement, leading to all of our further investigations of this most important substance.

I want to also mention my mother, a Chicago public school teacher, who was determined to broaden her children's experiences beyond the confines of a ghettoized environment. And to all my ancestors who have passed on and who saw it as their duty to correct and develop our behavior with strict rules about what behaviors were acceptable, those that were totally unacceptable and those that would not be tolerated.

Also to all of my Black Chicago public school teachers who, in the early 1940s, were determined that we as Black children were going to learn to contribute to our world, repeating to us endlessly, "You have to be ten times as good," subtly informing us [of] the conditions in an unjust society beyond the protection of our Black community experience; and to all of the Black people in the church.

I was baptized in the Olivet Baptist Church in Chicago—that's on the Baptist side of the family—and christened at the A.M.E. Church. But for all of those elderly people and older people who would monitor and watch our behavior, and if you got out of line they would say, "I'm going to tell your mother" or "I'm going to tell your grandfather" or take you to your grandmother or your grandfather.

Finally, to all of the African people who endured the horrors of captivity and enslavement, determined to survive so that we all can be here today to complete the work that the great Creator of the universe gave us, the cosmic assignment to perform in our time: to bring justice and peace to this planet and to the universe.[6]

The Impact of Wendell Phillips High School

Frances Cress Welsing's educational development was centered around the holistic influences that tapped into her intellectual gifts. It is clear that her family, at multiple levels, influenced her intellectual, educational, and social development. She grew up being nurtured in the all-Black Bronzeville community; attending and graduating from the all-Black Douglas Elementary School. In 1947, Frances entered the historic Wendell Phillips High School as a freshman. Phillips High School was established in 1904 and named after the nineteenth-century abolitionist, Wendell Phillips. (Coincidentally, Frances' father, Henry Cress, graduated from Phillips in 1916.)

From the beginning, Phillips always had a Black student population. However, in its early years, Jewish, Greek, Irish, and Swedish students were the predominant groups. As a result of the burgeoning escalation of the Great Migration, by the 1920s Wendell Phillips' student body had become predominantly African American. Wendell Phillips High School indeed became the pride of secondary educational opportunities for African American students in the Bronzeville community and served as an important anchor.

Phillips' iconic history is illustrous. In 1979, the alumni association created the Wendell Phillips Hall of Fame, which depicts throughout its hallways pictures and biographies of the countless achievements made by African Americans in their academic, athletic, and professional lives. Such notables as entertainer Nat King Cole, singer Dinah Washington, singer Sam Cooke, publisher John H. Johnson, banker Jacoby Dickens, and poet laureate Gwendolyn Brooks are among those celebrated in its halls from which current students and visitors draw inspiration.

The first African American high school basketball team that dominated in the Chicago Public League was from Phillips. Upon graduation, several of the Phillips basketball stars started the semi-pro team the "Savoy Big Five." Eventually, six of the players signed contracts with the newly created "Harlem Globetrotters" in 1926. Phillips High School has produced countless students that have gone on to become physicians, educators, architects, theologians, businessmen, and political leaders who have had major impacts in developing Chicago's rich African American history.

In talking with Frances' schoolmates, such as the accomplished accountant, Lester McKeever, the well-known educators, Wellington Wilson and Malcolm Hemphill, the poet/writer/social worker, Euseni Perkins, and her sister, Lorne (who graduated with Frances in 1951, as previously indicated), all testify that Frances was always a serious student and a curious seeker of knowledge. It is with this backdrop that Frances wrote her essay and was accepted into Antioch College in Ohio where she completed her bachelor's degree in 1957. Frances was then admitted to the historic Howard University College of Medicine, where she began to pursue her career in psychiatry. From all accounts, Frances was always an intense researcher who was constantly seeking answers to the critical issues impacting people of African descent and the conditions of African people worldwide.

Frances completed her medical degree in 1962 and then interned at Chicago's Cook County Hospital. In 1963, she began her general psychiatric residency at St. Elizabeth's Hospital in Washington, D.C., and went on to focus her career in the area of child psychiatry. She earned a fellowship in child psychiatry at Children's Hospital in Washington D.C., 1966-68. In 1968, she was appointed as assistant professor of pediatrics at the Howard University College of Medicine.

In 1970, the publication of her article, *The Cress Theory of Color-Confrontation and Racism (White Supremacy)*, caused a major controversy in the discourse of the academy. Frances always maintained, as did the Black activist community in America, that this was the reason that she did not receive tenure at Howard University in 1975. This, however, did not stop the continued work and contributions of Frances Cress Welsing.

Impact of Neely Fuller on the Work of Frances Cress Welsing

Frances Cress Welsing met Neely Fuller in 1967 at a party after an organizing meeting for the Black United Front of Washington, D.C. It was at this party that Neely Fuller and Frances connected, and Fuller began to share the ideas of his work that he had in his briefcase. Mr. Fuller had developed the first six handwritten pages—which grew to be more than 3,000—to become what is known as the *United Independent Compensatory Code/System/Concept,* copyrighted in 1969. Frances was so impressed with Fuller's ideas that she recruited a medical student from Howard University, the son-in-law of Margaret Burroughs (legendary founder of the DuSable Museum in Chicago), to type these handwritten pages and put them in a book format.

Neely Fuller was born on October 6, 1929, at the beginning of the Great Depression. During the Korean War, Fuller served in both the

Army and Air Force in the early1950s. Fuller carefully documented his experiences with racism and white supremacy that would ultimately become a textbook/workbook for thought, speech and/or action for victims of racism (white supremacy).[7]

Frances observed that "Fuller, the founder of the racism/counter-racism concept, was the very first victim of racism to understand it as a global system of organized behavior (thought, speech and action) for white supremacy domination in all areas of people activity (economics, education, entertainment, labor, law, politics, religion, sex, and war)."[8] In addition, Frances synthesized Fuller's work in the following manner:

> In other words, he recognized that all activity and behavior encompassed by the white supremacy system had and has its origin in the dynamic of racism. Additionally, Fuller understood that racism contained the seeds and origin of counter-racism, the behavior dynamic of liberation for the non-white victims of white supremacy. His work led me to question the necessity of the global white collective to evolve such a system of unjust behavior. The result was *The Cress Theory of Color-Confrontation and Racism (White Supremacy).*[9]

Finally, Frances wrote:

> Fuller observed that, contrary to most present thinking, there is only one functioning racism in the known world—white supremacy. He challenges his readers to identify and then to demonstrate the superiority or functional supremacy of any of the world's "non-white" peoples over anyone. Concluding that since there is no operational supremacy of any "colored" people, Fuller reveals that the only valid operations definition of racism is white supremacy.[10]

Through the association and mentoring of Frances Cress Welsing by Neely Fuller, a relationship emerged where they began to publicly make presentations together on the ideas of the origin of racism/white supremacy. Fuller explained these sessions as "code lectures and forums" which took place in and around the Washington, D.C. area, and on the campus of Howard University. This ignited great public discussion, responses, and dialogue that began to spread throughout the Pan African, Nationalist, and African-centered communities in the United States.

Because of her own deep family, community, and academic influences, and her intellectual curiosity, Frances was clearly impacted by the mentoring of Neely Fuller. In many of Frances' public lectures she often began with this statement from Fuller: "If you do not understand White Supremacy (Racism)—what it is, and how it works—everything *else* that you understand, will only confuse you."[11]

Frances Cress Welsing and the African Centered School of Thought

In the quest of African-centered scholars to create a "Black Social Theory," it is important that we define "African-centeredness."

> "African Centered"... represents the concept of categorizing a quality of thought and practice which is rooted in the cultural image and interest of people of African ancestry and which represents and reflects the life experiences, history, and traditions of people of African ancestry as the center of analyses. African-centeredness is therein, the intellectual and philosophical foundations upon which people of African ancestry should create their own scientific and moral criterion for authenticating the reality of African human processes. It represents the core and fundamental quality of the "Beingness" and "Becoming" of people of African ancestry. In essence, African-centeredness represents the fact that human beings, people of African ancestry, have the right and responsibility to 'center' themselves in their own possibilities and potential and through the recentering process reproduce and refine the best of themselves.[12]

It is in this context that we place Frances Cress Welsing's intellectual and scholarly contributions in the African-Centered School of Thought that emerged and had significant impact on the efforts toward developing a Black Social Theory. This African-Centered scholarship has informed us over the last 50 years through the writings of Cheikh Anta Diop, Jacob H. Carruthers, Asa G. Hilliard III, Marimba Ani, John Henrik Clarke, Théophile Obenga, Kobi K. K. Kambon, Wade W. Nobles, Amos Wilson, Chancellor Williams, Bobby E. Wright, Yosef ben Jochannan, Raymond Winbush, Linda Myers, Greg Kimathi Carr, Mario Beatty, Anderson Thompson, and many others.

The proliferation of Western thought has altered the lens through which we view the world. As Dr. Jacob Carruthers consistently pointed out in his writings, the African-centered intellectual and scholarly tradition seeks to:

> Advocate the restoring of the historical truth about Africa as the priority of African thinkers and activists, including Africans in the Diaspora.
>
> Advocate that there is a distinct universal African worldview, which should be the foundation for all African intellectual freedom.
>
> Overhaul the massive education and re-education of the African peoples of the world from an African perspective in the interests of African peoples as a necessary pre-condition for the freedom of the African mind and, subsequently, African liberation.[13]

Welsing's contributions clearly fall into this stream of thought.

Dr. Bobby E. Wright (one of Frances' early colleagues) explained in his seminal writings, as Dr. Carruthers described in his book, *The Irritated Genie*, "The critique of Black acceptance of white definitions and exposing of the falseness of the definitions themselves is essentially a reaction of negations. Such negation leaves a void which if not filled will absolutely depress the masses of Black people. Therefore, Wright forcefully emphasized the need for the development of a truly Black social theory. This is a very difficult assignment and cannot be accomplished by those brainwashed Black intellectuals who are awestruck by European theory and theorists."[14]

What Frances Cress Welsing contributed to the development of a Black Social Theory in the context of African-centered thought and an African worldview, was a theory that "determines the destiny of a people by establishing objectives and guidelines of their existence… it defines their relationship with other living things, it defines values and rituals, methods of childrearing and education… The ultimate achievement of a Black Social Theory would be the reintegration of a worldview Black culture."[15]

Within this framework we place Frances Cress Welsing as a luminary who leaves a legacy along with other African-Centered thinkers, scholars, and activists who, for the last 200 years, have been working to break the intellectual yoke of white supremacy. Further, her work to create an African-centered/Black Social Theory will endure within the African consciousness as we work to reclaim African civilizations, traditions, and cultures.

References

Carruthers, Jacob H. 1995. *The Irritated Genie.* The Kemetic Institute: Chicago, IL.

Cress Love, Lorne. One-on-one telephone interview on May 12, 2016.

Cress Welsing, Frances. "The Association for the Study of Classical African Civilizations 28th Annual Ancient Kemetic Studies Conference, March 19, 2011, Howard University, Washington, DC, Banquet with Frances Cress Welsing, M.D." *The Compass, Journal of the Association for the Study of Classical African Civilizations, Vol. 1, Issue 1.*

Cress Welsing, Frances. 1991. *The Isis (Yssis) Papers: The Keys to the Colors.* Third World Press, Chicago, IL.

Drake, St. Clair and Horace R. Cayton. 1962. *Black Metropolis: A Study of Negro Life in a Northern City, Vol. II.* Harper Torchbooks, Harper & Row, NY.

Nobles, Wade W. 1990. "Afrocentricity Def-Revised." The Institute for the Advanced Study of Black Family Life and Culture, Inc., Oakland, CA.

Stange, Maren. 2003. *Bronzeville: Black Chicago in Pictures, 1941-1943.* The New York Press, NY. ISBN 1-565840618-4

Worrill, Conrad. Notes from lectures by Dr. Frances Cress Welsing between 1992-2000. Personal archives of Conrad Worrill.

Worrill, Conrad. Notes from lectures by Dr. Jacob H. Carruthers between 1975-2003. Personal archives of Conrad Worrill.

Endnotes

1 Conrad Worrill,, Notes from lectures by Dr. Welsing between 1992-2000. Personal archives of Conrad Worrill.

2 Ibid.

3 St. Clair Drake and Horace R. Cayton, B*lack Metropolis: A Study of Negro Life in a Northern City, Vol. II* (New York: Harper Torchbooks, Harper & Row, 1962), p. 383.

4 Maren, Strange, *Bronzeville: Black Chicago in Pictures, 1941-1943* (New York, NY: The New York Press, 2003), xxxi.

5 Lorne Cress Love, Notes from a one-on-one telephone interview conducted by Dr. Conrad Worrill on May 12, 2016.

6 Frances Cress Welsing,, "The Association for the Study of Classical African Civi- lizations 28th Annual Ancient Kemetic Studies Conference, March 19, 2011, Howard University, Washington, DC, Banquet with Frances Cress Welsing, M.D." *The Compass, Journal of the Association for the Study of Classical African Civilizations* Vol. 1, Issue 1, 28-29.

7 Frances Cress Welsing, *The Isis (Yssis) Papers: The Keys to the Colors* (Chicago: Third World Press, 1991), ix.

8 Ibid., ix.

9 Ibid., ix.

10 Ibid., 2.

11 Ibid., Dedication page.

12 Wade W. Nobles, "Afrocentricity Def-Revised." The Institute for the Advanced Study of Black Family Life and Culture, Inc., Oakland, CA.

13 Worrill, Conrad. Notes from lectures by Dr. Carruthers between 1975-2003.

14 Jacob H. Carruthers, *The Irritated Genie* (Chicago: The Kemetic Institute: Chicago), ix.

15 Ibid.

CHAPTER 1

Economics and Global White Supremacy

Patrick Delices

> Black people are the mothers and fathers of civilization. We have the system of white supremacy because the children have taken over the house.
>
> —Dr. Frances Cress Welsing

Introduction

In "African Civilizations as Cornerstone for the Oikoumene," Dean Lawrence Edward Carter, of the Martin Luther King Jr. International Chapel, explains that the word *economics* is derived from the ancient Kemetic (Egyptian) word *uakhuimene* meaning, among other things, "the protection of the earth or its estate" by law or God.[1] According to Carter, from *uakhuimene* we get the Greek word *oikoumene,* meaning "the house of the inhabited earth," and the Greek word *oikonomia*, meaning "the law of house management" or "God's house management."[2]

It is through this lens that this chapter examines the historical evolution of economics and its psychological interpretations and ramifications. There have been many attempts to define economics. However, few scholars have captured the essence of the original meaning of economics or have juxtaposed it in the context of global white supremacy. Therefore, this chapter will also focus on providing an expository analysis of Welsing's theory as it relates to the field of economics and the various theories concerning the system of global white supremacy. Given that economics is a broad subject and global white supremacy is even broader, this chapter will discuss Welsing's ideas regarding global white supremacy within the context of economics as illustrated in land, labor, and resources.

Welsing, Economics, and White Supremacy

Dr. Frances Cress Welsing theorized in her *Cress Theory of Color-Confrontation and Racism (White Supremacy),* that the main reason behind the superior economic standing of whites globally is due to their deep psychological fear of genetic annihilation by Blacks. While complementing the historic-economic and cultural-historic theses on the origin of global white supremacy, Welsing's psycho-genetic theory serves as an antithesis to the popular universalist-economic supposition of white racism worldwide. To understand Welsing's claims, an introduction to the development of her worldview and theory is key.

In 1959, in the midst of a transition in U.S. educational policy from segregation to desegregation, Dr.Welsing was a medical student at Howard University. Also, in 1959, Fidel Castro's revolution in Cuba was successful, establishing it as the first communist nation in the Americas. Considering Castro's triumphant revolution, Vice President Richard Nixon of the United States and Premier Nikita Sergeyevich Khrushchev of the Soviet Union engaged in the Kitchen Debate, where they argued about the tenets of capitalism and communism. It was also during the same period that a sincere, charismatic, no-nonsense nationalist from the Nation of Islam, Minister Malcolm X, embarked for the first time to the continent of Africa and to the landmass that is now known as the Middle East.

During that same year, a "controversial" African-centered coeval of Welsing, Leonard Jeffries Jr., graduated from Lafayette College with honors. In 1959, as a first among equals at Lafayette College, Jeffries was also granted the prestigious Rotary International Fellowship to study abroad in Switzerland at the University of Lausanne.

During her tenure at Howard, Welsing encountered the works of the Black Marxist Oliver C. Cox, who wrote the classic text, *Caste, Class and Race*, and became familiar with his assertion that "there is no consistent theory of race relations."[3] Ironically, Cox's writings dovetailed notable events in the early 1960s where seventeen countries in Africa became independent from European colonial forces. It was during this period that France, Belgium, and the United States colluded to assassinate the first democratically elected prime minister of the Congo, Patrice Émery Lumumba, on January 17, 1961.[4] It could be said that, out of fear, three powerful white nations conspired to assassinate one Black man.

By 1962, Welsing had earned her MD in Psychiatry from Howard Medical School, while ruminating on Cox's assertion. However, Welsing was not the only scholar contemplating Cox's claim; that year, the Senegalese scholar Dr. Cheikh Anta Diop responded to Cox's assertion by publishing *The Cultural Unity of Black Africa,* which had an enormous impact on Welsing's view of race relations and color confrontations. In his book, Diop proffers the *Two Cradle Theory*.

The *Two Cradle Theory* argues that a severe glacial climate along with a harsh, isolated environment in Europe created a hyper-aggressive, individualistic, and xenophobic people who were nomadic and depigmented. These people, described as white, are often identified as the *Ice People* as they represent the *Northern Cradle*. Their mode of production (economic system) is centered on individualism.

In the universalist-economic model, the *Northern Cradle* is identified as the *Global North* (colonial and imperial nations of Western Europe, the United States, Canada, Australia, New Zealand, Israel, Hong Kong, Singapore, South Korea, and Taiwan). Even though Australia and New Zealand are geographically located in the Southern Hemisphere, they mimic the economic and cultural realities of nations in the Northern Hemisphere.

According to Diop, individuals who remained in the sun-drenched climate of Africa, were described as peaceful, cooperative xenophiles. This population did not lose their pigmentation and are identified as the *Sun People* from the *Southern Cradle*. Their mode of production (economic system) is centered on communalism. In the universalist-economic model, the *Southern Cradle* is known as the *Global South* (developing nations or underdeveloped nations in Africa, Latin America, the Caribbean, and some parts of Asia, where their economies and socio-political institutions have been negatively impacted by slavery, colonialism, and imperialism).

Scholar-activist Neely Fuller Jr. appended Diop's *Two Cradle Theory* by providing a contemporary economic and socio-political understanding of race relations, based primarily on the scientific method of observation. Fuller attempted to address Cox's theoretical assertion by providing a "functional statement on racism."[5] A decade after Cox's treatise regarding the paucity of race relations theories, Fuller published *A Textbook for Victims of White Supremacy*, which has been republished as *The United Independent Compensatory Code/System/Concept: A Compensatory Counter-Racist Code.*

Fuller's main thesis identified *Nine Areas of People Activity* (NAPA) within the system of white supremacy: economics, education, entertainment, labor, law, politics, religion, sex, and war/counter-war. Within these nine major areas, Fuller hypothesized that there was only one system of functional racism in the world: global white supremacy.[6] To counter or end global white supremacy, Fuller suggested that Blacks must first and foremost alter their economic philosophy and behavior. In his work, he presented actionable steps to counter or end global white supremacy.

Alternatively, Diop presented a theoretical framework that explained the anthropological origin of whites and their racist economic, socio-political, and cultural behavior. Fuller, unlike Diop, did not provide an anthropological basis for explaining the origins of racism. In examining economics within the confines of global white supremacy, Fuller reasoned that "various economic systems such as capitalism, communism, and socialism have been devised, used, and refined in the effort to achieve the primary goal of white domination" as exemplified in the infamous "Kitchen Debate."[7] Even Marxism, for Fuller and Welsing, would prove to be invalid as a theoretical framework within the universalist-economic ideology. Marxists believed that global white supremacy (racism) would dissipate with the rise of the working class and socialism.[8] Karl Marx and Friedrich Engels purported that capitalism and slavery were not immoral because they were "in the dialectical progression to a higher social order" which was "essential to the development of modern civilization."[9] Moreover, "Marx characterized African-Asian formations (MPA) as 'ephemeral,' transitory societies outside of the pale of historical revolutionary movement."[10] Diop states:

> Marx and others incorrectly analyzed the African-Asian state system and misunderstood the collective consciousness, the communal benefits, and the cooperative production, land use, and ownership. As a result, Marx referred to African-Asian production as "generalized slavery" in contrast to the private slavery of Greco-Latin states. He also believed that the closed village communities of MPA were the reasons for the stagnation of these societies. [11]

Thus, in a capitalist economic system, the "free" market economy is similar to a socialist market economy, where labor is free, cheap, and/or forced, which highlights the oppressive and exploitative nature of both (socialist and capitalist) economic systems fueling global white supremacy.

For Fuller, economics is the first element of NAPA in the "known universe" that "pertains to how all the time and all energy is used" and the "matter of how everything is handled—and to what end."[12] Furthermore, Fuller asserts, "economics does not simply mean acquiring, saving, and/or spending money. Economics is not a tool of money—money is a tool of Economics."[13] It is therefore Fuller's analysis that economics is an all-encompassing construct of everything—life, our house (the planet earth), and the universe (God's estate)—not just about currency.

Without giving Fuller any acknowledgement or credit, many prominent white economists in the twenty-first century referred to economics as the study of not only the economy, but more importantly, the study of life, the universe, and everything.[14] As an example, economist Tim Hartford of the *Financial Times* named his 2008 work, *The Logic of Life: Uncovering the New Economics of Everything.*[15] Similarly, economist Steven Levitt and journalist Stephen Dubner titled their popular book, *Freakonomics: A Rogue Economist Explores the Hidden Side of Everything*, while the economist Robert Frank published *The Economic Naturalist: Why Economics Explains Almost Everything.*[16] Unlike these white economists, Welsing gave Fuller full credit and acknowledgement regarding his socio-political supposition on economics and global white supremacy.

Inspired by the works of Cox , Diop, and Fuller, Welsing brilliantly synthesized all three theories: universalist-economic; cultural-historic (anthropological); and historic-economic (cultural-economic) into a psycho-genetic theory of racism. Welsing's understanding went beyond the ubiquitous psychological symbols of the economics of global white supremacy. Wesling introduced a comprehensive understanding of white supremacy as a destructive global psychological (cultural-economic) system.[17]

According to Welsing, she was "impressed by the concept of a 'system' of white domination over the world's 'non-white' peoples [that] could explain the seeming predicament and dilemma of 'non-white' social reality," which ultimately influenced her main thesis of The *Cress Theory of Color-Confrontation and Racism (White Supremacy)* in 1970.[18] To put in context Welsing's theory regarding the pathological and psychological need of whites to oppress, exploit, and exterminate non-whites globally, an analysis of the etiology of economics is crucial.

The Economic Etiology of Global White Supremacy

The worldwide collapse of global white supremacy looked promising as manifested in the decolonization of the *Global South* from the *Global North* in the early 1960s. However, global white supremacy would soon reposition and reshape itself in the form of neo-colonialism, neo-imperialism, and neo-liberalism. By promoting a universalist-economic theory to explain worldwide racism, many scholars thought the *North-South Conflict* (*Color Confrontation*) was mainly centered on the utility and domination of economics as expressed in land, labor, and resources. However, to understand the etiology of economics, one must examine the historical, political, and cultural underpinnings of the psychological evolution of economics under global white supremacy.

Economics originated in Africa, along with writing, speech, language, and other disciplines such as philosophy, psychology, religion, science, medicine, law, mathematics, and so forth. Dr. Jawanza Kunjufu writes: "The history of African economics does not begin in the United States of America. It does not start in 1619, but, rather 350,000 years ago when the first human was recorded to have lived in Africa."[19] Africa is not only the cradle of humanity and civilization, it is also the birthplace of economics, the knowledge and study of everything from our house (the planet earth) and God's estate (the universe) to the utility of life, land, labor, and resources, along with its behavioral practices regarding production, consumption, trade, capital/wealth accumulation, information/ knowledge, and rational/irrational human choices (decision-making).

At any rate, in *Civilization or Barbarism: An Authentic Anthropology*, anthropologist Cheikh Anta Diop states the following:

> Racial differentiation took place in Europe, probably in southern France and Spain, at the end of the last Wurm glaciation, between 40,000 and 20,000 years ago," where "the first inhabitant of Europe was the Grimaldi Black man, who was responsible for the first lithical industry of the European Upper Paleolithic period called Aurignacian industry."[20] Concluding that "the first White appeared only around 20,000 years ago, the Cro-Magnon Man—the result of a mutation from the Grimaldi Negroid due to an existence of 20,000 years in the excessively cold climate of Europe at the end of the last glaciation.[21]

Welsing, in her analysis of economics and global white supremacy, accepted the premise that during and after the Wurm glaciation, the pigmentation of some Black Africans started to deteriorate, especially as they migrated to and settled in Europe. The harsh experience of the Wurm glaciation, coupled with significant pigmentation and Vitamin D loss caused irreparable damage and trauma to the psyche of those Africans who migrated to what eventually became the region of Europe.

As an addendum to Diop's *Two Cradle Theory*, the central thesis of *The Cress Theory* asserts the following:

> White-skinned peoples came into existence thousands of years ago as the albino mutant offspring of black-skinned mothers and fathers in Africa. A sizable number of these Black parents had produced, rejected, and then cast out of the community their genetic defective albino offspring, to live away from the normal black skin-pigmented population, with the awareness of their rejection and alienation (akin to leper colonies).
>
> The white tribe's eventual migration northward, to escape the intensi-

> ty of the equatorial sun of the Southern Hemisphere, left the albinos eventually situated in the area of the world known as Europe—now recognized as the home of the white tribes. This early rejection of the albino offspring might be viewed as a prehistoric (pre-Western civilization) instance of parental rejection, child neglect, and abuse.[22]

However, according to Diop, the manifestation of an albino is a pathological occurrence, whereas the existence of a depigmented white is not a pathological occurrence because unlike the albino, the depigmented white became white normally by adapting to a cold climate.[23] Furthermore, notable scholar Vulindlela I. Wobogo in *Cold Wind From the North: The Prehistoric European Origin of Racism Explained by Diop's Two Cradle Theory*, makes the following inference: "Albinos have African features, morphology, and hair, and the mutation of these traits to those of whites must still be explained even if albinism were a prominent feature of the racial differentiation."[24] Welsing surmises in the *Isis Papers* that the albino African living in the extreme cold, hostile environment of Europe, developed a deep-rooted survival mechanism vis-à-vis a conscious and/or subconscious pathological narcissism, profound sense of self-alienation and anxiety, xenophobia, and an enduring fear of genetic annihilation. Welsing maintains that to survive the European developed an intense desire to enslave and exterminate non-whites while dominating their land, labor, and resources. They did this by engaging in abnormal and aggressive behavioral practices and irrational economic policies regarding production, consumption, trade, capital/wealth accumulation, and the production and distribution of information/knowledge which ultimately manifested into a system of global white supremacy.

The Economics of Global White Supremacy

The *Global South* has an abundance of resources in comparison to the *Global North*, but it is the *Global North* that manufactures the abundance of goods, while controlling the services and supplies. As such, industries in the *Global North* are capital intensive, while industries in the *Global South* are labor intensive. From 1492 to the present, industries in the European-American world can be described as capital intensive, where the economic activity requires emerging technology along with an indefinite amount of investments. Large amounts of capital, financial backing, and underwriting, underpinned by speculation are applied to process raw materials and manufacture goods by maintaining a high degree of production and profit margins, while keeping interest rates low. As a pernicious and enduring consequence:

> In a capitalist society that goes low, wages are depressed as businesses compete over the price, not the quality, of goods; so-called unskilled workers are typically incentivized through punishments, not promotions; inequality reigns and poverty spreads. In the United States, the richest 1 percent of Americans own 40 percent of the country's wealth, while a larger share of working-age people (18-65) live in poverty than in any other nation belonging to the Organization for Economic Cooperation and Development (O.E.C.D.).[25]

In warmer climates such as Africa, Latin America, and the Caribbean, economic activity required more labor than capital to produce goods. For example, raw materials harvested on the plantations (colonial labor camps) and extracted from the mines fueled the colonial economy, by free (slave) labor, illustrating how this type of production served as the bedrock of capitalism and global white supremacy.

In "American Capitalism is Brutal. You Can Trace That to the Plantation," Pulitzer Prize winning sociologist Matthew Desmond contends the following:

> Slavery was undeniably a font of phenomenal wealth. By the eve of the Civil War, the Mississippi Valley was home to more millionaires per capita than anywhere else in the United States. Cotton grown and picked by enslaved workers was the nation's most valuable export. The combined value of enslaved people exceeded that of all the railroads and factories in the nation. New Orleans boasted a denser concentration of banking capital than New York City. What made the cotton economy boom in the United States, and not in all the other far-flung parts of the world with climates and soil suitable to the crop, was our nation's unflinching willingness to use violence on nonwhite people and to exert its will on seemingly endless supplies of land and labor.[26]

However, before a worldwide European and U.S. American hegemony, Africa had a communal mode of production (economic system) that was rich in land, labor (people), and resources. In contrast, Europe had a feudal mode of production (economic system) and was scarce in fertile land, labor (people), and natural resources. History and economics took a turn with the beginning of the transatlantic slave trade and the expulsion of African Moors from the Iberian Peninsula. This transition provided Western Europe with a competitive economic advantage on the world stage.

In his classic tome, *How Europe Underdeveloped Africa,* Pan-African scholar and socio-political historian Walter Rodney states the following:

> Western Europe and Africa had a relationship, which insured the transfer of wealth from Africa to Europe. The transfer was possible only after trade became truly international; and that takes one back to the late fifteenth century when Africa and Europe were drawn into common relations for the first time along with Asia and the Americas. The developed and underdeveloped parts of the present capitalist section of the world have been in continuous contact for four and a half centuries. The contention here is that over that period Africa helped to develop Western Europe in the same proportion as Western Europe helped to underdevelop Africa.[27]

According to African-centered political scientist Dr. Leonard Jeffries Jr., starting in 1482, there was a fifty-year turning point in world economic history, which served as the decisive juncture for the development of Europe and the underdevelopment of Africa and the Americas. In his analysis, Jeffries proclaims that external economic factors such as slavery, colonialism, imperialism, and capitalism gave rise to a worldwide European and U.S. American hegemonic system. In his foreword to the late Pan-African historian John Henrik Clarke's *Christopher Columbus and the Afrikan Holocaust: Slavery and the Rise of Capitalism*, Jeffries articulates the following proposition:

> The fifty-year period from 1482 to 1536 A.D. has special significance

> for world history. During this period, the European's world was able to synthesize various economic, political, and cultural forces and lay the foundation for a global system of power, centered around materialism, capitalism, and imperialism. At the heart of the new global system of European-American materialism was super exploitation of the indigenous people of the Western hemisphere and the enslavement of Africans. As a result, two worlds collided and left us with a legacy of genocidal institutionalized White supremacy. African and Native American humanism lost out to the system of European materialism.[28]

Dr. John Henrik Clarke, in *Christopher Columbus and the Afrikan Holocaust*, advances a 200-year period (1400s–1600s) where the economic realities of slavery, colonialism, imperialism, and capitalism gave rise to global white supremacy and the false notion that whites are superior and Blacks are inferior. Nana Ekow Butweiku (Harold Dicks), a scholar-activist and intellectual contemporary of Dr. Clarke, builds on Jeffries' and Clarke's postulations by meticulously chronicling the sadistic behavior of Europeans within a 500-year turning point period (1400s – 1900s) in his classic, well-researched work, *500 Years of European Behavior: Its Effect on Afrika and African People*.

Ole Jorgen Benedictow, a Norwegian historian known for his work on the etiology of plagues, believes that the hyper-aggressive behavior of Europeans began with the advent of the bubonic plague, also known as the Black Death. From 1346 to 1353, the so-called Black Death killed an estimated fifty million Europeans (60 percent of Europe's population).[29] To survive and avoid the plague, much of the population had to ultimately leave western Europe. It is postulated that during this era, the aggression among whites mounted into the domination of other nations' land, labor, and resources. In the context of Welsing's theory, whites, in fear of genetic annihilation from the Black Death, escalated their violent behavior as historically demonstrated by their increase in wars, crime, religious flagellants, and the persecution of non-whites and non-Christians.[30]

When the military invasion of Europe began in the fifteenth century around the world, the economic rise of Europe was concurrent with the demise of Africa and the Native population of the Americas. As a result of the transatlantic slave trade, nearly 100 million innocent Africans perished, as the Native population in the Americas faced genocide.[31] From 1492 until 1508, it is estimated that three million indigenous groups in the Caribbean died due to European invasion.[32] Furthermore, throughout the Americas, it is estimated that the Europeans exterminated about fifty-six million Native Americans by 1600.[33] Thus, as European colonizers murdered a lot of Native people in various conflicts (color confrontations) and also by spreading disease (biological warfare), the indigenous population in the Americas was reduced by 90 percent in the century after the barbaric European raids of the Americas and the Caribbean in 1492.[34] Consequently, "European colonization of the Americas resulted in the killing of so many native people that it transformed the environment and caused the Earth's climate to cool down" which also resulted in not only "large-scale depopulation" but also "in vast tracts of agricultural land being left untended."[35]

On January 2, 1492, Abu Abdi-Llah (Boabdil), the African Moorish leader, surrendered to the Spanish monarchy. Following the expulsion of the Moors in Spain, Queen Isabella I of Castile sanctioned and financed Columbus' militaristic "voyages" to the Americas. This led to the African Moors becoming one of the first groups to be enslaved and transported to the Americas. Later that year, the first king of the Songhai Empire, King Sunni Ali (Ber) died. With his death came a series of internal conflicts in the western part of Africa which left the continent vulnerable to Arab and European enslavers. According to Jeffries, at that time, the global political economy started to shift permanently from a communal system to a capitalist system by way of mercantilism, slavery, colonialism, imperialism, and a plantation-based economy centered on the export of enslaved African captives, sugar, rum, molasses, tobacco, cocoa, and bullions.[36]

By 1482, the Portuguese, in search of gold, had established a trading fort known as Elmina Castle on the Gold Coast (present-day Ghana), and held captive Africans who would later be transported to the Americas. Rodney notes that "the ships of the Portuguese gave the search for gold the highest priority, partly on the basis of well-known information that

West African gold reached Europe across the Sahara."[37] The "Europeans were anxious to acquire gold from Africa because there was a pressing need for gold coins within the growing capitalist money economy" as "Europe allocated to Africa the role of supplier of human captives to be used as slaves in various parts of the world."[38] Within a few years, Portugal and Spain were in competition to seek riches (gold and silver) beyond the shores of West Africa. It was during this era of exploitation, that the balance of the global economy changed from communalism to feudalism to capitalism...Africa and the Americas became impoverished, as Europe became enriched.

In *Capitalism and Slavery*, the first Prime Minister of Trinidad and Tobago, Dr. Eric Williams, discusses in his thesis the fact that profit maximization led to the mass enslavement of Africans which led to an established psychological and institutional acceptance of slavery in the promotion of capitalism. Williams postulates that "slavery is not a product of Western capitalism; Western capitalism is a product of slavery."[39] Williams, like Rodney, adduces the universalist-economic thesis by incorporating the historic-economic proposition of capitalism as the main rationale and origin for slavery, racism, and global white supremacy. However, for Welsing, it was not necessarily economics but the deep psychological urge for genetic survival that motivated Europeans to kill and enslave other people as they stole their lands and resources.

As an addendum to the theses of Rodney, Williams, and Welsing, the late scholar Cedric J. Robinson advanced a notion of racial capitalism which challenged the Marxist idea that capitalism was a revolutionary negation of feudalism. Instead, capitalism emerged within the feudal order and flowered in the cultural soil of a Western civilization which was thoroughly infused with racialism. Capitalism and racism, in other words, did not break from the old order but rather evolved from it to produce a modern world system of "racial capitalism" dependent on slavery, violence, imperialism, and genocide. Capitalism was "racial" not because of some conspiracy to divide workers or justify slavery and dispossession, but because racialism had already permeated Western feudal society.[40]

Williams was the first scholar to identify and call this worldwide economic exploitation of trading human beings and raw materials the *Triangular Trade*, which is defined as a multilateral global trading system which involved enslaved human captives from Africa taken to the Americas in exchange for commodities that were then taken to Europe. Rodney, in agreement with Williams, observed the following: "the exploitation of Africa and African labor continued to be a source for the accumulation of capital to be reinvested in Western Europe" where "Europe became the center of a world-wide system and…it was European capitalism, which set slavery and the Atlantic slave trade in motion."[41]

By becoming some of the largest trading centers globally, Europe and the United States have continued to dominate international trade and transactional exchange (buying and selling) of goods. Rodney describes these as economic monopolies, by stating: "What was called international trade was nothing but the overseas of European interests" where "Europe had a monopoly of knowledge about the international exchange system seen as a whole, for Western Europe was the only sector capable of viewing the system as a whole."[42] The foundation of the capitalist system is in part the creation of whites' psychological obsession with power and sequestering the land, labor, and resources of people of color. This is clearly illustrated in their quest for gold from the Empires of Africa.

From 1000 to 1500 A.D., the majority of Europe's gold came from West Africa.[43] To provide a historical context for the expansion of trade and the burgeoning economic structure of the Europeans and eventually North America, it is necessary to go back again to 1482. During this era, Africa and the Americas were homes to the great empires of Ghana, Mali, Songhai, the Moors, Mayans, Incas, the Aztecs, and many more. Europeans invariably sought refuge from the harsh European environment and lack of resources through escalating trade with Africa. Valued minerals, particularly gold and silver, motivated the Europeans to expand their quests for more resources to augment their respective economies as detailed in New *Dimensions of African History* by Pan-African scholar John Henrik Clarke and Egyptologist Yosef Ben-Jochannan.

Therefore, the global travels of Africans and the knowledge of enormous gold reserves as displayed by Mansa Musa of Mali played a major role in attracting Europeans to Africa and the Americas, leading to war (color confrontation) and the destruction of planet earth, particularly throughout African and Native American lives and lands.

Gold from sub-Saharan Africa started to circulate heavily during the early fourteenth century, around 1324–1325. The historical record indicates that the increase in the circulation of gold was due to the immense wealth of Emperor Mansa Musa of Mali, who freely distributed his incalculable gold reserves to many people he met through his travels on the way to Mecca. It was the Emperor's philanthropy that brought European attention to Africa's wealth.[44]

Emperor Musa, who historically is considered to have been the richest person in the world, reigned over 2,000 miles of land. Musa's wealth outstrips the wealth of all billionaires in US dollars in 2019 including Jeff Bezos, Bill Gates, and Warren Buffet. As such, with a current net worth of roughly $400 billion today, Mansa Musa is "the richest person that has ever walked on this planet" where, "just for comparison: the richest person alive at the moment, the founder of Amazon, Jeff Bezos, is worth about $131 billion and Bill Gates, with his $ 96.5 billion is the second person on the list of the richest people."[45] Musa, who was a devout Muslim, went to Cairo, Egypt to Mecca. It was during this 4,000-mile pilgrimage that those who encountered his caravan of 60,000 were exposed to gowns of brocade and over 500 "slaves" bearing gold staffs.[46] The historical record indicates that while in Cairo, Musa spent so much gold on the poor that he caused mass inflation in the area.[47]

This journey literally placed Mansa Musa on the world map. Emperor Musa is included in the 1375 Catalan Atlas, one of the most important maps of Medieval Europe (see the following illustration). As the story goes, the news of his wealth spread across the Mediterranean and shaped European views of Mali as a place of splendor, wealth, and sophistication, which became the impetus for the Portuguese to begin its naval raids against the empire in the 1400s. Thus, it was during the fourteenth century that the local currency in West Africa were cowrie shells;

while, gold and salt were the main mediums of transnational exchange and international trade.[48] Gold was, and continues to be, valuable as it is used as a medium of exchange in the global market.

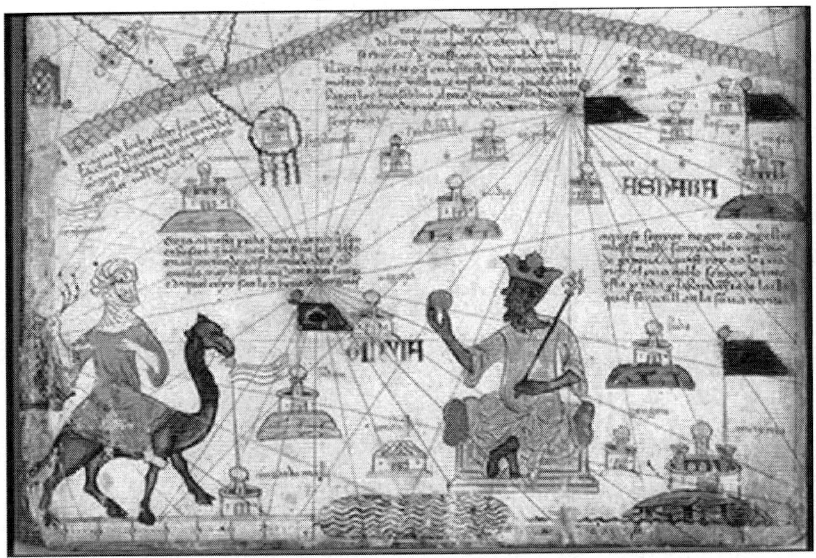

Emperor Mansa Musa of Mali holding a gold nugget.[49]

In his seminal work, *They Came Before Columbus*, Guyanese anthropologist Ivan Van Sertima states that it was the gold from Mali that funded West African merchants to explore the Americas before Columbus. Even with the fall of Mali, under the Songhai Empire, gold endured as the main product in trans-Saharan trade, followed by kola nuts and the selling and trading of enslaved African captives.[50]

In typical lectures about the transatlantic slave trade, it is not often mentioned that Switzerland and Norway played a major role. With regard to Switzerland, "Swiss banks, for example, owned as much as a third of the Compagnie des Indes, a French company that held a monopoly over the West African slave trade, while trading houses financed and did business with slave traders."[51] In addition, "Norwegians made up around 10 percent of the total crew serving on slave ships at any one time" where "Norwegians staffed slave forts on the African coast, sailed on the slave ships and carried goods produced by slaves back to Norway and the rest of Europe. The 'triangle' went mostly from Norway and Denmark to Ghana, then to Caribbean ports such as St. Croix and St. Thomas and back to Scandinavia."[52]

In reference to the convergence of other people's land, labor, and resources, variously usurped by the Europeans, the extent of such pillaging is not well known. For example, from 1503 to 1660, Spain embezzled so much silver and other precious metals from the Americas that it multiplied all the reserves of Europe by four.[53] It is often stated that the silver that was misappropriated from the mines of the Americas and the bones of the Native population that died laboring for the Spanish crown in these silver mines could have been used to construct a bridge from the Americas to Spain.[54] Black conservative economist Thomas Sowell cites:

> There is no question that the Spaniards' conquest in the Western Hemisphere, for example, not only brutalized the conquered peoples and destroyed viable civilizations, but also drained vast amounts of existing wealth in gold and silver from the Western hemisphere to Spain—200 tons of gold and more than 18,000 tons of silver—the result of the looting of existing treasures from the indigenous peoples and the forced labor of that same population in gold and silver mines. Nor was Spain unique in such behavior. But the question here, however is: To what extent can transfers of wealth explain economic differences between peoples and nations in the world today? Spain is today one of the poorer countries in Western Europe, surpassed economically by countries like Switzerland and Norway, which have never had such empires.[55]

In *The Ascent of Money*, historian Niall Ferguson also claimed that Spain became overly dependent on the Americas with the revenues that gold and silver generated by way of mercantilism and free, forced labor. Further, with a mercantile system, capital inflows were limited despite rapid economic expansion because European empires like Spain were dependent on the massive capital flowing from the Americas, where the colonies could only trade exclusively with its colonial empire. This created a financial and credit crisis that led to worldwide warfare, as illustrated in the American Revolution of 1776, the French Revolution of 1789, and the Haitian Revolution of 1804. The Haitian Revolution became the ultimate color confrontation between Blacks and whites as Haiti became the first and only successful "slave" revolution and Black republic in the Western Hemisphere.

To understand how Spain became one of the poorest countries in Western Europe—but not in the world—one must understand that, in capturing gold from the Americas, Philip II of Spain defaulted on Spain's debts. According to Ferguson, Spain was known as a sovereign default nation, the first nation to become delinquent in repaying its debts due to the high cost of operating overseas colonies, rising military expenditures and ship building costs, and the devaluation of gold. Consequently, speculators lost confidence in Spain's capital-intensive industries and venture capital colonial exploits as Spain started to lose its economic grip on its overseas colonies. From that point on, it became extremely difficult and costly for Spain to borrow money and remain wealthy.

Within the psychological context of Welsing's thinking, the European lust for gold in particular goes deeper than the economic value bestowed upon it; this appetite was motivated by the unconscious desire of whites to be Black. Gold is a radiant yellowish-brown (tan) precious metal that guarantees the value and utility of currencies (monies). Welsing makes the connection between the color of gold and melanin by presenting the following argument:

> I therefore theorize that because: 1) black and brown skin (melanin pigmented skin), with its natural oils, glistening and gleaming in the sunlight, looks like gold (as is attested to in the white supremacy culture by the frequent references to a "golden tan," meaning a golden brown or black color), and 2) that which was deeply desired more than anything else by the albino mutant's pigmented skin, then the metal gold (the only metal substance with lasting luster and a color that approximates the color tones of melanin pigment) became the deeply unconscious symbol of the most desired substance in the entire global white supremacy system/culture. Gold is then the symbol for melanin skin pigment in the white psyche. The possession of gold in the

white psyche is the unconscious equalizer for the absence in whites of melanin.[56]

Along with usurping land, labor, and resources, whites have engaged in monopolizing information and knowledge about themselves, Blacks, and the world at large by portraying themselves as superior and others as inferior. This has been achieved by seizing sole proprietorship of knowledge production and information dissemination. As the colonizers of information and knowledge, whites have employed information asymmetry (e.g. misinformation, propaganda, and gaslighting) as a useful tool to continue to achieve economic imbalance in our house (planet earth) and the God's estate (the universe). From a hegemonic perspective, Western epistemology is deemed to be scientific, universal, and based on truth, while all other forms of knowledge are viewed/portrayed as superstitious, not universal, and unscientific. Therefore, by monopolizing and colonizing information and knowledge, adverse selection overwhelms the decision-making process of non-whites within a global white supremacist economic market system. What follows is that people of color often make decisions about their NAPA based on the information or knowledge given to them by whites, which often leads to negative outcomes for people of color. Thus, whites not only colonized land, labor, and resources, but also information and knowledge, along with the minds (and hearts) of non-whites, to solidify not only their economic dominance, but also their genetic survival.

The late African-centered political scientist Jacob H. Carruthers refers to whites' colonization of information as an full-blown attack against knowledge in his scholarly work, *Intellectual Warfare*. In his critique, Carruthers refers to white and Black scholars who promote a Eurocentric worldview. This is done primarily through curricula, which is standardized and promotes the worldview of mostly white males. In essence, the promotion of the Eurocentric worldview and capitalistic system is not only intellectual warfare, but it is also a moral hazard. Whites have profited immensely by not fairly engaging contractually with Blacks, especially in international trade, given the unequal exchange of economics and knowledge which is based on manipulation, force, deception, and imperfect information.

To undergird the plausibility of Welsing's thesis regarding whites' psychological fear of being genetically annihilated by Blacks, it is important to apply her thesis from a historical-economic perspective. "Between 1492 and 1914, Europeans conquered 84 percent of the globe"; by 1919, "over 1.2 billion people out of a world population of 1.8 billion, which translates to 70 percent, resided in colonies, semi-colonies or dominions."[57] By 1966, direct colonial rule had dematerialized in most of Africa, Asia, Latin America, and the Caribbean where "only some thirty million people (mainly in southern Africa, together with several small islands and territories scattered throughout the world), amounted to considerably less than one percent of mankind, who remained under European or American rule."[58] Yet, as direct colonial rule exited Africa, Asia, Latin America, and the Caribbean, indirect colonial rule (neocolonialism, neo-imperialism, neoliberalism, and post-racialism) entered.

Map: "European Colonialism Conquered Every Country in the World but These Five" – Vox, 2015.

From the fifteenth century to the present, with the rise of the system of global white supremacy, Europe has dominated (i.e. colonized and/or enslaved) most of the world. As of 2015, roughly 95 percent of the world's landmasses, including the countless people therein, have been under the colonial control of Europe, except for five countries as illustrated in the map below.[59]

As a consequence of slavery, colonialism, and imperialism (global white supremacy), the total GDP (Gross Domestic Product) of the colonizers (Portugal, Spain, France, United Kingdom, Denmark, Netherlands, Germany, Italy, Belgium, and the United States) is (US) $30 trillion, with the GDP of the United States still growing at 54 percent of the above total at (US) $16.8 trillion.[60] GDP is the main indicator used to measure or determine the condition of a nation's economy based on economic output (all earned income and/or expenditures). GDP therefore indicates the economic size and health of a nation based on its monetary or market (total dollar) value for all finished goods and services that are produced yearly[61]. On that account, "conversely, at just US$247, South Sudan has the world's lowest GDP per capita, and many countries, predominantly in Africa, have a GDP per capita below US$1000. Based on UN and IMF figures, the United States has the largest GDP in the world at $20.4 trillion (IMF) and $18.6 trillion (UN)."[62]

Whereas GDP measures the production of goods and services within a nation, GNI (Gross National Income) measures the income of a nation's residents and businesses, even if the goods and services are produced outside of that nation. In comparison to Europe and the United States, where the average net wealth exceeds $100,000 per year, the top twenty poorest countries in the world, except for Haiti, are in Africa with a per capita of under $2,000 per year as illustrated below:

Liberia—GNI per capita: $710
The Central African Republic— GNI per capita: $730
Burundi—GNI per capita: $770
The Democratic Republic of the Congo—GNI per capita: $870
Niger —GNI per capita: $990

Malawi—GNI per capita: $1,180
Mozambique—GNI per capita: $1,200
Sierra Leone—GNI per capita: $1,480
Madagascar—GNI per capita: $1,510
Comoros—GNI per capita: $1,570
Togo—GNI per capita: $1,620
Gambia—GNI per capita: $1,700
Guinea-Bissau—GNI per capita: $1,700
Burkina Faso—GNI per capita: $1,810
Uganda—GNI per capita: $1,820
Haiti—GNI per capita: $1,830
Zimbabwe—GNI per capita: $1,850
Ethiopia—GNI per capita: $1,890
Chad—GNI per capita: $1,920
Rwanda—GNI per capita: $1,990[63]

Surprisingly and sadly, the home of the wealthiest person who has ever walked the earth is now one of the poorest countries in the world. In terms of global poverty, Mansa Musa's Mali now ranks twenty-two with a GNI per capita: $2,160.[64] Moreover, the first Black republic and the only successful "slave" revolution in the Americas to abolish both chattel slavery and colonialism is now the poorest country in the Western Hemisphere with a "GDP per capita of $870 in 2018 and a Human Development Index ranking of 163 out of 188 countries in 2016. Based on the most recent household survey (2012), over 6 million Haitians live below the poverty line with less than US$2.41 per day, and more than 2.5 million fall below the extreme poverty line (US$1.23 per day)."[65]

Not surprisingly, in comparison to the per capita income of the poorest nations in the world, President Donald Trump's cabinet is worth a total of about $14 billion. For example, Betsy DeVos, Secretary of Education, comes from a family worth more than $5 billion; Todd Ricketts, the co-owner of the Chicago Cubs and the CEO of Ending Spending is now the U.S. Deputy Commerce Secretary, his $5.3 billion fortune came from his father's business, Ameritrade. Linda McMahon, who is the Small

Business Administrator of the United States in the Trump administration, has family wealth worth of $1.2 billion; and Vincent Viola, who was being considered for Army Secretary, but withdrew, is worth $1.77 billion. Trump's selection for Treasury Secretary, Steve Mnuchin, has a net worth of $655 million, while Secretary of Commerce Wilbur Ross is worth $2.5 billion.[66] Thus, "when it comes to billionaire population[s], the United States dominates with 27 percent of the world's billionaires. Its total billionaire count rose [by 4 percent (705 billionaires) between] 2017 to 2018... Meanwhile, total billionaire wealth worldwide decreased by 5 percent to [equal] slightly more than $3 trillion."[67]

Given the massive generational wealth disparities and inequalities that have been produced by global white supremacy via slavery, colonialism, and imperialism, prominent scholar and activist Sandew Hira, in his *20 Questions and Answers about Reparations for Colonialism,* provides a detailed economic distribution of what is owed to us (descendants of our African Ancestors) in US$ trillions by way of reparations. As illustrated in the table below, Hira based his calculations in US$ trillions on the following factors: human injury and suffering caused by slavery and colonialism; the building of enterprise and the development of real estate on other people's property without payment; taking goods without payment; and non-remuneration for services rendered (labor).[68]

Sandew Hira's Reparations Calculation Table (US$ Trillions)

Region	Human Suffering	Rent	Stolen Goods	Unpaid Wages	TOTAL
Asia/Middle East	212	96		1,444	**1,752**
Africa	174	286		1,212	**1, 672**
South America	29,481	67,758	8,178	212,633	**313,050**
North America	25	4,438		148	**4, 611**
TOTAL	**29,892**	**67, 578**	**8, 178**	**215,437**	**321,086**

Conclusion

Global white supremacy is sustained by several factors, such as the environment, economics, psychology, culture, and genetics. As such, there are several theories that explain the origin of white supremacy and why whites dominate the global economic market. The *Cress Theory,* being perhaps the most tendentious and plausible theory, explains the origins of white supremacy and why whites have been successful in their economic domination of non-whites.

Welsing's theory on global white supremacy posits that whites subconsciously feel inferior to Blacks because of their recessive genetic makeup. According to the *Cress Theory*, it is this particular biological (genetic) factor that psychologically compels whites to act with extreme aggression toward non-whites, an inclination manifested from an unconscious rage that they cannot be Black due to a lack of melanin production (albinism). Within this context Welsing focused "on what possible motivational forces, operative at both the individual and group levels, that could account for the evolution of these patterns of social behavioral practice that function in all areas of human activity (economics, education, entertainment, labor, law, politics, religion, sex, and war)."[69] Further, to fully comprehend the psychological factors and economic forces that account for this global system as it functions, one must classify the symptoms and systematization of white supremacy as a worldwide disease or pathology.

Although Dr. Frances Cress Welsing was not an economist, as a psychiatrist and behavioral scientist, she, like a plethora of "classical economists," fully understood the relationship between economics and psychology, which she put to use by presenting and advancing psychological interpretations and analyses of economic behavior and motivation. Until her transition in 2016, Dr. Welsing never deviated from her original thesis regarding race relations (color confrontation) and the global system of white supremacy. Welsing's theory has generated much debate and has been useful in providing psychological explanations regarding the economics that we witness today at our house and in God's estate.

Endnotes

1 Lawrence Edward Carter, "African Civilizations as Cornerstone for the Oikoumene," in *Nile Valley Civilizations*, ed. Ivan Van Sertima (USA: Journal of African Civilizations, 1989), 14.

2 Ibid., 14.

3 Oliver C. Cox, *Caste, Class and Race: A Study in Social Dynamics*. (New York: Monthly Review Press, 1948).

4 In 1960, the seventeen African countries which declared their independence from European colonial forces included Benin, Burkina Faso, Cameroon, Central African Republic, Chad, Congo, Congo -DRC, Cote d' Ivoire, Gabon, Madagascar, Mali, Mauritania, Niger, Nigeria, Senegal, Somalia, and Togo. DRC gained its independence from Belgium; Nigeria from Britain; Somalia from both Britain and Italy; and the remaining countries from France.

5 Frances Cress Welsing. *The Cress Theory of Color-Confrontation and Racism (White Supremacy): A Psycho-Genetic Theory and World Outlook* (Washington DC: C.R. Publishers, 1970), 4.

6 Ibid., 4.

7 Ibid., 4.

8 Vulindlela I. Wobogo, *Cold Wind from the North: The Prehistoric European Origin of Racism Explained by Diop's Two Cradle Theory* (Charleston, SC: Books on Demand, 2011), 266.

9 Ibid., 265.

10 Leonard Jeffries Jr., "Civilization or Barbarism: The Legacy of Cheikh Anta Diop," in *Great African Thinkers*, ed. Ivan Van Sertima (New Brunswick: Transaction Books, 1989), 157.

11 Ibid., 157.

12 Neely Fuller Jr., *The United Independent Compensatory Code/System/Concept: A Compensatory Counter-Racist Code* (USA: Neely Fuller Jr., 2016), 59.

13 Ibid., 2 & 59.

14 Ha-Joon Chang, *Economics: The User's Guide* (New York: Bloomsbury, 2014).

15 Ibid., 15.

16 Ibid., 15–16.

17 In *An African Answer: The Key to Global Productivity*, international management consultant Edgar J. Ridley states that any symbol or symbolic thinking is based on myth and fiction; whereas, a symptom or symptomatic thinking is based on reality and truth (53 -54). For Ridley, thinking only symbolically is abnormal and is a mis- adventure neurologically; whereas, thinking symptomatically is a normal and natural way of thinking (53 – 54). Therefore, thinking only in terms of symbols creates a paralysis of analysis; whereas, thinking symptomatically provides us with a system analysis.

18 Frances Cress Welsing, *The Cress Theory of Color-Confrontation and Racism (White Supremacy)*, 4.

19 Jawanza Kunjufu, *Black Economics: Solutions for Economic and Community Empowerment* (Chicago: African American Images, 1991), 16.
20 Cheikh Anta Diop, *Civilization or Barbarism: An Authentic Anthropology* (USA: Lawrence Books, 1991), 13 -14.
21 Ibid., 15 – 16.
22 Frances Cress Welsing, *The Isis Papers*, 23-24
23 Edgar J. Ridley, *An African Answer: The Key to Global Productivity* (Trenton: Africa World Press, 1992), 58-60.
24 Vulindlela I. Wobogo, *Cold Wind from the North* (California: CreateSpace Independent Publishing Platform, 2011) , 295 - 296.
25 Matthew Desmond, "American Capitalism is Brutal. You Can Trace That to the Plantation," *The New York Times*, August 14, 2019, Retrieved from https://www.nytimes.com/interactive/2019/08/14/magazine/slavery-capitalism.html
26 Ibid.
27 Walter Rodney, *How Europe Underdeveloped Africa* (Washington DC: Howard University Press, 1981), 75.
28 Leonard Jeffries Jr., "Forward," in *Christopher Columbus and the Afrikan Holocaust: Slavery and the Rise of European Capitalism* by John Henrik Clarke (New York: A & B Publishers Group, 1993), 10.
29 Ole J. Benedictow, "The Black Death: Greatest Catastrophe Ever," History Today, March 3, 2005. Retrieved from http://www.historytoday.com/ole-j-benedictow/ black-death-greatest-catastrophe-ever.
30 Samuel K. Cohn, "The Black Death: End of a Paradigm," *American Historical Review*, vol 107, 3, (2002), 703–737.
31 John Henrik Clarke, *Christopher Columbus and the Afrikan Holocaust: Slavery and the Rise of European Capitalism* (New York: A & B Publishers Group, 1993).
32 Eric Williams, *From Columbus to Castro: The History of the Caribbean* (New York: Vintage Books, 1984).
33 Oliver Milman, "European colonization of Americas killed so many it Cooled Earth's climate", *The Guardian*, January 31, 2019. Retrieved from https://www.theguardian.com/ environment/2019/jan/31/european-colonization-of-americas-helped-cause-climate-change
34 Ibid.
35 Ibid.
36 Leonard Jeffries Jr., "Forward," in *Christopher Columbus and the Afrikan Holocaust*, 10.
37 Walter Rodney, *How Europe Underdeveloped Africa*, 77.
38 Ibid., 77.
39 Garikai Chengu, "How Slaves Built American Capitalism," Counter Punch, December 2015. Retrieved from https://www.counterpunch.org/2015/12/18/how-slaves-built-american-capitalism/
40 obin D.G. Kelly, "What did Cedric Robinson Mean by Racial Capitalism."

Boston Review, January 12, 2017.Retrieved from http://bostonreview.net/race/robin-d-g-kel- ley-what-did-cedric-robinson-mean-racial-capitalism.
41 Rodney, *How Europe Underdeveloped Africa*, 82 & 84.
42 Ibid., 75-76.
43 Henry Louis Gates, *Africa's Great Civilizations: Empires of Gold*, February 28, 2017. Retrieved from http://www.pbs.org.
44 Excerpts, Aine Caine, *Business Insider*, February, 2018.
45 *TopBuzz*, "10 Rich People From the Past That Make Modern Billionaires Look Small," August 19, 2019. Retrieved from https://www.topbuzz.com/a/6727049097292808709?app_id=1106&c=sys&gid=6727049097292808709&-impr_id=6731459399351601413&language=en&re- gion=us&user_id=6707019744992478213..
46 Jessica Smith-TED-Ed Lectures, May 2015.
47 Ibid.
48 The Metropolitan Museum of Art, 2000. Retrieved from www.metmuseum.org.
49 *Abraham Cresques, The Catalan Atlas of 1375*(France:*Bibliothèque Nationale de France*, 1373).
50 Ivan Van Sertima, *They Came Before Columbus* (New York: Random House, 1976).
51 SWI, "Switzerland Played Key Role in the Slave Trade," *Swissinfo.ch*, August 22, 2003. Retrieved from http://www.swissinfo.ch/eng/switzerland-played-key-role-in-the-slavet- rade/3472130
52 Philippe Diaz, *The End of Poverty*, 2008,. Retrieved from http://www.theend-ofpoverty.com/.
53 Philippe Diaz, *The End of Poverty*, 2008,. Retrieved from http://www.theend-ofpoverty.com/.
54 bid.
55 Thomas Sowell, *Wealth, Poverty, and Economics* (New York: Basic Books, 2016), 6.
56 Welsing, *The Isis Papers,* 204.
57 Jack Woddis, *Introduction to Neo-Colonialism*, (New York: International Publishers Company, 1968), 28
58 Ibid., 28.
59 Max Fisher, "Map: European Colonialism Conquered Every Country in the World but These Five," *Vox*, February 24, 2015. Retrieved from http://www.vox.
60 Hira, 20 *Questions and Answers about Reparations for Colonialism*, 77.
61 Ibid., 77.
62 *World Population Review*, "GDP Ranked by Country 2019." Retrieved from http://worldpopulationreview.com/countries/countries-by-gdp.
63 *World Population Review*, "Poorest Countries in the World 2019," August 27, 2019. Retrieved from http://worldpopulationreview.com/countries/poorest-coun-tries-in-the-world/.

64 Ibid.
65 The World Bank, *The World Bank in Haiti* (April 5, 2019). Retrieved from https://www. worldbank.org/en/country/haiti/overview
66 Aimee Picchi, "Donald Trump's Cabinet: $14 Billion of Wealth and Counting," *CBS Money Watch*, December 9, 2016. Retrieved from http://www.cbsnews.com/news/donald- trumps-cabinet-14-billion-of-wealth-and-counting/. See also http://www.cbsnews. com/pictures/donald-trumps-14-billion-cabinet/.
67 Hillary Hoffower, "The Top 15 Countries with the Most Billionaires, Ranked," Business Insider, May 12, 2019,Retrieved from https://amp.businessinsider.com/where-do-billion- aires-live-top-countries-ranked-2019-5,
68 Hira, *20 Questions and Answers about Reparations for Colonialism*, 74 - 80.
69 Frances Cress Welsing, *The Isis Papers*, 4.

CHAPTER 2

VOICES ECHOING CHANGE:

CHALLENGING THE WHITE SUPREMACIST EDUCATIONAL SYSTEM

Yaa Asantewaa Nzingha

> Black people must learn that no system of oppression ever maximally develops those whom the system is specifically structured to dominate. Such a system only permits the oppressed to survive so they can continue being oppressed. No system of oppression is structured consciously to destroy itself.
>
> —Dr. Frances Cress Welsing

As an educator, getting parents to understand the significance of Brother Malcolm X's quote, "Only a fool would let his enemy teach his children," and how it relates to Dr. Welsing's profound words above, has always been a challenge. Unfortunately, as a people, too often we believe that white supremacist institutions headed by white supremacist instructors are the answer to our survival, causing us to allow, even celebrate, having our oppressors/enemies teach our children. I cringe when I hear Black people boast about their child's acceptance to an Ivy League school; followed by headlines such as CNN's, "There must be something in the water at Elmont Memorial High School. For the second year in a row, an Elmont High School student has been accepted into all eight Ivy League schools."[1] Elmont is a predominately Black school. This statement blatantly suggests that Black youth are inferior and must ingest some magical potion to be accepted into the oppressors' racist institutions, supporting Dr. Welsing's analysis that "Inferiorization is essential to the process of oppression."

More disturbing are beliefs within Black communities that badges of honor have been bestowed upon them when their youth attend schools like Harvard, Yale, Princeton, Brown, Dartmouth, and others.

I remember my disappointment when I worked at an African-centered school and although they had a strong African revolutionary curriculum; its claim to fame was having one of its students accepted to Princeton. As I listened to this statement being delivered with "much pride," I feared that all the greatness that had been bestowed on this student would be destroyed at Princeton. A quote by Dr. John Henrik Clarke in his book, *Notes for An African World Revolution*,[2] reverberated in my mind; He aptly states:

> The crisis in African education is really a crisis in African self-confidence. Most of us who have thought seriously about the matter know that our former slave masters cannot afford to educate us. Powerful people never educate the victims of their power on how to take their power away from them. This simple fact eludes most of us, especially those African-Americans who call themselves scholars and leaders.

Craig Steven Wilder sheds light on the extent to which Ivy League schools were involved in enslavement in his book, *Ebony and Ivory: Race, Slavery, and the Troubled History of America's Universities.*[3] He writes: "The academy never stood apart from American slavery, in fact it stood beside church and state as the third pillar of civilization built on bondage." He supported this statement by referencing a flyer published in the May 12, 1755 issues of the New-York Post, Weekly *New-York Gazette,* and *Weekly Post-Boy* from Kings College (now Columbia University) advertising the sale of Black youth: "Two likely Negro boys and a girl, to be Sold. Inquire of William Griffith, Opposite Beekman Slip."

An article printed in *The New York Times*, January 23, 2017, entitled "Columbia Unearths Its Ties to Slavery," illuminates the many ways that the institution of human bondage seeped into the financial, intellectual, and social life of the university, and of the North as a whole.

In an interview with journalist and investigative reporter Amy Goodman, Wilder further discusses the involvement of Harvard, Yale, Dartmouth and Princeton in the slave trade. The following is a synopsis of Wilder's interview.

Harvard

At Harvard University, there is a house named after Increase Mather. The Mathers are part of the colonial history of slavery. As an early president of Harvard, Increase Mather, used an enslaved African—a person given to him by his parish—to run the business of the college. This enslaved African ran errands between the various trustees. Mathers writes in his diary that he sent his Negro to do various bits of work for the college.

By 1638, Harvard had an enslaved man living on campus, referred to as "the Moor," who was directly related to two slave traders. I imagine that is how he got to Cambridge. Right after the Pequot War (an armed conflict between the Native American Pequot and an alliance of English colonists of the Massachusetts Bay, Plymouth, and Saybrook colonies, in which the Pequot were defeated), the captive Pequots were taken to plantations in the West Indies where they were exchanged for enslaved Africans. Immediately following these events, "the Moor" appeared on campus and became part of the legend of early Harvard.

Yale

Yale has a very similar story. In 1701, when the founders were meeting to establish what was then the Collegiate School, they came from various towns followed by their manservants, or slaves. Enslaved people were present at the founding of the institution. Once established, the new business of higher education and the financial model for a successful college required tapping into "new sources" of wealth in the Americas: the slave trade on the plantations of the South and the West Indies. The first endowed professorship at Yale comes from the Livingston family of New York and New Jersey, one of the largest slave-trading families in what would become the United States.

Princeton

Betsey Stockton was an enslaved African owned by Ashbel Green, an early nineteenth-century president of Princeton. She was given to his wife by his father, Robert Stockton, as a wedding gift when she was very young. Ashbel Green eventually emancipated her, but she continued to live in the president's house and work there, and consequently, became famous as a biblical scholar. Eventually, she became a schoolteacher in New York and joined a mission in the Sandwich Islands (Hawaii), where her skills with language and religion became critical to the success of the mission.

Stockton was the founder of the first mission school opened to the common people of Hawaii. She learned the indigenous Hawaiian language and established a school in Maui where she taught English, Latin, History and Algebra. She also trained native Hawaiian teachers to take over upon her departure until the arrival of another missionary. The site of her school is the location of the current Lahaina Luna School. Stockton left Hawaii in 1825, returning to the mainland where she taught Native American children in Canada.

Dartmouth

At Dartmouth, the teaching of science in Hanover, New Hampshire began when the president's physician, the founder of Dartmouth, Eleazar Wheelock, dragged the body of a deceased, enslaved Black man named Cato to the back of his house, where he boiled the body in an enormous pot to free up the skeleton, such that they might wire it up for instruction. That act was not unusual. In fact, when medical colleges were established in North America in the 1760s (the first was at the College of Philadelphia, now the University of Pennsylvania, and the second was at King's College, now Columbia), part of what enabled their existence was access to corpses—people to experiment upon. It was precisely the enslaved, the unfree, and the marginalized who got forcibly volunteered.

Believing that racist white supremacist institutions serve our people well is ludicrous. We hand our children's minds over to the oppressors at an early age, starting in nursery school, believing that if they attend predominately white centers of education in predominately white neighborhoods, they will receive superior educations. This is a prime example of the thinking referred to by Neely Fuller and echoed by Frances Cress Welsing: "If you do not understand white supremacy/racism, what it is and how it works, you will be confused by everything [you think] you understand." This confused state of mind continues throughout elementary, junior high school, high school, and college, contributing to the belief that Yale, Princeton, Brown, and Dartmouth—schools built on the backs of our Ancestors—are far better for us.

Dr. Amos Wilson alludes to this state of mind when he concludes:

> Cultural continuity is maintained by educating children in the ways of 'their' culture. And they are educated in the ways of their culture to MAINTAIN their culture, to advance its interests, and ultimately to try to maintain its very survival. That is the fundamental reason people are educated. And as long as we are not educated to defend ourselves against these people then we are being incorrectly educated. Nothing else matters. Ultimately then, intelligence must be defined in terms of the degree in which it solves YOUR PROBLEMS. The nature of education today prepares you to solve THEIR PROBLEMS and not your own. That's why you study THEIR books, you go to THEIR schools, you learn THEIR information, THEIR language, THEIR styles, THEIR perceptions, so when you come out of school you can do a humdinger of a job solving European's problems, but you can't solve your own. And then you DARE call yourself 'intelligent?' C'mon. That's the height of stupidity.

In conversations with friends, former students, and family about white supremacy's impact on THEIR education and life. I was not surprised, but moved by much of what they had to say and their level of "self-analysis," and so I asked them if they would be willing to share their experiences in print. Not only were they willing, but also enthusiastic and eager, hoping their VOICES would inspire others to speak out and make change happen. The following are interviews which address their respective experiences.

Voices 1: Chalatise and Gene

"My husband and I came to Sankofa International Academy after many years of this Amerikkkan Fool System failing our son. We wanted more for him and believed in his potential. He was labeled throughout his elementary school years as "Special Education-Learning Disabled."

According to them, he had difficulty reading at his grade level and could not keep up in a mainstream learning environment. They convinced us, as they do many parents, that our child needed "special help" that he couldn't receive in the classroom. My son is from a loving, two-parent home where reading, writing, family discussion, and love are constantly reinforced. Little did we know that when he went to school, what was being taught at home was being brainwashed out of him. He was learning to be a victim of low expectations. He became withdrawn, and his self-esteem and confidence were being destroyed. We didn't know what to do or what alternatives were available to us.

We learned about Sankofa International Academy while watching *Like It Is*, a TV show hosted by Gil Noble. Sister Ollie McClean, the director of Sankofa, was on his show speaking about Black children being pipelined to prisons, coming to her school broken and self-defeated. After visiting the school, we took our son out of public-school and enrolled him in Sankofa. This was the best decision my husband and I ever made!

When he brought home assignments and discussed the details of his day, we were learning about our greatness along with him. He learned about his African culture, the origin of mathematics and science. He read novels that spoke to "his" life. He learned how to verbally express his ideas openly, with confidence. We saw our son bloom into his own greatness. He could articulate himself with poise and displayed strong presence.

After graduating from Sankofa, his current high school, Eagle Academy for Young Men tried to place Gene back into the Special Education system. They were trying to re-label him all over again without any valid reason. The explanation we were given was, his old records from elementary school reflected he was Special Ed. They didn't recognize Sankofa as an independent school. We contacted our Sankofa family and they, along with us, had them remove the Special Education label from his records.

Voice 2: Brandii

My experience comes from being the parent of a student in the NYC public-school system for seven-plus years. Among the many different challenges faced within those years that compromised the education of Black children, my most recent encounter involved a white history teacher during a parent-teacher conference. The school to which my husband and I send our daughter is predominately Black with a diverse set of teachers.

We were very concerned as to why our daughter had never brought any work home regarding her history and culture. When we inquired about work being assigned in the classroom reflecting our child's history, the teacher responded, "I do not have adequate knowledge about the Black experience and the history of Black people." She "advised" that our daughter bring a few suggestions to the table for her next class. Not only was her response offensive and unprofessional, it was clearly an example of white supremacy at its best. This instructor proved herself unqualified to teach Black youth. She consciously excluded and omitted the true history of almost every child in the class. In fact, the class was learning about a white abolitionist named John Brown, totally ignoring Black abolitionists such as Fredrick Douglass, Sojourner Truth, David Walker, Hetty Reckless, and John Mercer, to name a few, whose common names in Black and American history were not common in a class room full of Black children.

White supremacy has a huge impact in the school system for Black students. Black children feel inferior mainly because they rarely hear about people just like them excelling. Black history has and continues to be unapologetically erased from the American public-school system. Our children are deliberately being short-changed, and receive a minimal education when it comes to their own history. As parents we must organize, challenge the system, and insist on change.

> Education is indoctrination if you're white; subjugation if you're black.
>
> James Baldwin, ***No Name in the Street***, 1972

VOICE 3: ADELINE

Coming from Haiti as a child and growing up in America, I did not realize the effect of white supremacy on our education system until I was older. At this point I had already graduated from college. As I started to work in education it was very disheartening to see what was happening to our Black youth, especially the young men. The education system is grooming them for prison. They lack the self-esteem that comes with knowing who you are. As a result, these brilliant students are dropping out every day. Last year, while working in the Bronx as an assistant teacher for an elementary school where the student body is predominantly African, we started to learn a little about slavery. That was the first time I saw the students really engaged. Throughout the years it's been the usual European readings and histories. They were very excited and had so many questions. The children automatically turned to me with all their questions because I was the only African teacher in the classroom. It was hard because at first, I felt limited in what I could share, fearing that I would be called a racist by parents and possibly lose my job. Second, my white colleague might have reported me. I told the students to do their own research and tell me what they found. These young fifth grade minds needed answers to their questions and I failed them because it meant that I might not have a job next month, which also meant that I might not have food and shelter. The system is set up in such a way that it cripples you and backs you into a wall. I just hope those students hold that curiosity as they move forward in their education and do not accept as truth everything that they are taught. Every day is a challenge working in the education system.

VOICE 4: NATHCHA

I am a high school social studies teacher who is constantly in conflict with myself about teaching the true history of the world to my students versus just going along with the curriculum and teaching them about the achievements of people who don't look like them. As a "special education" social studies teacher, most of my students are Africans and Hispanics. Some years I may have one or two European children in my class. Although this is the demographic of students in my classroom, everything they see in the textbooks, lessons, and videos in social studies is about Europeans, apart from three or four historical figures or topics. I have to constantly bombard my students with images ofEuropean kings, queens, political figures, and leaders because this is what will be on the state test and these are the faces and places they will have to remember in order to score high.

I had this one student whom I taught for three years; I watched him slowly unravel over the years academically and socially. He would ask me from time to time, 'When are we going to learn about Black people?' 'Why don't we learn about Black people?' I didn't have a good answer for him. It hurt me deeply to know that he was begging to be taught about himself and there was willingness to learn about his past and about those who looked like him, but I couldn't deliver. I told him we would, but by the time we got to the topic of the Haitian revolution he had already checked out. All those months of sitting in the classroom and not learning about anyone who looks like him had already turned him off to learning the topics that followed.

He always sticks out in the back of my mind as one of the ones I let down—one of the ones I could've made a difference with, but didn't. I couldn't do it; I just couldn't get myself to stop thinking about the test and the consequences that come with teaching children about the true history of the world and the real contributions of African people in history.

When it's time for Black History Month I try to pack it in, and teach students as much as I can about African people and their contributions to the world. When students find out about the contributions African people made, the information comes into conflict with the information they have been taught in school throughout the years. They ask questions that I am afraid to answer, or must be careful answering, as to not say anything that will jeopardize my job. They ask me questions like, 'So, has everything we've been told a lie?' 'Do Europeans take credit for everything?' 'Why didn't they teach us this before?'These questions break my heart and a little piece of me at the same time, because I can't answer truthfully; I can't say, yes, many of the things you have been taught since elementary school and have read about in textbooks are distorted and a lot of the times are outright lies; I can't say, yes, Europeans did and still do take credit for many things in history that Africans did. I can't tell them they weren't taught the truth because we live in a global system of white supremacy and that means they must be taught that Europeans are the greatest people on the planet and that other people, especially Africans, have contributed little to nothing in history. If I answered truthfully, if I was honest about the reality of the world as it is, I would be in jeopardy of coming under attack from parents [and] administrators, and possibly, losing my job.

African children not being able to see themselves in a positive and powerful light in history contributes to the low self-esteem, distorted view of their self-worth, and lack of motivation that many of them have. The stress that comes with not being able to truly educate African children about the complete history and true reality of the world as it is today is not only harmful to the student, but also to the teacher. As a teacher, it has been very stressful to know that I know the facts of history, but cannot teach them. It has taken a toll on me physically, mentally, and spiritually. I am ashamed that, as a Black educator, I must participate in mis-educating those very children that I say I care about and the future depends on, and [I] can't teach them more for fear of losing my job and the life necessities that it allows me to obtain. The stress of being an African teacher and helping to mis-educate African youth feels like I'm participating in my own genocide. Many times, when I go to work I dread it. The only thing that helps me get through is sharing the bits and pieces of knowledge I can with my students. Many times, I feel like a coward because my ancestors expect more, even though some might say otherwise; but I'm working on letting go of the fear and making my ancestors proud.

Voice 5: Jahi

I was twelve years old when I walked into school with memos in my hand. It was a memo for each teacher I had during my seventh-grade year. In that memo, I did something almost unimaginable. I made a 'declaration.' It was in this declaration that I, politely but unapologetically, made known that I would no longer answer to the name Christopher Smith but was to be called Jahi Kassa Taquara. I can still hear some of the silent responses. Some teachers had their eyebrows raised, some their mouths open. Some grimaced. A few smiled. But even at that age, I was very clear that my declaration wasn't about making others comfortable. It was about me. It was about moving away from a pedagogy of conformity to embrace true education designed to bring forth the very best of who I was.

I came from a family that believed the prerequisite for believing in your greatness was in understanding your history. My mother didn't waste time filling my bedtime with stories of pumpkins, talking animals, and twinkling stars. My bedtime stories were essays written by Jawanza Kunjufu, speeches by Dr. Martin Luther King, Jr., and *The Autobiography of Malcolm X*. My grandmothers, who were filled with the "holy spirit," were also filled with conviction, as they did not hesitate to share with me the wisdom of their years and their stories of struggle. From their mouths I learned about the stinging assault of segregation, the brutal murder of Emmett Till, and the Civil Rights Era. These things I absorbed from the cradle. I grew up understanding the world I lived in. I understood the price of my color, but more so, I understood the necessity of thinking critically.

My early exposures to history and critical thinking led to my decision in choosing to change my name. I remember meeting my junior high school drama teacher for the first time. I was scared of her. Not in the way you fear a gun, but more out of reverence and respect. She set her expectations for her class in a very uncompromising and non-negotiable way. There was no room for the opinions of a bunch of twelve-year-olds. She made it known that her voice was the only voice of authority. I felt right at home. However, it was when she wrote her long name on the blackboard that I was captivated. I'd never heard a name like that before. Later that day I even went to the teachers' mailboxes to find her name on one of the boxes just to see it printed. Some weeks went by, maybe even a few months, before I finally found the courage to ask her about her name. "Excuse me, what kind of name is that?"

She took the time to explain it to me. It was an African name. 'Were you born in Africa?' She replied, "No, but I certainly con- sider myself an African." Here I stood, with the roots of my history planted firmly and deeply in Africa, yet I had a name that was entirely European. My mother always taught me that we bore the names of those who enslaved us. I remember thinking how horrible it was to be named after someone who hated and despised you. To be named after some- one who had no regard for your life or well-being. This teacher went on to say that she made the decision to change her name. I didn't even know that was an option. I asked her where she found her name and she provided me with three small books. I spent an entire week with those books. Finally, while at home under a dim light near my bed, I wrote down my new name: J-A-H-I.'

I told my grandmother that my new name was Jahi and she told me to wash the dishes. I never thought she took me seriously or really acknowledged it. One day, a package arrived at our front door. She told me to sign for it and open it. I opened the small leather box and there was a gold-plated watch. On the face of the watch, in gold letters, was my name, my African name: Jahi Kassa Taquara. I looked at my grand- mother and she smiled. I smiled too. Shortly after, my grandmother made her transition. At the time, I just couldn't understand how she could leave me. But over the years since her passing, I've come to believe that her giving me that watch served as an indication that all her work, her teaching, her guidance, and her love reached full circle. Providing me with that watch was her way of saying that I had finally passed the test, and that it was time for me to move on to the next level of my life, and time for her to move onto the next level of her life in 'glory.'

Voice 6: Dequi

I have worked as an educator and counselor in the New York City Department of Education for almost twenty years...I am of African-Cherokee-Shinnecock descent and dress in a way that speaks to my heritage. Several years ago, a white female principal at one of the first high schools where I worked said, about a year into my being at the school, that she didn't want me in her school. Her complaint was that I only worked with what she thought were African American students. She didn't know my students came from Belize, Guyana, Jamaica, Honduras, Dominican Republic, across this country, the Caribbean, South America, and Africa. Her limited conceptualization of students was skin color and, because theirs was dark, she thought them to be African American. This, along with her complaint that my clothes 'sent an exclusive message,' required a meeting with my union representative and program supervisor. Thanks to my students, their parents, my union rep, and program supervisor, I finished out the school year and was then transferred to another school. She barred me from entering the building so long as she was principal.

Voice 7: Jacquelyn

I was born and raised in a small Ohio town in which there were very few families of African descent. During my years in the school system, I experienced being the only Black student in every grade level except first and eighth. A sea of white engulfed me—white teachers, white book characters, white history. I learned about George Washington, Susan B. Anthony, and Thomas Edison; but the accomplishments of Harriet Tubman, Carter G. Woodson, Bessie Coleman, and other African Americans were never taught. The only mention of my ancestors in the history books was through the topic of enslavement. I remember sitting in a high school history class during a lesson on the Civil War. Students volunteered to read selections from the assigned chapter. When the section regarding enslavement was read, I felt embarrassed. At that time, I didn't know the greatness of my ancestors, and I didn't know how to seek out information on my own.

After graduating from high school, I attended an historic black college. It was there that my history was introduced to me. While taking a class called 'Negro Writers in America,' I read works by Richard Wright, Zora Neale Hurston, and other creative Black authors. While taking history courses, I learned the truth about the contributions of

African Americans that was denied to me during my education in a white environment.

After I completed my degree in elementary education, I was employed by an urban school district in Wisconsin and assigned to a third-grade classroom in a predominantly African American school—where Black History wasn't addressed in the curriculum. The knowledge I obtained during my college years inspired me to read and learn more about the achievements of my people. For my students to have good self-esteem and aspire to be the best, I knew they had to learn about the struggles, strengths, and accomplishments of the ancestors who came before them. To that end, I added a Black History lesson to my daily instruction.

Now, it never occurred to me that any parent would be uncomfortable with the teaching of Black History in my classroom. However, one day the mother of a white student told me that she was concerned that Black students might become upset and take it out on her daughter. I didn't get into an in-depth conversation with the mother. Thinking back on it, the mother's apprehension is a good example of the fear white people exhibit when they are not the majority.

Voice 8: Lori

I was seven years old in the second grade. Our white teacher Miss Thorne was executing her weekly, Monday routine: collecting money for milk and crackers. The crackers, wrapped in thick, dark chocolate, were shaped like half a ruler. Their rich smell floated over the room, making me determined to have my own treat. As my turn came, I proudly offered my change and asked for milk all week and five crackers each day. Indignant, Miss Thorne threw down her pen, yelling, 'This is not your money! You never have any! You must have taken it from your mother's pocketbook!'

I was hurt and humiliated before the class of 30 staring eyes. I felt alone. Most of the students were as poor as me, wearing worn, ill-fitting clothing, rundown shoes, never having a nickel for one morning treat. But they were mainly white and Miss Thorne had never treated them like this. She put my money in an envelope, sealed it, wrote my name on it and locked it in her desk drawer. Tears burned my eyes and turned my throat raw. She ordered me to my seat.

At dismissal, I ran all the way home to escape the shouts 'thief, thief' from my classmates. Crying and heartbroken, I told my mother and father how I had saved my nickels and dimes in my own pink bank shaped like a little beach pail. They were sympathetic and understanding. The next morning, I received more comfort when my mother said she would come to school later after chores were done.

When my mother walked into the classroom, Miss Thorne was obviously surprised. My mother explained, loud enough for all to hear, that my father gave me a small 'tip' each time I went to the store for his newspapers and magazines. My mother gave each of her children ten cents on special occasions such as birthdays, holidays, and visits with relatives. Visitors also gave me a nickel when they saw my excellent monthly report cards. As my mother spoke, Miss Thorne's thin, white face slowly turned from pale pink to bloody red. My mother turned to the class and announced, 'Loretta is not a thief. She has never stolen anything. I trust her completely.' Her parting thrust to Miss Thorne was: 'Be sure she gets milk and crackers for the next five days.' I felt vindicated and eventually rose to the top of the class in grades. Even Miss Thorne could not deny that accomplishment, and my classmates cheered me on. That was 82 years ago.

*****

Hearing and absorbing these VOICES—voices that had reached resolution, voices that were still confused and struggling, voices that felt ashamed and powerless, I recognized the urgent need, as an educator, to challenge the fear triggered by white supremacist brainwashing and work on what Dr. Welsing refers to as restoring "true mental health" to African people.

As a teacher, I took the opportunity to challenge this task by incorporating meaningful lessons into a curriculum otherwise designed to destroy our youth culturally, historically, mentally, and spiritually. A system designed to break them, annihilate their self-esteem, and make them, as Dr. Welsing would say, think they are "functional inferiors." This task was somewhat easy when I taught in an independent African school, but definitely a lot more challenging in the public-school system where I was fired for teaching Black youth that they were African.[4]

One thing I was highly aware of while employed at Sankofa International Academy, an African-centered Independent school, was the importance of starting the day strong. Every morning, the youth recited from memory all the countries in Africa, located them on the map, pledged allegiance to the red, black and green flag and praised the Ancestors. Every lesson during the day was designed to confirm their "African Greatness." This was a necessity because, as Dr. Welsing points out, "We're the only people on this entire planet who have been taught to sing and praise our debasement. 'I'm a bitch. I'm a hoe. I'm a gangster. I'm a thug. I'm a dog.' If you can train people to demean and degrade themselves, you can oppress them forever. You can even program them to kill themselves and they won't even understand what happened."

It was crucial that the students understood the power of resistance, personal and historical, and developed a clear perspective of who resisted, not only in America, but worldwide. It became clear to them that, unlike Europeans, Black youth did not have to worship fictitious superheroes such as Batman, Superman, Catwoman, and so on. Our people have "authentic" superheroes: Malcolm X, Patrice Lumumba, Yaa Asantewaa, Harriet Tubman, Khalid Muhammad, Nat Turner, Gabriel Posner, Denmark Vesey, and others. We have brothers and sisters incarcerated, political prisoners who are "superheroes," such as Sekou Odinga, Jalil Muntaqim, Assata Shakur, Move 9, Russell "Maroon" Shoatz, Veronza Bowers, Abudullah Majid, Mutulu Shakur and numerous others who fought and died for many of the benefits we enjoy today. It was mandatory that Sankofa students clearly understood the necessity of studying their heroes. They delivered oral presentations weekly to reinforce the magnificence of African cultures and African people; and to emphasize that they did not need to identify with the fallacious heroes of white supremacy. Assata Shakur states it clearly when she exclaims,

"No one is going to give you the education; you need to overthrow them. Nobody is going to teach you your true history, teach you your true "heroes"; if they know that, that knowledge will help set you free."

Public-school, compared to the African-centered independent school, was quite a different experience. Although I received little support from the administration and most staff members at JHS 113, a public-school in Brooklyn, N.Y. where I was the drama instructor, it did not deter me from teaching truth and resistance. I often read Langston Hughes' article, 'The Negro Artist and the Racial Mountain,' published in *The Nation* in 1926, as a reminder of white supremacy's hold on the mind of the Black artist. Hughes declared,

> One of the most promising of the young Negro poets said to me once, "I want to be a poet not a Negro poet," meaning, I believe, "I want to write like a white poet"; meaning subconsciously, "I would like to be a White poet" meaning behind that, "I would like to be White." And I was sorry the young man said that, for no great poet has ever been afraid of being himself. And I doubted then that, with his desire to run away spiritually from his race, this boy would ever be a great poet. But this is the mountain standing in the way of any true Negro art in America—this urge within the race toward whiteness, the desire to pour racial individuality into the mold of American standardization, and to be as little Negro and as much American as possible.

I revisited Langston Hughes' article when I was having a conversation with my Godchild, Farrah Gray, and asked him his sentiments about educating Black youth today. He responded, 'Black youth must be taught a knowledge of self because if they don't know who they are, anyone can name them and if anyone can name them, they will answer to anything.' Ironically, I realize at the age of 69, much has stayed the same.

I instinctively followed Dr. Welsing's lead when she stated strongly in *The Isis Papers*, "I won't rest until Black children are taught to love themselves as themselves." I was assiduous about the importance of educating my students concerning love for self [and] culture, which brings a sense of empowerment. This indoctrination became apparent when the students organized a boycott in 1997 of a bodega near their school after one of their peers was apprehended and put in a choke hold for allegedly stealing a bag of potato chips. Although the school security and principal appeared on the scene promptly, the owners refused to release the hold until police arrived and found no evidence of theft. This was one of several incidents of false accusations from the bodega against JHS113 students. After several days of planning and estimating approximately how much money the bodega made monthly from the students, we moved from the planning stage into the action phase, and boycotted the store. With mostly students from my drama department and a few "educators" (most teachers were afraid to join the boycott), we arrived an hour before morning classes started to protest in front of the store and stayed an hour after dismissal to continue our objection to the bodega's policy of harassment. During the first week, the owners of the bodega stood in the door of their establishment laughing at the students as they chanted and carried signs condemning their mistreatment. Week two, they laughed less and were not so amused when they saw how much of their income came from these very protesters, a crucial fact we became aware of in our planning. By weeks three, four and five they were not laughing at all. Week six had them at the entrance of the school requesting a meeting with whomever oversaw the protest. The principal informed them she would meet with the responsible parties and get back to them. I formed a committee made up of students, the administration, and myself to address the concerns of the bodega. We disagreed on how the concerns should be handled. The administration wanted to make a list of demands the bodega would comply with to end the boycott. By now the boycott was in its eighth week and the owners were strongly feeling its effects. I suggested we continue the boycott to force the closure of the store and set an example for other businesses in the area. The administration felt the students should experience the "victory" of compromise. I felt a compromise would not represent victory, but defeat.

After several meetings and twelve weeks later, the principal contacted the bodega owners and presented them with a list of demands they eagerly accepted. Along with many of the students who protested, I was disappointed with the decision; but, due to school policy, we complied yet silently continued an "unofficial" boycott. As the universe would have it, the bodega lost so much money during the boycott they could not recover and were forced to close. The students that participated in the boycott were eleven, twelve, and thirteen years old at the time. They are now in their late twenties and early thirties.

I was approached recently by a former student who was involved in the boycott who said, 'I learned a lot from you in drama class, but I will never forget us shutting down that bodega. It showed me we could make change happen. We had power. Until then, I never believed it was possible.' At that point, I realized this student understood what Dr. Francis Cress Welsing meant when she said, 'If Black children and Black people as a whole are ever to be developed fully, Black people themselves will have to enact that development.' The student realized the role that she and her classmates played by taking responsibility in bringing about change and combating white supremacy.

No matter how difficult the task, we must recruit African-thinking educators into the public-school system and find a way to instruct them on how to strategically teach subject matter that combats white supremacy and educates, not just students but parents. According to the National Center for Education Statistics (2015), there are 7.7 million Black students in the U.S. public-school system. So often when I talk to concerned Black educators and conscious community members about the improper education our public-school youth are receiving, they reply aggressively, 'We need our own schools!' Yes—they are right—but, unfortunately, we don't have our own schools and the few we do have are not equipped to handle 7.7 million students. If we had enough independent schools to house approximately 1000 students each, we would need 7,700 schools in addition to the ones we now have. That equals at least 154 independent schools in each state. It would be a phenomenal amount of work, but not an impossible task.

Meanwhile, what do we do with 7.7 million youth while we organize to make African-centered schools a reality? In the same 2015 report, The National Center for Education Statistics reveals that out of the 3,385,200 public-school educators in the U.S. only 230,193.6, or about

7% are Black. Therefore, we must reach those educators who are willing to challenge the white supremacist system, train them and organize to protect them[selves] when they come under attack by the powerful and entrenched bureaucracies. To successfully accomplish this, we need to have in place organizations on the national, state, and local levels ready to assume this responsibility. These organizations should include educators of the same mindset, attorneys, parents, community activists, and social media experts who can disseminate information immediately.

Another alternative is to encourage African-centered homeschooling. An estimated 220,000 African American children are currently being homeschooled, according to the National Home Education Research Institute. In an article published in *The Atlantic*, February 17, 2015, Ama Mazama, a faculty member in the African American Studies department at Temple University in Philadelphia, discusses how she began homeschooling her three children twelve years ago and realized quickly that there was little research on Black homeschoolers. Mazama wrote:

> Whenever there are mentions of African American homeschoolers, it's assumed that we homeschool for the same reasons as European-American homeschoolers, but this isn't really the case, she said. Because of the unique circumstances of Black people in this country, there is really a new story to be told.

In a report published August 26, 2012 in the *Journal of Black Studies*, Mazama surveyed Black homeschooling families from around the country and found that most chose to educate their children at home, at least in part, to avoid school-related racism. Mazama calls this rationale "racial protectionism" as a response to the inability of schools to meet the needs of Black students.

"We have all heard that theAmerican education system is not the best and is falling behind in terms of international standards," she said. "But this is compounded for Black children, who are treated as though they are not as intelligent and cannot perform as well, and therefore the standards for them should be lower." Mazama found that schools rob Black children of the opportunity to learn about their own culture because of a "Euro-centric" world-history curriculum. 'Typically, the curriculum begins African American history with slavery and ends it with the Civil Rights Movement,' she said. "You have to listen to yourself simply being talked about as a descendent of slaves, which is not empowering. There is more to African history than that.' Mazama's studies show that Black parents who choose to homeschool often teach a comprehensive view of African history by incorporating more detailed descriptions of ancient African civilizations and accounts of successful African people throughout history. This allows children to 'build their sense of racial pride and self-esteem,' she said.

Meanwhile, Cheryl Fields-Smith, an Associate Professor in the Department of Educational Theory and Practice at the University of Georgia, cites similar motivations among Black homeschoolers. 'The schools want little black boys to behave like 'little white girls' and that's just never going to happen. They are different,' she said. 'I think Black families who are able to homeschool can use homeschooling to avoid the issues of their children being labeled 'trouble makers' and the suggestion that their children need special-education services because they learn and behave differently.'

Regardless of whether our geniuses are in public-schools, private schools, home schools (and they only work if the home school is African- and Resistance-centered), or independent schools, we must work diligently to make sure that neither the oppressor, the oppressor's children, or any of his followers interfere with the liberation of our youth's minds. It is our responsibility to find ways to reach them inside and outside the system. Lacking a 'degree' in education cannot be used as an excuse 'not' to educate. We must study, read, gain the knowledge, digest it, live it, and create ways to disseminate it to our youth via after-school activities, book clubs, cultural sleepovers, lectures, the street corner, and in other settings. Instill in them their African cultures, their Greatness. Imbed in them the words of Dr. Frances Cress Welsing and make 'change' happen: Black Children are our most valuable possession and our greatest potential resource. Any meaningful discussion of the survival or the future of Black people must be predicated upon Black people's plan for maximal development of all Black children. Children are the only future of any people. If children's lives are squandered, and if the children of a people are not fully developed at whatever cost and sacrifice, the people will have cosigned themselves to certain death. They will be destroyed from without and from within by the attack of their own children against them. And they may be destroyed by both.

Endnotes

1 CNN, April 06, 2016.
2 Clarke, John Henrik. *Africans At the Crossroads: Notes for An African World Revolution.* Trenton, New Jersey (Africa World Press, Inc.1991), 55.
3 Wilder, Craig Steven. *Ebony and Ivy: Race, Slavery and The Troubled History Of America's Universities.* New York: Bloomsbury Press, 2013.
4 Winbush, Raymond A. *Should America Pay? Slavery and The Raging De- bate On Reparations.* New York, N.Y. (Harper Collins Publishing Company 2003), 299-314.

CHAPTER 3

NOTHING ELSE BUT CONFRONTATION: HOW FRANCES WELSING'S *CRESS THEORY* INSPIRED PUBLIC ENEMY'S FEAR OF A BLACK PLANET

Chuck D & Harry Allen

INTERVIEW HELD MAY 6, 2016 IN NEW YORK CITY

The following interview was conducted on May 6, 2016, in Roosevelt, Long Island, New York. The building was once his family home, but has since been converted to offices and studios.

HARRY ALLEN: What is *Fear of a Black Planet* about?

CHUCK D: Paranoia. It was speaking to the issue that there's already a world of color; human beings are all hues, colors, shades, or whatever. Yet in traveling around the world, I still found out that there was this favoritism, this concept of purity, versus everything else being contaminated with color. And so, I kind of looked at the whole thing, white supremacy, as being the fear of a Black planet.

And then later on, being introduced, through you, to Neely Fuller Jr.; getting introduced, through you, to Dr. Frances Cress Welsing, along with what myself and Griff was reading, [the question became] What was the gist of all this paranoia? What was the gist of the hatred…hatred, being fear? What were they scared of? Why if I say "Black," then all of a sudden, cats are on they heels? What was this unwritten code in the Black community, when a Black person says the word "white," they'll start to whisper it, like they're not supposed to say it?

HARRY*: Sotto voce.* Soft voice.

CHUCK D: Yeah. "Take the bass outta your voice when you say 'white.'" And when you say "Black"— damn, why you sayin' "Black" so loud? Silly little shit like that, you know and having discussions about it.

And then coming off the heels of the response from *It Takes a Nation of Millions…* in 1988, going into 1989, and seeing people on they heels about Blackness: "Black, Black, Black, Black, Black, Black, Black…," not only coming out of people, but at unbelievable, massive volumes and decibels. Hearing all the stuff that was kinda like spewing out in response to that. That was an interesting beginning, and starting place, to write about fear of a Black planet.

HARRY: Why did you make the album?

CHUCK D: My contract was to deliver albums. And you gotta write and deliver something. And it was a great idea at that particular time. Also, musically and culturally, we wanted to make something totally different than what had been [heard] before. So when everybody was expecting another nationalist, fist-throwing *It Takes a Nation of Millions to Hold Us Back* —in baseball, we call it the curveball to the fastball: an off-speed pitch to get you on your heels.

And that was the plan. To actually put it together lyrically and musically was the challenge.

HARRY: Your debut album, *Yo! Bum Rush the Show*, was released in 1987 to good critical acclaim, with sales between 300,000 and 400,000 copies. Your sophomore album, however, *It Takes a Nation of Millions to Hold Us Back*, was another matter entirely. Released in 1988, it was certified platinum a year later. Today, it is widely regarded as one of the most important and transformative entries in the history of recorded music.

CHUCK D: We knew that much when we was making it.

HARRY: What do you mean?

CHUCK D: We wanted to make a *What's Going On*. We wanted to do something thorough.

HARRY: When you say "we wanted to make," these were conscious thoughts and discussions you were having.

CHUCK D: Of course. Because the album-oriented format was relatively new to rap music and hip-hop. The albums had been done before, but never done with necessary seriousness.

Before, rap albums were collections of singles. The majors wasn't gonna touch rap music, and hip-hop was hard for them because it was a singles-oriented music. All the way up to '86. Then, when Run-DMC's Raising Hell happened, it was like heads started to turn and said, "Well, this is an album."

So it didn't behoove them financially to get into a business where they had to sell singles. They had to sell albums, and they just could not see how albums could actually fit into the agenda of moving high volumes of this new configuration they had planned called CDs. This is something they had to move for seventeen, eighteen dollars, or fifteen, twelve dollars wholesale.

And at that particular time, none of us knew that they needed a very practical plan to sell these CDs, that they needed albums, and the practical plan is that singles would not work selling this new technology. We didn't know that at the time. All we knew is that there was a vibe, there was a soul, there was a feeling with this music.

Now I think—this is also in retrospect—that our Long Island upbringing, from the '60s and the '70s, made us subconsciously know that this combination of soul, R&B, blues, smashed into what little or a lot that we knew about rock & roll, guitar-driven music, would actually mesh and find a home. And I think our Long Island panoramic view of the city, but still being in Long Island, surrounded by the apartheid of white communities, allowed us to have this overstanding; something that allowed us to make a record that just didn't fit into urban feeling. It resonated. It said a lotta different things.

I think also we came at a fortunate time, being ten years older than most people… [We] grew up in the '60s and '70s with stations like WABC, which had great curating DJs talking at fast speeds, bringing you James Brown and Steely Dan, Jefferson Airplane, and Sly and the Family Stone, and Aretha Franklin, and Janis Ian, and Carol King, and Wilson Pickett all in the same hour.

That was something I think was subconsciously driven into us; a "smash-up mode" of how we're gonna make some music. Things that ain't supposed to go together, we're gonna make it work and make it fit, in a DJ-type of mode. It allowed us to say, we're gonna make these types of records, that actually feel good, that we understand. We didn't know it at the time, but we knew what hip-hop was, and we knew what hip-hop hadn't done yet.

HARRY: What hadn't it done yet?

CHUCK D: It hadn't accepted all the other aspects of music as legitimate pieces of its future.

HARRY: What aspects?

CHUCK D: Let's take Run-DMC's famous story of using "Walk This Way," but as soon as the guitars come in, they was outta there. Well, Rick Rubin says no, keep the guitars in. The future was the total: all the instruments and the music, but putting that soul to it, like a DJ.

It was almost like the speed of how DJs operated in the '60s, kinda matched where we wanted to go with a rap over music, in the '80s and '90s. If you heard Chuck Leonard talking over the tail end of The Beatles' "We Can Work It Out," it's almost like he's rapping to a beat as he's going into a commercial talking about Palisades Amusement Park, or Raceway Park. These commercials, even, were driven into our heads. I mean, they all had a rhythm. And they had voiceovers over the rhythm.

I grew up hearing a guy like Marv Albert, not only announcing basketball games but on the radio announcing hockey games. Which is an impossible speed to master: a rhythm, while a little puck is zooming on the ice, and you're hearing Marv Albert going play-by-play. A lotta times people say, "Oh man, you got your style offa Marv Albert." But a lotta people think it's the NBA basketball games. Yes, but only to a certain degree. Hearing him on WNBC doing Ranger games and hockey was art. I couldn't comprehend it. He was so fast. Almost like an auctioneer.

So those were some of the things that were in our subliminal.

HARRY: Ranger games.

CHUCK D: Ranger games.

HARRY: So what was your plan for albums, after *Nation of Millions*?

CHUCK D: I didn't have one in '89. I had one for 1990. *Fear of a Black Planet* didn't have a title, but in checking out Dr. Welsing and people like Steve Cokely and Neely Fuller, and what was happening in New York at the time, the idea was to have a political conversation. The sonics weren't figured out yet; even the politics were sketchy. But it totally wanted to be a "local-global" record. "Global," based on our experiences of what we had seen, and what we had learned about the American story from the outside looking in. "Local" dealing with where we were from, with the whole misunderstanding of Blackness in New York City, especially during the third Black Renaissance that you was a part of, Harry.

HARRY: "The third Black Renaissance"?

CHUCK D: New York City. You know: You had the Black Renaissance in the '20s, and later on, you had the '50s, '60s. And then you had—

HARRY: There's one in the '80s with, you know, Spike (Lee, filmmaker) and—

CHUCK D: Yeah, yourself, and—

HARRY: Stuff at *The Village Voice*, Black Rock Coalition. All that—

CHUCK D: Rap music, The City Sun, WLIB, David Dinkins.... You know, all these things converged.

HARRY: And police violence.

CHUCK D: And police violence. And "Enough of this Blackness scarin' the fuck out of us!" (chuckles)

So that was the way we went into making the record. We knew that people was waiting and sitting on the fastball of another *It Takes a Nation*. We knew we were not gonna make a record better than that, because you can repeat the techniques, but you cannot repeat the time. You have to reflect the time. And that's what we wanted to have *Fear of a Black Planet* do. It had to reflect the global time that we was thinking and seeing, but also acting locally. So it had a little bit of what we was dealing with locally, Eleanor Bumpurs and that type of stuff. *Fight the Power* being out in '89 helped handle that. It had a local but a global resonance.

I'm telling you, think about going to Serbia, Montenegro, and the Yugoslavian collapse, and talking to somebody in Zagreb on how much they fuckin' hate a fuckin' Serb. Cats looking alike, and they got all the hip-hop gear on, and they're listening to you and Ice-T. Makes you like, OK. It's sort of similar to trying to talk to a Crip about a Blood in South Central, but it's woven with all kinds of other shit that's cultural and religious, and...wow, it's deep. But, at the end of the day, these guys'll stop fighting and in the same fucking arena, along with mercenaries, have us play *Muse-Sick-n-Hour Mess Age*, which was probably one of the biggest records ever in Eastern Europe, because it was the first record that was performed in Eastern Europe after the collapse of the Berlin Wall. Before that, everything was, quote-unquote, "black market."

For example, when the Iron Curtain was still up, we'd play Berlin. East Berlin would hear the radio stations, get news of the concerts, and the kids would line up at the wall with guns pointed at 'em, but they never could go to the concert. So they had been hearing this shit from the biggest hip-hop group of their particular time, from '87 up to '92, '93, over the radio. They get the radio, but you can't go to fuckin' West Berlin to check out the show where Public Enemy is playing, doin', "Fight the Power." So when the wall came down, and the shit opened, them muthafuckas…man. In Hungary, I remember we played Budapest for the first time, I think this was 1994, with Ice-T. Do you know they had busloads? Chartered buses—like how old people go to casinos. They had 16 buses coming from the former Yugoslavic republics, all the Balkans, Russia, coming into Budapest to check out the fucking gig, playing in Estonia. "Fight the Power" meant a lot to them at the time. It was like, Yo, man, everything was fucking dark. We had to do everything behind closed doors, religion or anything….

HARRY: This is what people would say to you?

CHUCK D: Yeah. Shit was deep.

HARRY: I remember having the great privilege of rolling with you. I remember we were in the Netherlands. I caught this on video. There was a sister. She was…

CHUCK D: From Suriname?

HARRY: From Suriname. And I remember us all sitting around her and talking with her. And I'm videotaping this. I don't know how you knew her, or how much of this went on, on a regular basis, when you guys move around. Like, how much of it was perform, and then talk to the locals afterwards about racism?

CHUCK D: It happened on a regular basis. All of us did it.

HARRY: Why?

CHUCK D: 'Cause we were old enough to have a sense of ourselves. We were not caught up in, "This is what this rock or rap band has to do in order to maintain popularity." When you're on the road, if you're not gonna be drinkin', and smokin' and in the club, and "makin' it happen," and "makin' it pop," or gamblin', and shit like that, you have to do something. We got 24 hours a day. You wanna get rest, but with me, I also wanted to be able to soak up a story.

I wanna be able to get: Who the hell am I talking to? Why is it different, here, than right across the river, in Austria? Why is it different here, where you got people from Suriname but at the same time, your people were actually from French Guiana? What's the difference between French Guiana and Suriname?

You know what I'm saying? This narrative may be discussed in history, or discussed sociopolitical-wise. But how often is it gonna be discussed in rap fuckin' music? Somebody might come off and say, "Frantz Fanon said this in 1959," but one thing for damn sure: Nobody said this shit in rap music.

HARRY: Why were you interested?

CHUCK D: I don't know. It's how I was raised. I was always curious about geography, people, places, and things. My mother and my father were never afraid to go anywhere.

HARRY: What do you mean?

CHUCK D: When we had to go somewhere, my dad could go anywhere. I mean, you know, like places upstate where other people would go, "I don't know if it's Black people up there."

HARRY: Sunset towns.

CHUCK D: Yeah. My dad would never be intimidated by that. "OK, we'll be the Black people, then, I guess." We'd go and have a good time.

HARRY: Intrepid spirit.

CHUCK D: And never in no "kowtow and bow-down" type of way. It'd be like, he goes in as a man, my moms is a woman, we're the kids, and we're gonna have a good time in this place that's untraditional for Blacks to go. Very clear about that. Very clear. Like, you're a human being, don't be afraid to go anywhere. My dad could go in a Klan meeting and damn near have them serving buffet...(chuckles) I swear to God.

HARRY: By doing what? What is it that he would do? Just be himself, you mean?

CHUCK E: Be himself, but he had a combination of and a balance of strength and candor, and humility all at the same time.

HARRY: Interesting. Very interesting. I see that in you. All of that. All the stuff that you named.

CHUCK D: Well, I'm only half the man my father was.

HARRY: Chuck, with these experiences, talk about writing the lyrics for *Fear*. What was your general process, and how did it change, or how was it modified?

CHUCK D: Well, I can say from "Welcome to the Terrordome," it was about the curveball. And the first curveball in *Fear of a Black Planet* was hopin' that Flavor came through.

In 1989, Flavor was sayin' how he wanted to write this cut, and this cut, and this cut. I said, fine, you can write every cut that you wanna do. But I want you to specifically write about this: "911 Is a Joke." I gave him the title, and I said write about how emergency systems in the Black community are always fuckin' late or don't come at all. And he disappeared for a year. And came back with it.

HARRY: He did a really good job, by the way.

CHUCK D: Keith and Eric did the track. It's the funkiest shit I ever heard in my life.

HARRY: I was there the night you finished it.

CHUCK D: As Hank [Shocklee] began moving on to other projects, and kinda stepped away from the Fear project a little bit, Keith became a glued force with Eric. That's when I first got the shit on "Terrordome." Keith came in with the body of it, and I had spent all year gathering sights and sounds from massive tapes, many of them given to me by Davey Cook—lectures from his radio show. Then they had guys like Thomas Todd. He had voiceovers I would mark off and categorize. And then also tapes of different songs, parts, samples. I kept my books and I would just itemize them.

HARRY: This was actually your research/composition-writing process.

CHUCK D: All damn year of '89, as I was sitting, riding buses by myself—I would not ride with the crew with so much tension among members on the bus. I would take Greyhound and just have the tapes. I listened to a lot of Sly Stone—a lotta Sly Stone—especially his first album, *A Whole New Thing*, that nobody'd heard at that time; his album failure, so to speak, with CBS. And I was just listenin' to it, listenin' to that album and categorizing things. I remember listening to the Motortown Revue and what Berry Gordy did to record and capture these live concert performances at the Fox Theater or the Graystone Ballroom.

HARRY: What was your goal, with all of this?

CHUCK D: Well, my goal was to see if I could tie the narrative of whatever record I'm gonna do with vocal samples in a way that I did on *It Takes a Nation*. For example, on *Don't Believe the Hype*, that whole, "Now, here's what I want y'all to do…for me," that's Rufus Thomas at Wattstax. So, what I kinda did was find the vocal samples, 'cause I was writin' the lyrics.

It's all interwoven. The album, *It Takes a Nation*, is interwoven with the concert tape that I brought back from London, right, and also the narrative from Wattstax. So we kinda took London and Wattstax to put together, right. And "Wait a minute! ... Brothers and sisters, I don't know what this world is coming tooooo!" So when people talk about an international record, our whole thing to capture territory was done on *It Takes a Nation* in the first five seconds.

HARRY: Absolutely.

CHUCK D: When 10 years later, they start talkin' about, "What do you think about this international aspect of hip-hop," I'm like, "We said that in '88."

HARRY: So weird hearing that back then. You start a record talking about London...

CHUCK D: No. Start a record talking about London like (makes sound of a huge crowd's roar). People were like, "Public Who? Here?" So, our whole thing was to make somebody go,"What the fuck: Where they at? And they doin' what?"

HARRY: Interesting.

CHUCK D: How do you think that somebody would have felt in London? Number-one group for the last two years, where they said they're not even on the hip-hop radar. Hears that shit for the first five seconds. It almost brings like an emotion rising out of you, because that record—not to speak any blasphemy, or whatever—but that record, at the first ten seconds, became an epiphany. It almost became a religion in the culture for people in Europe.

HARRY: Explain.

CHUCK D: I can't. I can't explain. All I know is that we don't take credit for it, I don't take credit for it, we shouldn't take credit for it, because whatever happened, it happened to come through us, and we did it, and it came through us from some other place.

HARRY: It's a moment.

CHUCK D: It's a moment. And that's what I said: When people wanted *It Takes a Nation* or *Fear of a Black Planet* to come back, I said, you can mimic the techniques. You can't capture that fuckin' moment in time, where it was bold enough to scream and spit at everything in the 360s (laughs). It was a moment in brilliance and madness all at the same damn time. And we can't take credit for that. You know, that was a thing of the moment, and it was some higher order. I remember playing in Philadelphia, and when they raised the Public Enemy backdrop, man…I mean…

HARRY: What was the backdrop?

CHUCK D: It was the Public Enemy stencil letters and the logo.

HARRY: "PUBLIC ENEMY" and the target.

CHUCK D: Yeah. Fuck the explosions. Fuck the pyro. Just a curtain with a big-ass fuckin' logo. I remember cats…

HARRY: ***Chuck sticks a fist in the air, imitating the crowd response at the sight of the backdrop. Suddenly, he drops his head, and begins weeping. I look away, not quite sure how to act. I've known Chuck since 1982, and this is the first time I've ever seen him cry. He's emotional for about 10 seconds, before speaking, through tears, his voice a bit hoarse…***

CHUCK D: It was amazing, man. (tries to compose himself) I mean, I was kinda looking,'cause I was on the side, looking out there…

HARRY: I get it. I get it. It was everything you believed in, in that moment. Everything you believed in, crystallized in that moment.

CHUCK D: (nods, emotional) Couldn't take credit for anything.

HARRY: Exactly. Completely out of your hands.

CHUCK D: I didn't have nothin' to do with that. I had a little to do with it, but…this is the first time I got emotional, Harry, but I'm, you know, I'm with you, so I could feel like this…

HARRY: Man, I'm ready to start crying too.

CHUCK D: The banner went up, and I seen Black people just standing... (his voice fades out again with emotion) It wasn't offensive to anyone. It was just, "This is good. This is good."

HARRY: Right. "This is where we're supposed to be."

CHUCK D: Yeah (pauses, takes a few minutes, and slowly returns back to his normal self). It was the same feeling I got, Harry, I think it was '73 or '74 and the Nets were playing the San Antonio Spurs in the ABA playoffs. And Dr. J, who was from Roosevelt, donated funds to the Roosevelt School athletic program.

And I remember: When they played the national anthem—this is '73, '74—you looked around, and the brothers in 'fros did not fuckin' get up outta their seats. I mean, you're looking at rows and rows of people just sitting there (laughs). It's like, "Are you fucking kidding me? Like, yo, man...." So, that statement...

HARRY: That's the antipodal moment to what you just described.

CHUCK D: Exactly. That's what brings the emotion, 'cause it was...15 years later...

HARRY: What you did corrected that ABA moment. That was a complete correction.

CHUCK D: That was amazing, man. It was amazing. It was Philadelphia, man. So, the next time we came around, which was like the end of fuckin' summer of '87, "Rebel Without a Pause" obliterated the town. Obliterated Philadelphia. It became the Philadelphia anthem for like, fuckin' 10 years. Like, no record got close... Well, I should say five years, and then Wu-Tang, later on....It was an anthem.

HARRY: When you saw that backdrop go up, did you react as emotionally as you just did?

CHUCK D: I couldn't watch it. I went backstage.

HARRY: Did you cry?

CHUCK D: I didn't cry. I had a show to do (laughs)… I better not cry…

HARRY: You actually removed yourself from it, because it was too emotional?

CHUCK D: No, I was focused on, "Now, I gotta fuckin' mash this place out." I mean, what the fuck: I'm lookin' at this person rise up, and I'm lookin' at fucking 20,000 people in the audience! I got a job to do. I'm thinking about, "OK, don't fuck up." You know? So, in hindsight, looking back at that moment…

HARRY: You realize the glory of it now.

CHUCK D: Oh, yeah. But back then, it's like, "You got a job to do. You could end up being a buster here."

HARRY I so get it. I so get it, and I wish I had been there.

CHUCK D: It was amazing, man. 'Cause this same place, in the Philadelphia Spectrum, I'd seen on TV so many times. Dr. J, who's our hometown hero, this was his house.

HARRY Wow. Too many correlations and loops.

CHUCK D: But "911 Is a Joke" was Flavor comin' through. When Fear of a Black Planet already was formed, "911 Is a Joke" was the curveball to introduce that album, and take all pressures off me. Remember: Terrordome was being scrutinized, and then they said, "Well, here's the Fear of a Black Planet, so we gotta go through these lyrics. Let's see what every song got to say." And, with "911 Is a Joke," it was, like, a joy. It was brilliant.

HARRY: It was.

CHUCK D: It brought in Chuck Stone as the director for the video, and…

HARRY: Samuel L. Jackson…

CHUCK D: …Me, who really, seriously hated, and to this day hates, doing music videos—

HARRY: You make a brief appearance in it.

CHUCK D: And you see I'm smilin'. It was the easiest Public Enemy record ever.

HARRY: High reward, low investment.

CHUCK D: High reward, and all I gotta do is…I just showed up and—

HARRY: Walked out. (*laughs*)

CHUCK D: Jam Master Jay was in the video.

HARRY: That's right.

CHUCK D: And the Afros, Hurricane, Hank, and Flavor. I remember one day I was asleep. I was knocked out. And I heard Downtown Julie Brown say, "And then, by the way, here's Public Enemy with their latest hit, '9-1-1 is a Joke!'" It was Flavor by himself and S1s. And I was like, "This is fuckin' great. I'm winnin'…and I'm in bed!" (cracks up) "And Flavor's doin' all the work!" I loved that piece.

HARRY: Chuck, talk about Flavor. Talk about the role he plays in Public Enemy. Like, as a person, but even more symbolically. Talk about why he's there.

CHUCK D: Number one, why he's there: He's there to take the front as I take the back. It was almost like, I wanna be the star, but behind the star. (chuckles) I'm a front person, but I don't wanna be the front person. But if the back front person…

HARRY: Why don't you want to be the front person?

CHUCK D: 'Cause I don't want the fuckin' attention, I don't want people looking at me, I want—

HARRY: But you're the lead vocalist.

CHUCK D: And? Who said that the lead vocalist wants the most attention? I think I have the best voice. So what that got to do with shit else? My thing is OK, I will dominate the sonics and the sound of it. But I was always willing to share the space in the stage. If "STAR" is the thing that has to come out of it, then I'm willing to be one letter of "STAR," or maybe two letters of "STAR," instead of all four letters.

HARRY: That's very interesting, because here's my next question: In a quote-unquote paramilitary, Black-consciousness group, why not just get a co-vocalist who's also paramilitary and Black-conscious?

CHUCK D: 'Cause he won't sound as good as me (chuckling). If they come that way, they'll have lyrics, but they ain't gon' sound as strong as me. People can say what they want. The only point I bring in this is I could be louder than anybody, ever. And my voice is gon' last stronger and longer than most people, ever. So, they gotta come with lyrics, they gotta come up with flow, they gotta come with a dynamic.

They could have the sound man say "Turn it up," with a lotta technological equipment. But I ain't never really needed any of that shit.

HARRY: If you're gonna get a star that you can be behind, you need someone for people to look at, and Flavor definitely gives you something to look at.

CHUCK D: No, better than that: More than look at, you can't take your eyes off him.

HARRY: Can't. Right. Yes.

CHUCK D: And you might not be able to take your mind off him.

HARRY: Right. But I always thought of it as "a spoonful of sugar helps the pro-Black medicine go down" kind of thing.

CHUCK D: Maybe.

HARRY: That PE without Flavor is a lot of liver. But with Flavor in it… well, I think the best kind of pictorial representation of what I'm saying is on the album artwork. If you look at the back of *Fear of Black Planet*, that great picture by Jules Allen, you guys are all there, doing geopolitics. And Flavor's off to the side with his hands in his pockets, flashing a big cheesy grin at the camera, his head cocked to the side…. (*laughing*). Like, what the hell's he doing?

CHUCK D: The world has become Flavor Flav.

HARRY: Indeed, indeed. Chuck, a lot has been made of Public Enemy's approach to production. That typically means how they utilize sampling. What kinds of soundscapes do you think sampling made possible? And by this I mean, how would you describe them in terms of Black music, or its history?

CHUCK D: Well, I've always said that rap music makes up for its lack of traditional arrangement and notes with a sense of reminding. Say we're taking something from Wattstax. When it came down to us making this patchwork of sounds, not only the sounds are there—the sights are there, the attitude, the atmosphere—but we put it together in a story that people could say, whoa, OK, there's something about this that makes me remember the moment. And a lot of this is based on feel.

HARRY: What do you mean?

CHUCK D: I remember many a time if Eric ["Vietnam" Sadler] said, "This is the note," Hank says, "Well, fuck the note." And I'm saying, "Well, a vocal could bridge the note to the point where it could not hide the note, but kinda morph the note."

HARRY: Are there any examples, specifically, you could think of?

CHUCK D: Everything's an example, because not everything can be put in sheet music. Sometimes you have something "stab" out. How you gonna write a stab that comes out of left field that happens to be a grunt? How you gonna put a grunt on a piece of paper? Some of this shit is impossible under that traditional way. I think there'll be future ways of musical and lyrical notation, but I think that there's a lotta this stuff that was innovative, at that particular time. There's not a lot of instruments being played on *Fear of a Black Planet*. It's all—I would say 99%—sound collage.

It changed after *Apocalypse '91*. And also the '90s ushered in the beginnings of the one-man producer. Which I've never had a fuckin' liking for. But it is the way it is, man.

HARRY: When you put together Wattstax as your own concert, you're creating a fiction.

CHUCK D: Mm-hmm. But we created a fiction that would also place itself in someone's imagination. I think imaginations were prepared better back then.

HARRY: All right. So, that leads exactly to what I wanted to ask you about: The Bomb Squad's production style was granular and particulate, and this was in part because of the production techniques and tools that you were working with…

CHUCK D: Right.

HARRY: You're putting these small pieces of sound together, a bit at a time. And so, I was thinking: This has a very subtle political effect and meaning, in at least two ways. One way is this: by having to build whole records out of very short pieces of other ones, it made you have to do a lot of searching, sorting, and qualifying. And the result is a kind of "talented tenth" approach to recorded sound.

You're saying these are the very best we have in terms of voices and performances, their quality and the statements that they're making. It's like, everything is kind of *ultimate*—in terms of tone and urgency. It's almost like a master chorus, or choir, that you're presenting. So that's one thing.

The other thing is, because you drafted so many voices and other sounds into the service of your own, there's this resultant field effect. And by "field effect," I mean, when you think about it, it's almost as though what you're suggesting is that all of those other records are really about this subject—the fear of a Black planet, which Dr. Welsing hypothesized was *a*, or *the*, driving force behind white supremacy. It's like you're saying that that's what all those records you sampled are really about. Or it is to that they are pointing.

CHUCK D: Right. Right.

HARRY: And this is an effect that occurred by you bringing them into your service. It's something that happened because you make them all kind of sing with you, in a certain sense.

CHUCK D: Yeah. And the sequence of that record, man…matter of fact, the sequencing of every record after, from that record on, was always hell. But it had to be done.

HARRY: It was hell because of the work that you'd made for yourself? And it was hard to top it or to do it again?

CHUCK D: Nah, I wasn't tryin' to top it. It's just that you wanna try to do it right. It's almost like when a cinematographer edits while they shoot. It's that same type of thing.

HARRY: Umm, wow. It's recursive. It's folding in on itself.

CHUCK D: I mean, the sequencing of "Brothers Gonna Work It Out" is very clear. 'Cause the sequencing of it goes kinda like it was written, they kind of puzzle into each other. You know, "Drop it!" (sings a few bars) So the sequencing of it rides through. And that's how it was made. The sequencing was probably done before the songs were finished. (sighs) The sequencing was probably done before the song started.

HARRY: So, you had to build a song around the sequence that you'd built.

CHUCK D: Right.

HARRY: Oh, we gotta get into that some other time. That's way too much. My mind's blowing, because one, "Brothers Gonna Work It Out" is probably my favorite track from the whole album.

CHUCK D: Right.

HARRY: And it's because, as I've said, it's a prayer. I hear it as a prayer. *You* know when I say "prayer," I'm not saying that lightly.

CHUCK D: So, were you surprised when the Million Man March happened in 1995, and people were using that line: "In 1995 / You'll twist to this / As you raise your fist to the music / United we stand / Yes, divided we fall / Together / We can stand tall"?

HARRY: I didn't know that.

CHUCK D: Yeah, that third verse…I was inspired also by that "Raise your fist to the music" from that time I saw that brother get up and stand with all those people in Philadelphia.

HARRY: It's the only record on *Fear* whose title is a promise.

CHUCK D: (thinking) Right.

HARRY: I want to finish making this point, about the political thing…. It's a kind of synthetic thing, this pointing. When you make a record about global white supremacy and you get this chorus of voices, and you have them reacting to your voice, it creates this subliminal, artificial, political meaning: That these records are really

all about this subject.

CHUCK D: Separately, they might not tell that story.

HARRY: Yes. But together they do, in this arrangement. It's like when you have a painting on the wall of a person looking straight ahead, but their eyes follow you around the room.

CHUCK D: Right.

HARRY: They don't really. But it's just an illusion. So, this is the political point. This is what's significant.

Neely Fuller Jr.—whom you've met, and who was a big influence on Dr. Welsing, and has been a big influence on me of course, and everyone—his position, in so many words, is this: If the system of white supremacy is the dominant system on the planet, which he holds it is, that means everything is *about* white supremacy. Which means everything points to it. And everything is a response to it—everything. There's nothing that isn't. That computer. You. Any record you make. Anything I say. These are all responses to the system of white supremacy. So it's almost like there's this other aspect of sampling, in the way you sample, that it's actually a comment. You're *making* these voices about white supremacy... *because they actually are*. And you're just kinda turning them that way, in that direction. Pointing them.

This is the thought that I had when I was considering what this means when you sample. And you said, rap makes up for its lack of melody with its sense of reminders. When you said that, I'm like, That's *what* it's reminding you *about*.

CHUCK D: Let me tell you, man. *Fear of a Black Planet* had to be coded in a way. 'Cause that text on the album cover shoulda been, "The Counterattack on White Supremacy." We called it, "Against World Supremacy."

HARRY: I didn't like that, back then when you did it, and I asked you about it. And you said at the time, "Well, it's against any kind of supremacy." But it almost read like you backed off; like you couldn't do it, or you were scared to, or you—

CHUCK D: It was a combination. It's like, "I already got this explained, I don't need to be defendin' that one fuckin' line." Especially after '89. You say "white supremacy" now, even in social media, and you gotta whole group of white people that feel offended. I'm like, "Yo, why you attachin' yourself to white supremacy, anyway? You have to spend too much time educating them. And they're not used to Black people educating them on anything. Unless it's like, "You know what: I'm gonna let you educate me on culture. But I'm only givin' you fuckin' 10 minutes." (laughs) "And then, nigga, I ain't listenin' to anything else you got to say." Wow.

So it's that type of vibe, and especially in 1990, man: I don't need to get into a year explaining whatever.

HARRY: You know, I would read a lot of your interviews, and think, "Chuck, why don't you just kinda go in and *say* it?"

CHUCK D: 'Cause you ain't gotta be there (chuckles).

HARRY: Right. You were having a whole bunch of conversations, and you just had to make a judgment as to, "Is this a conversation I can have, or *want* to have?" Especially coming off of, "Jews are the majority of wickedness around the globe," or whatever.

CHUCK D: To teach, coming from a Black man's perspective, you gotta understand that there ain't a lotta open minds and ears that are gonna try to hear you out teaching anything. It's almost like white supremacy is basically I guess, a civil way of saying, "Nigger, you can't teach me about fuckin' shit." Basically.

HARRY: Yes.

CHUCK D: I remember I was watching *Eyes on the Prize*, and it had in Selma, this cop, I guess, and this protester. And the protester's up there talking, like, "Oh, we're not gonna fight you, we're gonna pray for you." And the cop said, "Yeah, whatever, nigger, but I doubt if your prayers could get above your head." (laughs) "Your prayers can't get above your head!" Like, wow.

One thing about them crackers: They had comebacks that you had to stop and freeze for a minute, like, "Damn: That's a hell of fuckin' line."

HARRY: They work on it.

CHUCK D: I know!

HARRY: The whole system's working on it.

CHUCK D: You come eloquent, and they'll come back with some cracker shit. And you be like, wow, the only way I can come back at this is—

HARRY: *To eliminate the system of white supremacy*. That's it.

CHUCK D: Mm-hm. Ain't none of that "Fuck you, white boy." Ain't none of that shit.

HARRY: That's all part of the system.

CHUCK D: Yup.

HARRY: That's *in* the system. The system's built to take that.

CHUCK D: Waitin' for you. Yup.

HARRY: Like, "honky" is *not* the opposite of "nigger."

CHUCK D: By no means.

HARRY: "Nigger" has got backup. "Honky" does not.

CHUCK D: Right. I tell people the definition of "cracker." I said,"Man, you understand there are people walking around, proud with 'cracker'..."

HARRY: Proud to be crackers. Calling themselves crackers.

CHUCK D: Yeah. And that they came from a legacy of cracking the skin open with the crack of a whip—

HARRY: Cracking skulls—

CHUCK D: You know? "'Cracker'? I'm the head-cracker here, boy." So when you say "nigger," niggers are on the fuckin' end of that; at the bottom of that list, boy. So, *Fear of a Black Planet* was answering to all this in sound, sight, style, and story.

HARRY: I call the opening of that album probably the greatest ever made, certainly the most overwhelming. To hear that in 1990, all people could do is just fall on their knees and worship, almost.

CHUCK D: All of that shit was a collage. Davey D was a part of delivering me a large part of that. Bill Adler's in it.

HARRY: Here's what I want to know: When you put that together, what is it that you wanted people to experience? Somebody in 1990 was getting that cassette or CD for the first time, and they're putting it in their stereo. What is it you wanted them to experience?

CHUCK D: Not to take the fucking cassette out. And not to fast-forward.

HARRY: How did you come up with the cover idea?

CHUCK D: I just thought…I don't know…the eclipse of something. Something being eclipsed. That's it.

HARRY: That was the drive for you.

CHUCK D: Mm-hm. And the letters, I sketched it on some kinda napkin, or something. I was influenced by Hildebrandt, who did the posters on Star Wars.

HARRY: Yes. Yes, *Star Wars*. It has that shape.

CHUCK D: Never saw *Star Wars* in my life.

HARRY: Or any of the *Star Wars* films.

CHUCK D: Or any. Somebody gave me all that shit, the trilogy in the Blu-ray case last year, but it was too crazy for my daughter to watch. I attempted to watch one of them. My wife has watched *Star Wars*, they know what it's all about. I never seen one [episode of] *Star Wars*.

HARRY: I remember you saying how B.E. Johnson turned the *Fear of a Black Planet* cover art in, and you were completely not expecting what he gave you back.

CHUCK D: I was awestruck. A lot of things were going on. So all I know is, when I got it, it was like, wow. (sighs, almost with reverence). I couldn't believe that something was lifted from a napkin, and he just…

HARRY: It was what you wanted, in your mind, but better. When you saw it, it must have been, like, "I'm gonna win. I'm gonna win." It did go platinum, didn't it? Of course, it went platinum. It's nearly double platinum now. One point seven million, I think, is where it is.

CHUCK D: I don't see how fuckin' 15 million people don't have it, but (laughing) I guess I don't understand why they have 56 million fuckin' Justin Bieber albums. I don't know one Justin Bieber song.

HARRY: "Sorry."

CHUCK D: I don't have any idea what that fucking song is.

HARRY: How did you come up with the title for the album?

CHUCK D: I don't know. *Star Wars* had something to do with everything, but I don't know….

HARRY: It sounds kind of *Flash Gordon*-ish. Like a movie serial, like (*assumes dramatic radio-announcer tone*) "Next week: *Fear of a Black Planet*." It's got that kind of feel. Were there second or third runners-up for the title?'

CHUCK D: No. *Fear of a Black Planet* was actually it. See, "It Takes a Nation of Millions to Hold Us Back" came out of a line from "Raise the Roof," on Yo! Bum Rush the Show.

HARRY: But why did you pick that for *Fear*?

CHUCK D: I have no idea.

HARRY: That's so odd! Because usually you have very specific ideas about stuff like this, especially titles.

CHUCK D: I probably forgot.

HARRY: Well, as we all know, the notion for a *Fear of a Black Planet* was inspired by the ideas of Frances Cress Welsing. It's a reduction of the concerns from her 1970 essay, *The Cress Theory of Color-Confrontation and Racism (White Supremacy): A Psychogenetic Theory and World Outlook*. And you also dramatize these ideas on the title track to the album, *Fear of a Black Planet*.

CHUCK D: Right. Exactly. That's one thing I do remember.

HARRY: How well did you know Dr. Welsing?

CHUCK D: Not at all. I think I met her once, if that. I met her actually through you and her works. And after you had suggested it, I also thought taking it on as being an answer to all that shit in '89. I could take on—I remember this clearly—the scientist version of the truth, and have that as a backing statement, as some backup to all the bullshit I experienced by people not knowing enough about racism. Taking that on, like, OK: This is the truth of the matter.

HARRY: At one point, I wanted to create a Public Enemy "advisory council," of people like her, Dr. Ben, and others, but you were against it. I think you believed it would take too much out of doing PE. Like, people wanted to hear you speak, not them, and that it would either dilute the message, or it would make it confusing as to who'd said what.

CHUCK D: I think also we had to get on with business as usual, as a group. I think it was almost like, I had to deliver this record, and my group could not just not do anything.

HARRY: Did you meet her at the Race Relations Institute, at Fisk?

CHUCK D: I don't recall.

HARRY: I once asked you, years ago, how does your own music sound to you? And I've never forgotten your answer. You paused for a second, you said, "*It sounds good.*"

CHUCK D: OK. So, what are you asking me for now: An updated answer?

HARRY: Yes, kind of, but not about your music. You spoke about this a little bit earlier: I wanted to ask you how your voice works, as an effect, sound, or instrument in a Public Enemy record.

CHUCK D: How my voice works?

HARRY: How does your voice work? What is the role of your voice, from your perspective, in terms of a Public Enemy record? I mean, obviously, to say the words, but, like, is there a larger idea, or goal, or aesthetic?

CHUCK D: Right, right. I think that the best uses of my voice is as a producer produces me. I mean, with early PE records, Hank was creating a template of how to make it work in the mix. I didn't necessarily pick tracks that moved me. I'd rather be told that this is the track that we gonna have to go at, and I'm gonna attack this track. This is the track that I have, and just being able to go with the flow of the production, and then being used as an instrument.

HARRY: It almost sounds like you're saying you put yourself at the service of the producer, as opposed to having your own ideas about your voice and how it should sound.

Well, at 44 seconds, "Meet the G that Killed Me," is the shortest track on *Fear of a Black Planet*. It's also the only track that features Frances Cress Welsing's voice.

CHUCK D: Right.

HARRY: I always thought that Dr. Welsing's speaking voice had a really unusual, kind of lyrical quality. I don't know if you saw her 40th Day Ascension Ceremony in February.

CHUCK D: No, no.

HARRY: They live-streamed it from the Union Temple Baptist Church in Washington D.C. They had all these people talking about Dr. Welsing, and there was a point at the end...

CHUCK D: They invited me, but I think that was around the time my dad...

HARRY: It was February 11th, so...

CHUCK D: Three days after.

HARRY: Three days after your father's passing. Yeah. Well, there you go.

CHUCK D: Yeah. I don't even remember that period clearly.

HARRY: What I was going to say is that they had everybody give their presentations, and then at the end, they had a part where they played a recording of her speaking. It was her giving a kind of benedictory speech, at an event she'd attended. And I remember listening to her voice, and...

CHUCK D: You heard her ringing it.

HARRY: I'd forgotten how beautiful it sounded. It had this sing-song quality to it that I thought was very pretty, very feminine, very Southern, and very Black. I just remember thinking how much I

loved her voice. And I thought that on "Meet the G that Killed Me" you countered her vocal, magically, with these carillon bells. She says, (*sing-songy*) "Every Black person...," and you've got these bells doing the same thing melodically. I wanted you to talk to me about the voices of Black women. And I'm thinking here of Dr. Welsing, but I'm also thinking of that honeyed, "What's your latest hit, brother?" right before *Fear*'s title track.

CHUCK D: Yeah, that's a woman who was a DJ in Mobile, Alabama, and actually was one of the first commercial radio stations: WAOK in Mobile.

HARRY: She said that to you?

CHUCK D: Yeah, 'cause she was giving us one of our first interviews. She says, "What's your latest hit, brother?"

HARRY: Beautiful. She sounds kinda like Dr. Welsing, in the tempo of her voice.

CHUCK D: She was, you know, a middle-aged woman, laid back in the cut, got that Mobile, Alabama, thing goin' on, which is similar to New Orleans. Mobile broke a lot of rap records. They used to have a guy down there by the name of the Mad Hatter. And Mad Hatter always used to have some rap records up in the charts. And they always used to report it in the middle of the—um, what was the radio magazine? *BRE. Black Radio Exclusive.*

HARRY: That's right.

CHUCK D: So when we finally went to Mobile in '87—with LL Cool J, Stetsasonic, and Doug E. Fresh, Whodini, and Eric B. & Rakim—this sister actually gave us an interview, and I taped it and brought it home.

HARRY: You don't remember her name, or her show's name?

CHUCK D: I'm pretty sure we could look her up.

HARRY: That might be good to find. I'm also thinking of people like Sister Souljah, whose voice you really used as an instrument; like a dissonant kind of trumpet, on Terminator X's "Buck Whylin.'"

CHUCK D: "WE ARE AT WAR!" "Come on!"

HARRY: Even stuff she says, the little statements: It's almost like it's going off—not tempo—but off-key….

CHUCK D: 'Cause she was hittin' notes that males couldn't hit.

HARRY: And when I think about women's voices in your records, I even think of your mom, whose voice I've always loved, and it's got this laugh in it.

CHUCK D: I never used my mom's voice in a record.

HARRY: That would be interesting.

CHUCK D: I never used my dad's voice in a record.

HARRY: I guess you still could. But say something about the voices of Black women.

CHUCK D: I would just say this: Collectively, there's no other moving force like Black women when they're actually grouped together in harmony.

HARRY: In action, you mean, or in speaking, or…?

CHUCK D: All of the above, or all of the below. I mean, how we would use it in production would also depend on a lotta different factors. But individually, it was about finding the right voice for the right moment.

HARRY: You have 3 children. All of them are females.

CHUCK D: Yes.

HARRY: PE has always been seen as a very male, even macho, kind of group, and sometimes has been charged with being misogynist.

CHUCK D: Mm-hm. By who?

HARRY: Oh, I don't know. It's a word you often see floating around, for various reasons.

CHUCK D: "Misogyny."

HARRY: Yeah. How have your daughters related to this album, and to your music, in general? Or more so, what role do you think your music has played in shaping their thinking?

CHUCK D: Well, my youngest daughter— she's turning 5, May 9th—doesn't know it exists. But the weird thing is—it's really strange—the other day, she was going, "Fight the power, fight the power." She's very aware of, "Public Enemy, Public Enemy." She's more aware of Public Enemy and "Fight the Power" than my oldest daughters were at that age. I don't know. Maybe they wasn't. Maybe they was. I don't know. But it's weird: She was like, "Fight the power." A five year old.

HARRY: You made a surprised face.

CHUCK D: Oh, hell yeah, I was surprised. Surprised a lot. I didn't think she even knew.

HARRY: How about your older daughters? How has your music shaped their thinking as adults?

CHUCK D: I think they've gotten it later on.

HARRY: What did they get?

CHUCK D: They're gettin' the importance of it, I guess, the social accountability. The thing is, they've seen me in "facets." They've grown up in a surrounding of this being overstood by their friends. But then they've never seen me…

HARRY: At work?

CHUCK D: Well, they've seen me at work, but they've never seen me at work while being at home. Like, I'm just spittin', and they're going, "You know Dad, we gotta go," and, "Who's gonna pick me up and drop me off at dance school?" That type o' shit. The magnitude of it, they knew, but they was kinda like, "Well, my dad is like this, but he could just as well be pushing a car outta the ditch." (chuckles) You know what I'm saying? Like, regular shit.

HARRY: What do you see as missing in today's Black music?

CHUCK D: In today's Black music? (pauses) Groups and teams.

HARRY: What do you mean?

CHUCK D: Too individualized. Too many individuals.

HARRY: What's wrong with that?

CHUCK D: What's wrong is if you're not Prince—if you're not one person, like Stevie Wonder—who can do it all, and do it all very well. Doing it without a group. We've seen the disappearance of groups, we've seen the disappearance of teams.

HARRY: Teams of?

CHUCK D: Musicians and artists.

HARRY: What's the difference between teams and groups? I'm not clear what you mean.

CHUCK D: A team is actually something that might be putting your music together, as opposed to one person. A group is maybe an act, and it's just like one person or two people trying to entertain. I think that's what is missing today. I could be wrong, but that's what is missing to me.

HARRY: One of the things I've detected in you is a type of satisfaction, and even pride, regarding the number of tours you've done, and the countries you've visited. What are the current stats?

CHUCK D: One hundred four countries, 104 tours.

HARRY: How did they match up like that?

CHUCK D: I don't know. They just actually ended up at the same place.

HARRY: What country do you most want to go to, that you've not been to, yet?

CHUCK D: Um…India?

HARRY: Fascinating.

CHUCK D: And we've gotten offers to [play] India.

HARRY: I think one thing your work shares with Dr. Welsing's is a concern with and focus on *globality*; that is to say, a planetary viewpoint.

CHUCK D: Yeah.

HARRY: *Fear of a Black Planet*, it's about a planetary viewpoint.

CHUCK D: One thing I've learned: In my mind, I don't say I'm a citizen of any fucking government or country anymore. Not that I ever was, but….

HARRY: You're a citizen of what, would you say?

CHUCK D: The booty! (laughs) Nah. Just the earth.

HARRY: To what degree, do you think, have Americans—particularly Black Americans—failed to develop a global outlook?

CHUCK D: Slavery has conditioned us into not recognizing, understanding, learning about how important the diaspora is. And I've always—well, not always—but the last 20 years, especially, I've resorted to the fact that you're a slave here on this Earth, as a Black person, if you don't connect with the diaspora. That's where we can at least seek a little bit more help from the rest of the diaspora; people of color, especially Black folks around the world, in order to make us seem like we're an abundant majority, instead of a minority that's at everybody else's benefit, and at our expense. I mean, for example, "Fear of a Black Planet" is a simple statement that says, we're not a minority, we're a majority, if we're gonna go by those primitive rules of "one drop of Black blood makes you Black."

HARRY: Or we could become [a Black planet], it seems like it's almost saying.

CHUCK D: How? We could never become one, scientifically.

HARRY: No, I'm just saying the words "Fear of a Black Planet" seem to suggest a fear of what might happen. It's either fear of what already exists, or fear of what's coming.

CHUCK D: Oh, OK.

HARRY: I'm not sure how you meant it. If you meant fear of what's already there.

CHUCK D: We usually have both meanings, you know. I mean, It Takes a Nation of Millions to Hold Us Back was clearly a, you know, double entendre.

HARRY: How?

CHUCK D: It takes a nation of millions to hold us back. There's millions of us that could hold ourselves back, or it takes a nation of millions of others to hold us back.

HARRY: Sure.

CHUCK D: "Fear of a Black Planet" is different. I don't think it has a double meaning; I think it's just like based on the fear of white annihilation.

HARRY: "White genetic survival" was the term that Dr. Welsing coined.

CHUCK D: Which was the whole reason why white supremacy made Blackness seem like it had the cooties.

HARRY: When you look back, what do you see as the shortcomings or failures of Public Enemy?

CHUCK D: (thinks) Not going to South Africa in the early 1990s.

HARRY: Is that it?

CHUCK D: Well, there's plenty, but I probably can't name 'em all.

My failing is not having 10 books by now. Because if I had 10 books by now, I wouldn't have to regurgitate and try to come up with shit when I know that I wrote this. It's like keeping a journal of thoughts in a timeline. I got, what: Three-and-a-half, four maybe? But I should have had 10 by now, maybe even 15. I should've moved into publishing when I turned 40. Now I'm 16 years in, approaching 60. So I could do a lotta catch-up now.

My writing has atrophied since 2010, especially, because of gadgets. I spend my time writing, and it's all on tweets. It's the perfect thing for me to write. I got into a mode where I thought, if I write, people don't have the wherewithal to read, or the time. And you shouldn't get into that mode. You should write anyway. Do it anyway. And I just got into thinking, well, if I write all this, who's gonna read it?

HARRY: Books are forever. People who read your books might not even exist yet. Their parents may not even exist yet.

CHUCK D: I know. But I'ma write more Terrordome blog posts. Gonna be shorter, sweeter, to the point, but more consistent.

HARRY: Last question. It's kind of long to set up, so I'll just read it to you: "In her lifetime, Dr. Welsing was often shunned. She was allegedly denied..."

CHUCK D: She was shunned by who?

HARRY: "She was allegedly denied professional positions and appointments. Her ideas were often incorrectly characterized by those attempting to explain them..."

CHUCK D: Figures, right?

HARRY: "...[Its] conclusions were often looked upon as kooky or outlandish by her peers." I can recall doing an interview once with a person putting forward psychological concepts about racism. And when I saw the relationships of this person's ideas to the ideas of Dr. Welsing, and I raised that point, this guest forcefully and silently began to shake their head "No." I stopped and asked what was wrong, and they told me, basically, that they couldn't afford to have their ideas associated with the Cress theory.

CHUCK D: Wow.

HARRY: When Welsing died, *The New York Times* did not run an obituary. And I have to check if *The Washington Post* did. But I think in all of this, she learned to press forward, despite this widespread kind of passive-aggressiveness against her. People kind of—you know, to use your term—treated her like she had the cooties, because of the kind of ideas she was putting forth. And I think it took a toll on her, in kind.

CHUCK D: You think so?

HARRY: I think it did. But I think she was also deeply appreciative for genuine acclaim and recognition she received when she got it. For example, I'll never forget the way she beamed, actually, at the Race Relations Institute when I presented her with a *Fear of a Black Planet* gold record plaque that you'd made for her.

CHUCK D: And you got that one to her.

HARRY: I got that one to her, and she was in front of a crowd, and she wasn't expecting it.

CHUCK D: You got pictures of that?

HARRY: I don't know. I hope so. I don't know. I was up…

(Chuck points his finger and makes shooting sounds)

HARRY: I was up front handing it to her-

CHUCK D: Now you got bullet holes.

HARRY: (*laughs*) I was up front handing it to her. I hope somebody was taking pictures.

CHUCK D: You hope.

HARRY: I know people were smiling and applauding her.

CHUCK D: I was totally, definitely, not in the picture.

HARRY: You were on your way there. That's why I didn't have you do it.

Anyway, I say all of this about Dr. Welsing, because I'd like you, please, to comment—

CHUCK D: She had a great gray afro, later on.

HARRY: I know (*pauses*)…a really good sister. It's really hard to believe she's not here anymore.

CHUCK D: Yeah.

HARRY: Really good sister, man.

But, I say all this because I'd like you, please, to comment on that aspect of race work: The lonely part.

How do you connect to what I've just said about Dr. Welsing, if at

all? That is, this lonely part: This part of putting these ideas out, having people treat you like the things you're saying don't make any sense, ignoring you. And you're still trying to get it forward, but you're not getting whatever it is you think you should.

CHUCK D: You don't care about enemies. You group your family, you group your community, and you please them, and fuck off, everybody else. And that eliminates the pressure and the frustration. You only really get frustrated by those who you think are your friends, that are really kinda your enemies, but that you thought were your friends.

HARRY: That's a big part of it, though: The question of who's your friend, and who's your enemy. Sometimes people don't reveal themselves as your enemy until way in.

CHUCK D: That's the chess game.

CHAPTER 4

Dr. Welsing, Entertainment, and Racism/White Supremacy

Anthony T. Browder

> Black people are going to have to stop finger-popping and singing. Black people are going to have to stop dancing and clowning. Black people are going to have to stop laughing and listening to loud radios. All of these behaviors, and many more, have absolutely nothing to do with addressing the challenges and conditions of the open warfare continuously being waged against the Black collective.
>
> (The Isis Papers, p. 183)

Entertainment is used frequently as a means of shaping people's perceptions of themselves and justifying their mistreatment of others. During the early twentieth century, entertainment in the form of novels such as *The Clansman*, films like *Birth of a Nation*, and radio programs like *The Amos 'n' Andy Show* were created to instill a false sense of superiority among White Americans and to justify their mistreatment of Black Americans. Unfortunately, many Black Americans also bought into these stereotypes and believed the lies they read, saw, and heard.

The negative perceptions of Blacks, created and perpetuated by the white entertainment industry, helped shape and sustain the racist environment into which Frances Cress was born on Chicago's South Side in 1935. Fortunately for young Frances, she was raised in a household and community that was led by strong "Race Men and Women," who understood that creating and instilling positive perceptions of Blackness could serve as an antidote to minimize the effects of the racism which ran rampant in the city, the nation, and around the world.

Throughout her long and illustrious career, Dr. Welsing's love for Black people never diminished, and she dedicated her life to our emotional, cultural, and mental well-being. This was evident in the relationships she forged with her patients and the thousands of people to whom she lectured in forums in the U.S. and around the world. Dr. Welsing taught Black people that self-love and self-respect had to govern all aspects of our lives if we were to be victorious in the war against the global system of racism/white supremacy. She chastised and scolded us when it was necessary, but never stopped loving us. She reminded us that we were the "mothers and fathers of humanity" and had as our "cosmic responsibility the resolution of the problem of injustice in the world." She never strayed from the values instilled in her during childhood. Perhaps that is why she became a child psychiatrist, so that she could pass on to children (young and old) the wisdom to help them navigate the harsh, cruel world that awaited them.

We thought that she would continue to be a source of inspiration for many years—but on New Year's Day 2016, that belief was shattered when we learned of her sudden hospitalization. Aftershocks of sadness spread around the world when Dr. Welsing's transition was confirmed, and people began to contemplate the extraordinary loss to the world.

As family and friends came to terms with the reality of losing one of the most fearless defenders of African people, we were confronted with many unanswered questions. How should we honor Dr. Welsing? How should we preserve her legacy for the generations who never knew her? How should we ensure that the racist/white supremacist society that feared Dr. Welsing in life would not succeed in erasing her legacy or minimizing her impact so as to relegate her to the dustbin of outdated Black radicals? How should Dr. Welsing be remembered and what would she want us to do in her absence?

Anyone who regularly heard Dr. Welsing speak would know what she wanted because her message was precise, clear, and consistent. She stated her position decades ago and stood her ground, never wavering from her prime directive:

> [L]et us get about the business of Black problem-solving, beginning with the problem of Black oppression under white supremacy. First and foremost, let it be the responsibility of every Black person to know and understand how the dynamic of white supremacy domina-

> tion is expressed in all areas of people activity: economics, education, entertainment, labor, law, politics, religion, sex, and war.
>
> (The Isis Papers, p. 161)

On examination, it is clear that the theories about the relationship between Black people and white people promulgated by Dr. Welsing in *The Cress Theory of Color-Confrontation and Racism (White Supremacy)* have been, in reality, more factual than theoretical in recent years. It is undeniable that Black people have been engaged in a protracted struggle against the forces of racism and white supremacy for more than 500 years. That struggle has been unrelenting, despite the brief periods of apparent progress and the passage of laws that gave the illusion of progress in "race matters." A cursory examination of American history quickly reveals that slavery, colonialism, Jim Crow, segregation, discrimination, miseducation, integration, gentrification, the "War on Drugs," and "The New Jim Crow" are variations of the same state-sanctioned terrorism meted out by whites against Blacks to maintain the system of white domination.

As with most conflicts, a skilled aggressor develops battle strategies and contingency plans long before the first assault. Dr. Welsing frequently used chess as a metaphor to describe the battle strategies used by whites in the ongoing war against Blacks and other people of color on the planet. Indeed, the best military strategists understand that the first battle is fought in the mind, and the first casualty of war is always the truth. In any effective military campaign waged in a theater of war, the enemy must be made to appear subhuman in the minds of the oppressor and the oppressed—and the more subliminal the messaging, the more effective the brainwashing.

Propaganda campaigns play a major part in any conflict. They are devised to fabricate perceptions that would be projected into the subconscious minds of subjects and push them into unreal worlds where they would become disconnected from reality and more easily manipulated. Once a population has been physically dominated, the psychological attack must continue in order to maintain control over the descendants of the subjugated. This method of control has been used effectively in the United States as described by Tom Burrell, the dean of Black advertising, in the introduction of his book *Brainwashed*:

> ...[O]ne of the greatest propaganda campaigns of all time was the masterful marketing of the myth of black inferiority to justify slavery within a democracy...Thomas Jefferson—propagandist extraordinaire, chief strategist, and creative director, along with other powdered-wig power brokers—sold the idea of white supremacy to the masses—all the masses...[It was] an effective marketing campaign... aimed at convincing both master and slave that blacks had always been and would forever be mentally, physically, spiritually, and culturally inferior.[1]

Entertainment and Information as Tools of Oppression or Liberation

Controlling the means of communication—the historical and contemporary narrative—is a necessary first step in any act of war and, once a population has been conquered, entertainment can become an effective means of maintaining control over a conquered people. For the purposes of this paper I have chosen to use the definition of entertainment as it appears at www.freedictionary.com:

> Entertainment—an activity that is diverting and that holds the attention.
>
> Amusement, diversion, recreation—an activity that diverts or amuses or stimulates;
>
> Beguilement, distraction—an entertainment that provokes pleased interests and distracts you from worries and vexations.

If Black oppression is to be eliminated under white supremacy, Blacks must first examine how entertainment has been used as an instrument to beguile and distract Black people and keep us singing, dancing, drinking, drugging and partying when we should be addressing the immediate threats to our individual and collective lives. Entertainment, according to Dr. Welsing, intersects with all areas of people activity because it shapes how economics, education, labor, law, politics, religion, sex, and war are viewed within the psyche of Black people, thereby determining how we respond to them. For example, through television, radio, and magazines, the entertainment industry has influenced and undermined the economic habits of Blacks by brainwashing us to believe we can buy our way out of a perceived inferior status by virtue of the cars we drive, the liquor we drink, the name brands we wear, and by mirroring the scripted lifestyles of reality stars, athletes, and entertainers.

In order for Black people to understand how entertainment has been used as an effective tool within white supremacy, they must first understand how symbols are used to convey and amplify messages of white superiority and Black inferiority. Dr. Welsing devoted an entire chapter to symbols in *The Isis Papers,* stating that "complex symbols" are embedded in "musical notes...written and spoken words." And that:

> Once the symbol is formed, it is capable of acting upon the brain-computer, which receives it as an energy or data message. This message [is] carried forth in any area of human activity [and acts] as powerful undetected persuaders, and thus, as powerful determinants of behavioral patterns.[2]

Since every form of entertainment is comprised of "patterns of symbols, logic, thought, speech, emotional responses, and perceptions"[3] embedded in the images, music, and words that are uploaded (consciously or unconsciously) into the minds of people being entertained, one would do well to realize that all information contained in every form of entertainment can either free or oppress minds.

*****

Entertainment is certainly not limited to radio, television, and film; it also encompasses print media (newspapers, magazines, and books) and the ever-expanding digital mediums of CDs, DVDs, videos, video games, the Internet, Facebook, Twitter, texting, and more. While the modes of entertainment have changed dramatically in recent decades, its impact has not and, no matter what form entertainment has taken throughout the ages, it has always been an effective means of shaping personal and public perceptions of self and others.

Control through the use of communication is not new. Since the invention of hieroglyphics over 6,000 years ago, words, whether printed on papyrus or carved in stone, have long influenced thought and behavior. With the advent of the printing press in 1440, the ability to reach and influence the masses increased exponentially. Once powerful rulers realized how easily they could manipulate public opinion through the strategic use of a few carefully crafted sentences (and images), they soon understood that words (and images) were more powerful than any weapon forged by man. The invention of radio and motion pictures in the 1890s, and television in 1929, gave those in power more powerful tools with which to impose their will on the unsuspecting masses under the guise of entertainment. With the advent of digital technology, never before in the history of mankind have so few people been able to exploit the masses so quickly, effectively, and thoroughly.

Communication technology combined with psychology are a proven lethal force in shaping the speech, thought and action among Black people.

The strategic use of psychology and technology to shape public opinion was developed by Edward Bernays—an early pioneer in advertising, marketing, and public relations during the first decades of the twentieth century. Bernays was the nephew of Sigmund Freud and used many of his uncle's theories to "control and regiment the masses to our will without their knowing it"[4] by using a scientific technique he referred to as the "engineering of consent." He defines "engineering consent" as the art of manipulating people. It maintained that entire populations, which were undisciplined or lacking in intellectual or definite moral principles, were vulnerable to unconscious influence and thus susceptible to want things that they do not need. This was achieved by linking those products and ideas to their unconscious desires. Bernays wrote the book *Propaganda* in 1929, in which he advocated for the manipulation of public opinion by government regulators and special interest groups. This is an example of what Dr. Welsing referred to in her writings; how the system of white supremacy utilizes the power of external influences, and the need to be constantly vigilant.

Techniques to engineer consent of the unsuspecting masses have greatly improved since Bernays' pioneering work, due to advances in the fields of neuroscience and neuroanatomy. Behavioral scientists, who apply theoretical concepts which are borne out of the white supremacist framework, have known that the brain is an associative organ that is programmed by the data it receives through the senses. This explains why Dr. Welsing often referred to the mind as a "brain/computer" which is being constantly programmed by external stimuli. Dr. Carla Schatz, a Stanford University neurologist, summed up the complex process of sensory data input and neuro-interconnectivity with the simple statement, "Neurons that fire together, wire together." Dr. Schatz understood that all data hardwired into the brain is stored deep within our conscious and subconscious mind. Cellular biologist Dr. Bruce Lipton, author of *The Biology of Belief,* provides startling new insights into the power of the subconscious that should be of particular interest to every person of African ancestry. Dr. Lipton stated:

> ...people are aware of conscious beliefs and behaviors, but not of subconscious beliefs and behaviors...the fact is that the subconscious mind is a million times more powerful than the conscious mind and that we operate 95 to 99 percent of our lives from subconscious programs.[5]

Although *The Biology of Belief* was written 24 years after *The Isis Papers*, we can appreciate Dr. Welsing's early understanding of the power of the subconscious mind when she wrote:

> ...perceptions, words, ideas, concepts and theories that are repressed or channeled into the unconscious level of the brain-computer becomes an entire world of ideas treated as though they never existed in the form of concrete reality.[6]

The art of shaping public opinion has been enhanced by recent scientific advances, such that a basic understanding of neuroscience, advertising, and marketing is crucial if we are to engage effectively in the process of "Black problem-solving" and understand the role entertainment plays in shaping our subconscious thoughts. The strategic use of entertainment as a psychological tool in the oppression of Black people is certainly not new. Frederick Douglass provided a first-person account in his 1845 autobiographical *Narrative*, which described how entertainment was used by oppressors to control Africans in America. Douglass wrote that whites gave enslaved Africans time off between Christmas and New Year's Day and encouraged activities such as "playing ball, wrestling, running foot-races, fiddling, dancing, and drinking whiskey." The Africans had to buy whiskey from their enslavers because they would "make bets on their slaves, as to who can drink the most whiskey without getting drunk; and in this way they succeed in getting whole multitudes to drink to excess."[7]

Douglass understood that sports, entertainment, singing, dancing, and intoxication were tactics used by enslavers to get the enslaved to accept an inferior status by reveling in momentary periods of frivolity throughout their lives, until they died and found relief in the afterlife. The creation and maintenance of slavery was dependent upon the enslavers creating permanent conditions of oppression and terror, such that their victims would welcome any brief respite from back-breaking labor and joyously look forward to the day when death would free them from a life of bondage. Once these activities became normalized, after years of repetition, they were ingrained into the cultural consciousness of the enslaved and embraced as valued traditions that were passed down from generation to generation. Such conditioning is now called "behavior modification," "social engineering" or "brainwashing." Whatever the terminology, its effects are real and have been scientifically validated.

Dr. Carter G. Woodson summed up the effects of negative programming in his 1933 publication, *The Mis-Education of the Negro,* when he wrote, "If you control a person's thinking you don't have to worry about his actions. You don't have to tell him to stand here or there, for they will find their proper place and stay in it." In other words, whomever programs content for the consumer determines the quality of life of the consumer—until the consumer changes the program.

The Welsing/Shockley Debate: Launching a Gold Era of Agitation Propoganda

In 1974, Dr. Welsing appeared on the nationally syndicated television show, *Tony Brown's Journal*. Her appearance on that program helped launch a golden era of positive African-centered information and entertainment that spread, via the airwaves, around the nation. The image of an articulate Black woman, sporting a large Afro, wearing a red, black, and green stripped dress and intellectually castrating a Nobel Prize-winning white supremacist on national television, shattered the negative stereotype of inferiority that had been programmed into the psyche of Black people. It was a bold display of *agitation propaganda* that shocked Shockley to his core and probably scared the hell out of many whites watching the broadcast.

Tony Brown's Journal introduced Dr. Welsing to a new audience that was inspired by a Black woman who self-identified as a psychiatrist/behavioral scientist and who resided in the Albert Einstein camp of "determinacy." Throughout her long career as a healer and strategist for countering the effects of the global system of racism/white supremacy, Dr. Welsing developed a strategy of "direct linear thought" that allowed her to "move continuously forward in a straight line process, from problem perception and depth analysis to proposed conclusive modes of problem solution."[8] This line of reasoning led Dr. Welsing to the inescapable conclusion that there was a "unitary cause of the many complex forms of behavior, knowledge of which would enable prediction of expected consequences."[9] By seeking out and identifying "the interconnections that exist between seemingly isolated disconnected behavior-energy phenomena in Western culture," Dr. Welsing devised a "Unified Field Theory (of) Psychiatry" that enabled her to transcend more Eurocentric theories of racism/white supremacy than her fellow psychiatrists and behavioral scientists—Black or white.

That edition of *Tony Brown's Journal* went "viral" long before the term was popularized by the Internet, and it showed the effects of what Tom Burrell called *positive propaganda programming*: "(T)he strategic planning and placement of words and images. The right words, in the right place, at the right time, have exponential value."

The astute communicator that he was, Tony Brown was probably aware of the impact the show would have on his viewers the minute Dr. Welsing walked into the studio. Mr. Brown was the first Dean of Howard University's Schools of Communication and he was hired by Cathy Hughes, the first female general manager of Howard's newly acquired radio station, WHUR-FM. Ms. Hughes and Mr. Brown both understood, even then, that the power of the media helped to shape the rise and expansion of positive messaging for the Black community in the 1970s. Ms. Hughes eventually left WHUR and went on to establish the Radio One media organization, which now owns over 65 radio stations in nine urban markets throughout the U.S. and is headquartered in suburban Washington, D.C. Dr. Welsing was a frequent guest on Ms. Hughes' flagship station WOL and regularly provided analyses of events affecting the lives of African Americans, within the context of countering the system of racism/white supremacy.

Positive Propaganda in Washington D.C., 1980–2000

The effectiveness and tremendous impact of positive propaganda programming was evident throughout the Washington Metropolitan Area between 1986 and 1996, when a coalition of Black-owned and operated media outlets (WOL, WPFW, and WDCU radio stations; *The Washington Informer*, *Capital Spotlight*, and *Afro* newspapers; and WHMM-TV, Howard University's PBS station) began airing shows and writing articles about African and African American historians and scholars. These activities led to Washington, D.C., becoming the hub of the African-centered movement, and much of this activity was set in motion by a 30-minute weekly television program called *For the People*, which was broadcast on the South Carolina Educational Television (SCETV) network in Columbia, the state capital. *For the People* was created and hosted by Listervelt Middleton in 1977, with the intent of showcasing interviews with local Black South Carolinians who were often ignored by the mainstream white media.

Mr. Middleton's early interviews featured local African American residents, but he struck gold when he interviewed historians Chancellor Williams (born in Bennettsville, SC) and John G. Jackson (from Aiken, SC). Both scholars discussed their landmark publications, *The Destruction of Black Civilization* (Williams) and *Introduction to African Civilization* (Jackson), which were classics within the Conscious Community but soon became popular within the wider community after their appearances on the show. To watch Mr. Middleton ask probing questions of Williams and Jackson; listening to them discuss little known aspects of African, American, and world history, transformed the conscience of Black people who had been conditioned to believe the lie—that Black people made no meaningful contributions to world culture and civilization.

Howard University's WHMM-TV began broadcasting *For the People* on Sunday mornings and repeated the program Sunday and Wednesday evenings. Buoyed by the favorable feedback he received from viewers in the Washington Metropolitan Area, Mr. Middleton expanded his talent pool to include interviews with Black scholars who lived outside of South Carolina. In 1987, Middleton featured a series of thirteen 30-minute interviews with Professor Asa G. Hilliard III, *Free Your Mind: Return to the Source*, which became the most watched program in WHMM-TV history. Dr. Hilliard's interviews reinforced the positive programming of the earlier interviews with Drs. Williams and Jackson, and he provided new evidence of the indigenous African origins of ancient Egyptian civilization. This was the first time in television history that Black folk had a program where they could talk openly about the African influences on world civilization and how this history had been largely ignored or falsified by racists within academia and the media—and it was broadcast without commercial interruptions.

Mr. Middleton added an additional series of interviews with Egyptologists, historians, social scientists, and Black intellectuals such as Dr. Welsing, Yosef Ben-Jochannan, John Henrik Clarke, Dona Richards (Marimba Ani), Amos Wilson, Ivan Van Sertima, Cheikh Anta Diop, Charles Finch, and dozens of other African-centered scholars who seldom, if ever, received positive, mainstream media exposure. One of the highlights of *For the People* was the show's 1987 trip to Egypt with 1,000 African Americans, where Middleton broadcast interviews with scholars in the shadow of the pyramids and other ancient monuments. While speaking at a tribute for Mr. Middleton at Howard University on January 23, 1993, Dr. Welsing shared with the audience that she was "addicted to *For the People*," and frequently discussed topics raised on the show during her monthly lectures at the Cress Welsing Institute as well as regular appearances on WOL. During one radio broadcast, Dr. Welsing said that she found the program to be such an effective tool for transforming the consciousness and behavior of the people who watched it, she begin prescribing it as a form of behavior therapy for some of her patients. This was agitation propaganda at its best—using positive entertainment as a means of individual and collective liberation.

During this same time, a group of West Coast scholars began hosting annual Melanin Conferences featuring presentations by psychiatrists, psychologists, educators, scientists, and historians, who brought to the public's awareness the importance of a "civilizing molecule" called melanin. The speakers provided evidence proving that melanin was more than the substance which gave skin color; it was described as a *chemical key to Black greatness* and our direct line of communication to The Creator and the Ancestors. The annual Melanin Conferences made rock stars out of Frances Welsing, Richard King, Carol Barnes, Wade Nobles, Asa Hilliard, Patricia Newton, Na'im Akbar, Hunter Adams, and others. The atmosphere generated by this new wave of Black Consciousness infused the air with energy, and had the same empowering effect as the Civil Rights and Black Power Movements of the 1960s as it spread across the United States, Caribbean, and Africa.

Dr. Welsing's Influences on the Entertainment Industry

Dr. Welsing's bold and consistent message about the Black condition influenced younger generations of artists like *Public Enemy* and the release of the Welsing-inspired album, *Fear of a Black Planet*, in 1990.

This release is considered by many in the entertainment industry as one of the most significant hip-hop recordings of all time. Each track on the album raised awareness on issues of race/racism/the system of white supremacy and encouraged listeners to "Fight the Power." The raps reflected the popularity of the growing African-centered Movement and introduced a new generation to the works of Dr. Welsing and the power of seeing their world through African eyes.

Greater public awareness of Dr. Welsing's teachings resulted from the 1991 publication of her magnum opus, *The Isis Papers: The Keys to the Colors*. It established the framework through which the public would examine and discuss racism/white supremacy as interpreted by a Black psychiatrist with a deep understanding of the subject and long-standing commitment to her people.

Elements of Dr. Welsing's theories made their way into a scene of the 1992 film *Boomerang*, featuring Eddie Murphy, Halle Berry, and an amazing supporting cast of African American entertainers. The Welsing-inspired scene in *Boomerang* took place as actors Murphy, David Alan Grier, and Martin Lawrence played pool. Lawrence explained to his friends that the green pool table represented the earth, the colored balls the colored people on the planet who were taken out one by one by the white cue ball. The game was "won" when the cue ball knocked the black eight ball off the pool table/planet. Murphy and Grier thought Lawrence was off his rocker for believing such absurdities; they reacted as many did upon hearing Dr. Welsing's analysis. It was a wonderful piece of satire which indicated to observant viewers that Welsing's theories were being mainstreamed by a few courageous souls in the entertainment industry.

Reactions to the Cress Theory and *The Isis Papers*

Newton's Third Law of Motion states, for every action there is an equal and opposite reaction. A racist system would not sit idly by and allow Black people to liberate themselves without serious consequences. The first counterattack occurred around 1990. Some viewers objected to "anti-Semitic" comments supposedly made by Dr. Welsing and Dr. Ben (Jochannan) on *For the People*, which prompted the management at SCETV to threaten the show's cancellation. The Washington, D.C., community pushed back by going on the airwaves of WOL and encouraging listeners to call and write letters of support for Middleton. Our counterattack was successful and *For the People* continued. The following year, Dr. Leonard Jeffries came under attack for a speech he gave in Albany, New York. Shortly thereafter, other Melanin scholars and intellectuals in the forefront of the African-centered Movement were attacked in the mainstream media, while others in academia were threatened with denial of tenure. Throughout this difficult period a supportive community provided physical, financial, and moral support to those under attack on the front line.

Today, as we survey the conditions of African Americans across the country, we can see that many Black communities are in crisis. Predictions of the emergence of a "post-racial" society following Barack Obama's presidential election have given way to a resurgence of overt racism and an unprecedented rise in police murders of Black people. Predominantly Black urban centers like Washington, D.C., Harlem, and Chicago have been transformed into urban homestead communities of young, upwardly mobile whites. There is a deep and palpable sense of despair. One can only imagine where Black people would be today if more of us had read *The Isis Papers* and understood how prophetic Dr. Welsing was when she wrote:

> The length of time required to neutralize global white supremacy will be "inversely proportional" to 1) the level of understanding of the phenomenon; plus 2) the evolution of self-and group-respect, the will, determination and discipline to practice the appropriate counter-racist behaviors—on the part of the non-white victims of white supremacy. Thus, the 21st century…will be a time perhaps of great devastation. But, undoubtedly, it will be a time of great change. And the most critical factor in that change of circumstances will be non-white people's ever increasing understanding of the behavioral phenomenon of white supremacy as a global, terroristic power system. [10]

The Task Ahead

In a world devoid of the physical presence of Dr. Welsing, the challenge the Black community now faces is how best to use the vast array of communication devices available to us to educate and empower the masses, instead of allowing our attention to be diverted from critical issues by mindless entertainment. We have seen in recent years how social media has been used to focus world attention on local and international issues of critical importance and motivate masses of people to confront injustices head-on.

Many Millennials have had their lives transformed after discovering online lectures of Black scholars and intellectuals whom they were never exposed to during their years of formal education. This newfound knowledge has led to the development of a new generation of filmmakers with access to cameras and editing equipment, which has allowed them to produce documentaries, on shoestring budgets, that are exposing people to knowledge of ancient and contemporary Black history and culture. Segments of the *Hidden Colors* series have exposed hundreds of thousands of people to Dr. Welsing, who was featured in Volumes 1 and 3 of the series.

As the popularity of this genre increases, we can expect to see documentaries exploring all areas of people activity and inspiring Black people to become the agents of their own mental and physical liberation. It is the hope that Black entertainers of the future will adopt codes of behavioral conduct for developing "Black self and group respect" and produce material devoid of Black people: name-calling, cursing, squabbling, gossiping, snitching, being discourteous and disrespectful, robbing, stealing, fighting, and using and selling drugs to one another [11] This is the mindset that must be developed if Black people are to save themselves. Dr. Welsing has shown us the way, and if we are pensive, we can hear her saying:

> Instead of engaging in our past practices of complaining, moaning, crying, groaning, begging, clapping hands and singing "We Shall Overcome" when confronted [by the] death-causing, life-stultifying

problems posed by white supremacy, Black people in the U.S. must dissect and analyze those problems to the core. With this knowledge, Black people can take the necessary steps to eliminate the problem. [12]

Endnotes

1 Tom Burrell, *Brainwashed: Challenging the Myth of Black Inferiority*, (Smiley Books, 2010), p. xii.
2 Frances Welsing, *The Isis Papers*, (Third World Books, 1991), p. 40.
3 Ibid., p. 78.
4 Edward Bernays, *Propaganda* (Routledge, 1928) p. 71.
5 Bruce Lipton, *The Biology of Belief* (Hay House, Revised 2008).
6 Frances Welsing, *The Isis Papers*, (Third World Books, 1991) p. 59.
7 Frederick Douglass, *Narrative of the Life of Frederick Douglass, an American Slave*, 1845.
8 Frances Welsing, *The Isis Papers*, (Third World Books, 1991), p. 153.
9 Ibid., p. 42.
10 Frances Welsing, *The Isis Papers*, (Third World Books, 1991), p. i
11 Dr. Frances Cress Welsing Memorial Page, *Facebook*.
12 Frances Welsing, *The Isis Papers*, (Third World Books, 1991), p. xvii.

Chapter 5

Laboring within the Mind Fields of Global White Supremacy

José V. Pimienta-Bey

For more than three hundred and fifty years, people classified as "whites" have implemented a highly aggressive socio-economic and political system known as Global White Supremacy (GWS): a system which is arguably the most dominant aggregate of social power on the planet. I often identify it as Global Eurocentric Hegemony (GEH) as well, since the people(s) to whom it is primarily attributed are Europeans. Dr. Frances Cress Welsing dedicated some 50 years of her life trying to explain the destructive impact and primary impetus for GWS/GEH. Dr. Welsing theorized that most whites possess a genetic fear of people of color in general, and towards Blacks in particular. Her "Cress Theory of Color-Confrontation and Racism (White Supremacy): A Psychogenetic Theory and World Outlook," utilized her training in psychiatry to determine the motivation behind the highly pervasive and influential GWS/GEH system.[1] Dr. Welsing's explanations concerning the long legacy of violent oppression endured by people of color at the hands of whites, have most often been embraced by more "conscious" or African-centered circles. Although our late, great elder held credentials as a highly-educated, rigorously-trained psychiatrist, public allies—Black or otherwise—were typically hard to come by. Over the course of her life, many Black "intellectuals" and academics rejected Welsing's psychogenetic framework as it relates to racism. I however, am not amongst them. I have regarded Welsing's theory worthy of serious consideration from my first reading of her work nearly 30 years ago.

Labor, which is the focus of my chapter, represents one of the nine areas of human activity first identified by Neely Fuller Jr. over 40 years ago. The others include: economics, entertainment, education, law, politics, religion, sex, and war. Welsing complemented Fuller's work, theorizing that the historic confrontations between Europeans and the indigenous peoples of Asia, Africa, America, and Australia, have primarily been driven by a psychological awareness amongst Europeans of their numerical minority status and recessive genetic vulnerability.

Dr. Welsing wrote in her 1991 classic, *The Isis Papers: The Keys to the Colors*: "The goal of the white supremacy system is none other than the establishment, maintenance, expansion and refinement of world domination by members of a group that classifies itself as the white 'race.'"[2] Welsing expanded upon Fuller's initial thesis, which had suggested that the word "race," had "little biological validity but it translated more correctly as 'organization,' the sole purpose of which is to maintain white domination and world control."[3] "White" as a racial classification only came into global use around four centuries ago, traversing the globe with British expansion. However, since that time, it has become a color-based term used generally to identify persons of European ancestry.

Fuller's more recent works continue to expound upon what he and Dr. Welsing started. Fuller continues their efforts to awaken people of color to the ongoing impact and dangers posed by GWS/GEH. His latest work, *The United Independent Compensatory Code/System/Concept: A Compensatory Counter-Racist Code*,[4] has a chapter which specifically highlights the area of labor as it relates to the Color-Confrontation Theory which he and Welsing pioneered. Fuller writes:

> In a socio-material system dominated by Racists (White Supremacists) all "jobs" that are established and/or maintained by White people are dominated (either directly or indirectly) by those White people who practice Racism (White Supremacy). No person can be hired, fired, promoted, and/or get "in trouble" on a job unless it is the will of the White Supremacists.[5]

Fuller points out that under such a system, a non-white person can never truly be an autonomous "supervisor," since they are only granted such titles under the watchful control of the GWS/GEH system.[6]

Fuller goes on to assert that the perception of the racist (white supremacist), within such a constructed societal reality, is that whites alone are the most important and competent ("superior") workers within "the known universe."[7] Further, their most vital work is to "establish, maintain, expand, and/or refine, the practice of racism (White Supremacy)."[8] Like Welsing, Fuller asserts that "deceit, direct violence, and/or the threat of violence" are components inherent to maintaining the GWS/GEH system.[9]

Welsing's training as a physician and behavioral scientist were integrated into her explanations of GWS/GEH. Consequently, she sought a "treatment" or means to combat it. For example, in her classic *The Isis Papers,* she outlines the concept of "counter-racist psychiatry," which she defined as:

> ...patterns of logic, thought, speech, action, emotional response and perception consciously practiced by the victims of white supremacy (racism)—with the objective of eradicating racism at the global level. Functionally speaking, for the victims of white supremacy, this means to act in a self/group-respecting and supporting manner in all areas of people activity, despite the specific conditions of racist domination and oppression.[10]Welsing maintained that any submission to or co-operation with GWS/GEH were "signs of individual or group mental illness or self-negation."[11]

In *The Isis Paper*s, she wrote:

> Black people throughout the world live under the power of the white supremacy system of total oppression and domination, implying the absence of any true power to determine ultimately what happens to their individual and collective lives. [12]

Welsing added: "Ultimately there is a disturbance in problem perception... Black people in the U.S. reject the conscious recognition of the global white supremacy system."[13] This has resulted in "a collective Black floundering and an *ideological* vacuum and disorientation," with the "powerless arguing and squabbling amongst themselves ... [as Blacks] compete with one another for white supremacy jobs."[14]

Today, many such "White Supremacy jobs" can be seen within the Prison-Industrial Complex, another component of the GWS/GEH system that is firmly invested in an ongoing incarceration of non-whites. Michelle Alexander's powerful work, *The New Jim Crow: Mass*

Incarceration in the Age of Colorblindness,[15] does a superb job of outlining just how profoundly racist (anti-Black and Brown) the U.S. criminal justice system is. It is a multi-billion-dollar business, where corporations use prison labor to avoid paying decent, livable wages.[16] Most of the prison system's money came following President Nixon's proposed "War on Drugs" in the 1970's. Alexander explains:

> The drug war is largely responsible for the prison boom … and there is no path to liberation for communities of color that includes this ongoing war. So long as people of color in ghetto communities are being rounded up by the thousands for drug offenses, carted off to prisons, and then released into a permanent undercaste, mass incarceration as a system of control will continue to function as well.[17]

Alexander shows how White Supremacy is part of a historical continuum. She cites the short-lived successes of the early Populist movement led by a white Southerner named Tom Watson. Following the Civil War, Watson's Populists managed to unite poor and working class whites and Blacks, who had been exceedingly burdened by a severe agrarian depression of the 1880s–90s. Alexander explains: "The Populists took direct aim at the conservatives, who were known as comprising a party of privilege, and they achieved a stunning series of victories" throughout the South. [18] However, the conservative white oligarchs counterpunched, and utilized various tactics including "fraud, intimidation, bribery, and terror" in order to break up the alliances between white and Black labor.[19]

By the time it was over, even the presumed stalwart of labor unity, Populist leader Watson, declared: "Populist principles could never be fully embraced by the South until blacks were eliminated from politics."[20] Even "Northern [White] liberals" cast aside "their dark-skinned allies" and bowed to the conservatives.[21] Many poor whites lost out economically as a result of the broken alliance. For them, Alexander explains, "the racial bribe was primarily psychological."[22] The collapse of Populism, like several other failed alliances between white and non-white labor, illustrates that there is more to consider than just "class" conflicts. Such historical truths should compel us to consider Welsing's work.

For Welsing, the real obstacle which Blacks have faced in securing jobs and/or resources in general, is not predicated upon class struggle. She cites that "there is no "*fantasized* Black middle class versus the fantasized Black lower class;" as "class" itself "does not refer to income alone but to actual existing power."[23] Welsing rejected Marxist explanations of labor relations because she judged them to be incomplete for having customarily denied any recognition of deeper psychological motivations found within so many people who have chosen to identify as white. Welsing states:

> This attempted escape into Marxist doctrine falsely comforts some Blacks (as it did many Semites in Europe). In accepting this doctrine, they are convinced that there are some whites (the workers) who wish to unite with non-whites out of a supposed common interest.[24]

For Welsing, Black Marxists essentially fail to consider the "survival psyche of all who accept classification as white."[25]

Neely Fuller's 2010 publication, the *Compensatory Code/System and Codified Word Guide*, and his revised and expanded 2016 edition, both serve as corrective "workbooks" for mitigating GWS/GEH's destructive power. In his discussion of labor, Fuller contends that the very use of the terms "labor" and "laborer" must be used "with caution."[26] Fuller asserts that the system of White Supremacy is always seeking ways to reduce the worth or value of non-white labor. This is particularly true when one notes the classic Western characterizations of "skilled" and "unskilled" labor.

Fuller poses a profound question, "How, exactly, can any labor that produces a constructive result be correctly regarded as 'unskilled'?"[27] Fuller argues that "White Supremacists (Racists)" have typically called labor either skilled or unskilled in order to sustain the perception that the labor of white people (often referred to as "skilled" labor) is valued more than the labor of non-white people (more often referred to as "unskilled").[28]

Fuller even advises that the term "Labor Union" be used with caution. He writes: "What, exactly, is a 'union of labor' for? What, exactly, is a 'union of labor' against?"[29] Fuller argues that any truly united

"Union" of workers, should seek to achieve justice for all labor/workers, not just one group. Western history shows us that within the labor movement, Black workers were systematically removed or excluded from receiving the benefits and protections of labor unions.

In his 1994 work, *Black Labor, White Wealth: The Search for Power and Economic Justice*, Claud Anderson outlines just how much of the inequity we see today is linked to the legacy of chattel slavery. But Anderson recognizes that the problem goes beyond physical bondage. Anderson writes that Black people:

> ...have further handicapped ourselves by some of our own beliefs and behaviors. Our dogged pursuit of integration is one example. In so doing, we have destroyed our communities, diluted our numerical strength and become dependent upon others. We have been further handicapped by our inability to practice group economics in a capitalistic democracy.[30]

Fuller and Welsing's thesis can clearly be seen in Anderson's argument. To date, Blacks have largely failed to manifest a global union of Black or Pan-African labor in response to GWS/GEH.

Drawing in large part upon the insights of Du Bois, Harold Cruse wrote in his 1988 work, *Plural, but Equal: Blacks and Minorities in America's Plural Society*: "It became demonstrable that the class origins and affinities of the black elites were *nonnationalistic*."[31] Anderson's conclusions are also in agreement:

> We [Blacks] have always been a key capitalistic element in the national empowerment plans of others—as a source of free or cheap labor. Yet, we have never had a national empowerment plan of our own. We have never used our collective intellectual resources to create a national plan with explicit policies and strategies for our own economic and political gain.[32]

Although I agree with Anderson's essential argument regarding the need for a national empowerment plan, I would argue that only an *international* empowerment plan would be effective in countering GWS/GEH. Additionally, Anderson fails to acknowledge that there was such a "plan" by and for African people, and the plan resulted in action.

The Honorable Marcus Mosiah Garvey founded the Universal Negro Improvement Association (UNIA) and African Communities League at the beginning of the twentieth century, some 50 years after the 13th Amendment was passed. Garvey laid the groundwork for tangible international empowerment for all people of African descent. Furthermore, his UNIA organization would influence other movements such as the Moorish Science Temple and the Nation of Islam.

As our late, great elder scholar John Henrik Clarke stated in *Marcus Garvey and the Vision of Africa*, "[T]o call the movement he brought into being a 'back-to-Africa movement' is to narrow its meaning. This was only one aspect of his movement. Marcus Garvey's plan was for total African redemption."[33] His organization was strategically multi-dimensional, and this generated fear and consternation among Western powers. Garvey wrote within the UNIA's 1914 Manifesto, that one of his primary objectives was "To conduct a worldwide commercial and industrial intercourse."[34] Garvey understood that any improvement in the conditions of Black labor anywhere, would unequivocally be tied to the fate of Africans everywhere. Garvey and his adherents recognized the interdependent and interconnected fate of Africans globally: something which Dr. Welsing understood as well.

Garvey tried to empower Black/African labor in places like Liberia, a country essentially created in the 19th century by the United States. Liberia was one of only three "independent" African countries at that time. The other two were the British-established Sierra Leone and the Christian kingdom of Ethiopia. The late Black psychologist Amos Wilson explained in his monumental 1998 book, *Blueprint for Black Power*, that "the skullduggery of White businessmen" undermined Garvey's efforts. Wilson points out that white-owned companies like Firestone Rubber, with the helpful "machinations of the U.S., British, and French governments," were able to summarily abort any such efforts which threatened the economic and political domination of whites within Africa.[35]

Presently, it is still the case that no organization that has succeeded in improving socioeconomic conditions for the majority of Black people on a global scale. The reasons for such limited success, including Garvey's earlier catalytic movement, can be attributed to the relentless tactics of GWS. And many proponents of GWS have been comfortably headquartered within the United States. One only need reference Rosewood, Florida or Tulsa, Oklahoma, to see a few classic examples of the desecration and decimation of unified and self-supported Black townships.

Fortunately, Wilson—like Welsing—argued that GWS can be effectively challenged. Wilson's approach promoted the rediscovery, revitalization, and refurbishment of movements such as Garvey's. However, Wilson cautioned that the "Black leadership establishment," could actually hinder Black autonomy and socioeconomic progress, as he recognized that Black leadership was all too often an expression of the GWS system.[36] Although his voluminous *Blueprint for Black Power* largely emphasized conditions within the U.S., Wilson's arguments regarding the "segmented labor market" still have international applications which apply to the African Diaspora.

The glaring wage gaps between non-whites and whites further invigorate Welsing's work. In a January 7, 2016, article entitled, "Racial, Gender, Wage Gaps Persist in U.S. Despite Some Progress," author Eileen Patten of the Pew Research Center points out that among full and part-time U.S. workers, Blacks in 2015 earned just 75% as much as whites, with white women earning 83% as much as white men. When gender, race, and ethnicity were combined, all groups, except Asian men, lag behind white men in terms of median hourly earnings.[37] Hourly wages for Black men were $15, Hispanic men $14, and white men $21. Asian men earned $24, beating out white men by $3. The hourly wages of Asian and white women ($18 and $17, respectively) were higher than both Black and Hispanic women ($13 and $12), as well as Black and Hispanic men.[38] In addition, while white and Asian women have reduced the wage gap with white men significantly over the past four decades, Black and Hispanic men "have made no progress in narrowing the wage gap with white men since 1980."[39]

For those who believe that education or experience are the primary reasons for such scathing discrepancies, the research proves otherwise.

College-educated Black and Hispanic men still earn only 80% the hourly wage of their white male counterparts. Similarly, the statistics also show that white and Asian college-educated women, only earned 80%. Black and Hispanic women with a college degree were last, earning only about 70% of the hourly wages of "similarly educated" White men.[40] In addition, when Blacks were surveyed about "fair" treatment in the workplace, 64% said they were treated "less fairly" than whites. This compared to 22% of whites and 38% of Hispanics. Lastly, 40% of Blacks said their "race or ethnicity" made it more difficult for them to succeed in life, and 20% of Hispanics said the same. This compared to only 5% of whites. Asians were not reported in this survey.[41]

The Economic Policy Institute identified that such wage gaps were due to "discrimination and growing earnings inequality in general."[42] The EPI report identified "discrimination" as one of the "the primary reasons for America's huge racial gap in pay."[43] The report also recommended holding a summit to address the disparities in the salaries of Black college graduates.

In short, non-white labor in the U.S. is strongly affected by an overarching system of GWS, with a patriarchal foundation. Welsing's assertion that this is an expression of white genetic fear consistently maneuvering to prevent the rise of organized non-white economic power, must again be considered. What is also intriguing here, is that the only people of color who have managed to outmaneuver white dominance when it comes to wages and labor, were Asian men. The control of Black (and Brown) labor and economic wealth does appear as a GWS priority. But white concerns about Asian labor ("Yellow peril") are still part of the historical record. Welsing tells us that white hostility has been directed towards "all peoples with the capacity to produce melanin. However, the most profound aggressions have been towards Black people, who have the greatest color potential and, therefore, are the most envied and feared in genetic color competition."[44]

The once popular work of the early 20th-century Harvard educated historian Lothrop Stoddard, represents one of the clearest and strongest examples in support of Welsing's theories. In his book, *The Rising*

Tide of Color Against White World Supremacy (1921), Stoddard offered his fearful assessment of the world. Following Russia's defeat by the Japanese, Stoddard declared that millions of "colored minds" in both "Africa and Asia [were] thrilled with joy and hope," as "the legend of white invincibility lay, a fallen idol, in the dust ... That [White] supremacy was no longer acquiesced in [sic] as inevitable."[45] Stoddard's concerns again echoed the idea that ALL non-whites must be contained and controlled globally by whites. This further translates into maintaining white control over the entire earth's natural resources, including human labor, since such resources are necessary for sustaining life itself.

In his book, *Confessions of An Economic Hit Man*,[46] John Perkins explains that bribery, intimidation, and assassination were (and oftentimes still are) the keys to success in the Western global business system which he describes as akin to "slavery." He writes:

> Today, we still have slave traders. They no longer find it necessary to march into the forests of Africa looking for prime specimens ... They simply recruit desperate people ... to produce the jackets, blue jeans, tennis shoes, automobile parts, computer components, and thousands of other items they can sell in the market of their choosing.[47]

He continues:

> The modern slave trader assures herself (or himself) that the desperate people are better off earning one dollar a day than no dollars at all ... She [or he] also understands that these desperate people are fundamental to the survival of her company, that they are the foundation for her [or his] own lifestyle.[48]

When one looks at the primary beneficiaries of the various international companies, it is easy to see White Supremacy in action. Those defined as white remain its greatest beneficiaries, in spite of being the world's statistical minority. Asians represent the world's majority people, and even the present tensions between China and the U.S. in the areas of labor and global economic power can be seen within the framework of Welsing's argument.

So, what is China's role or place in Welsing's theory as it pertains specifically to Black people? How will China impact labor conditions within the developing world in general, and African countries in particular? In a June 13, 2017 *Financial Times* article by David Pilling, He points out that the China-Africa relationship is "shifting the commercial and geopolitical axis of an entire continent that many western governments had given up on."[49] Jing Gu, Director of the Centre for Rising Powers and Global Development in East Sussex, says: "To have 54 African [nations as] friends is very important for China."[50] Still, the article does report that some Africans are suspicious, and cites their complaints about Chinese companies employing too few locals, and paying scant regard to the environment. But overall Pilling admits, "there is a begrudging recognition that China has mostly benefited Africa."[51]

According to Pilling, there are roughly one million Chinese entrepreneurs who have settled in Africa. China is also the sixth largest lender to African countries. China's businesses are involved in extracting African mineral wealth, timber, oil, gold, and even illegal ivory. Chinese trade with African countries has soared from $10 billion in 2000, to $220 billion in 2014. Even a country like Ethiopia, whose natural resources are severely limited in comparison to many other African nations, has been the second largest recipient of Chinese loans. Financing for roads, dams, railways, and manufacturing plants topped out at more than $12.3 billion, more than twice that of "oil-soaked Sudan and mineral-rich Congo."[52] Of the UN Security Council's five members, China also has the largest number of UN "peacekeepers" on the African continent, with more than 2,000 troops."[53]

Pilling reports that "although China presents risk," most Africans say "it brings tangible benefits in finance and engineers. More importantly, it brings choice."[54] Previously, African governments had been "locked in often unproductive relationships with foreign donors who…brought billions of dollars in aid" and "a ruinously prescriptive Washington consensus of market-based development and reform."[55] Zambian economist Dambisa Moyo agrees with Pilling's assessment and sees great benefits for Africans.

Moyo says that Beijing is transforming the continent with big projects which have brought dams, airports, seaports, railways, and telecommunications networks to "even the most obscure" parts of Africa.[56] Pilling adds that Beijing's official policy of non-interference has also impressed many Africans. Leaders from Angola to Zimbabwe were particularly "fed up with lectures from former colonial powers about human rights and democracy."[57] China has been far less authoritarian and patronizing than the U.S. and other Western/European countries, something which many Africans appreciate.[58]

Interestingly enough, the "Centre" run by Director Jing, identifies African countries as "*Rising Powers*."[59] The use of such language infers a level of Chinese respect for developing countries within Africa. China's President Xi Jinping even addressed African labor and political leadership when he said China "offers a new option for other countries and nations who want to speed up their development while preserving their independence."[60] If China continues to share her own "miracle" with other "Rising Powers," this will allow for greater empowerment of labor within many non-white nations, thereby threatening GWS/GEH. The little known and rarely discussed Bandung Conference, held in April 1955, witnessed African and Asian nations working together to establish a "Third Force" in response to GWS. Current events may move the non-white world to renew such efforts.

In her brilliantly multidimensional work, *Yurugu: An Afrikan-Centered Critique of European Cultural Thought and Behavior*,[61] Marimba Ani reminds us how a European minority of less than 5 million controlled and held hostage over 21 million Africans and 3 million other people of color, within South Africa. The indigenous Africans could not vote, buy or sell land, live where they chose, move around freely, nor labor/work where they wished. Additionally, Africans could not hold public office, and this meant that they were politically powerless under the existing governmental system."[62] Africans represented 72% of the population; but were "relegated to 13% of the land" known as "Bantustans."[63] Europeans (Blankes/Whites) were 16% of the country, yet they held control of 87% of the land. Not surprisingly, Africans earned 29% of the country's wage, while Europeans earned nearly 60%. During the 1980's, the USA (Union of South Africa) only spent $178 per African student, and $1,323 per European student. The desired effect was to leave Africans as an ill-equipped and highly dependent labor force within their undeniably overt white supremacist system. The sad reality is that the histories of the United States of America and most Western nations abound with such actions taken by whites to limit, control, or destroy non-white labor opportunities and economies. In another work by Ani, "The Implications of African-American Spirituality," she contends: "the determining structure of the Western metaphysic is that of power, control, and destruction."[64] Both women, Ani and Welsing, reached similar conclusions, although they had taken different paths.

Welsing's psychogenetic theory and its connection to labor have been manifested in Libya. Libya went from Africa's wealthiest country to a failed state openly involved in the sale of captive Africans. Harvard research fellow Garikai Chengu reminds us that Libya was one of the "most modern and secular states in the Middle East and North Africa with the highest regional women's rights and standards of living."[65] Mainstream Western media and politicians largely demonized Gaddafi.

Chengu suggests that "Perhaps, Gaddafi's greatest crime, in the eyes of NATO, was his desire to put the interests of local labor above foreign capital and his quest for a strong and truly United States of Africa."[66] Chengu makes this argument because he took the time to study the effect of Gaddafi's policies, and how they worked to increase the value of African labor. Gaddafi's use of the nation's oil wealth to allow Libyans free health-care, free education, free electricity, and interest-free loans was raising the value of Libyan labor specifically, and African labor in general. Gaddafi's attempt to establish a more technologically advanced infrastructure and economically empowered African continent solicited fear in the minds of White Supremacists world-wide. Consequently, we shouldn't be surprised when journalists such as Neil Clark point out that Western backed "Extremists" and "blatantly racist, death squads" were tremendously influential in creating the "mess" in Libya.[67]

The anthropologist Michael Bradley argued in his controversial 1978 work, *The Ice Man Inheritance*: "Our [White] works and values reflect aggression. Our technology is aggression against the natural world."[68] Bradley's statement raises some interesting questions related to Welsing's theory. Doesn't the "natural world" include Black, Brown, Red, and Yellow peoples? Africans (Blacks) are, after all, the genetic mothers and fathers of humanity. What could be more "natural" than being Black, or being a person of color? Bradley's comment alludes to the West's historic aggression towards the more melanized ("natural") peoples of the earth. Psychologist Edward Bruce Bynum goes as far as to argue that "White identity development" has been like "an autoimmune disease" wreaking havoc upon the "body politic" and threatening the world itself.[69] Bynum's analogy fits well within Welsing's own assessment.

Finally, I think that it is important to point out that for all its injustice and inequity, the good doctor still defined GWS as the only "functional" form of racism. Welsing understood that since its purpose was to preserve "white-ness," its objective of self/group preservation would seem reasonable within that context. The obvious problem is how catastrophic this outlook has proven to be in relation to non-whites and the world at large. That is why Noel Ignatiev, founder of the *Race Traitor* journal, has declared: "Treason to whiteness is loyalty to humanity."[70]

Conclusion

Over some four centuries, people classified as white have employed a highly aggressive and confrontational system known in recent decades as Global White Supremacy (GWS). GWS requires that all theories and systems of political and economic organization establish, ensure, and expand upon white domination over the entire earth. This system has functioned as the most dominant aggregate of social power on the planet. In the realm of "Labor," non-white workers/laborers have found themselves violently oppressed and exploited by whites in ways that have gone well beyond simple financial profits. This has been especially true when the labor has been Black. Dr. Welsing's life work offers vital insight into what has driven such destructive behaviors and tendencies amongst whites.

Dr. Welsing held to her convictions and unselfishly shared her mind-opening scholarship with countless audiences regarding the unfathomable impact of Global White Supremacy. I believe that the hour compels us to not only celebrate the profound contributions of our late elder, but to earnestly dedicate ourselves to greater study of both white and non-white behaviors. I am convinced this is vital if we are to effectively address the scathing challenges and inequities related to not only Black labor, but all non-white labor worldwide. I maintain that our committed reflection upon and application of Dr. Welsing's work is the crucial first step towards ensuring not only economic survival, but the survival of humanity itself.

Endnotes

1 Welsing, Frances Cress MD. *The Isis (Yssis) Papers: The Keys to the Colors*. (n.p; C.W. Publishing, 1991), 1.
2 Welsing, *The Isis (Yssis) Papers,* 3.
3 Ibid.
4 uller, Neely, Jr., *The United-Independent Compensatory Code/System/Concept: A Compensatory Counter-Racist Code*. (Washington, DC: NFJ Productions, 1984) 2016.
5 Ibid., 131.
6 Ibid.
7 Ibid., 132.
8 Ibid.
9 Ibid.
10 Welsing, The Isis (Yssis) Paper, 53.
11 Ibid.
12 Ibid., 154.
13 Ibid.
14 Ibid.,155.
15 Michelle Alexander. *The New Jim Crow: Mass Incarceration in the Age of Colorblindness* (New York, NY: New Press, 2012).
16 Ibid., 219
17 Ibid., 220.
18 Ibid., 34.
19 Ibid.
20 Ibid., 34.
21 Ibid.
22 Ibid., 35.
23 Welsing, *The Isis (Yssis) Papers*, 156.
24 Ibid., 158.
25 Ibid., 158.
26 Fuller, 2010, 190.
27 Ibid., 190-1.
28 Ibid.
29 Ibid.
30 Claud Anderson, *Black Labor, White Wealth: The Search for Power and Economic Justice* (Bethesda: PowerNomics Corp of America, 1994), 6.
31 Harold Cruse, *Plural But Equal: A Critical Study of Blacks and Minorities and America's Plural Society* (Quill, William Morrow, 1987), 388, 389.
32 Anderson, *Black Labor, White Wealth: The Search for Power and Economic Justice*. 6.
33 John Henry Clarke and Amy Jacques Garvey . *Marcus Garvey and The Vision of Africa* (Black Classic Press, 2011, [Reprint from 1973]), p.4.

34 Ibid., 6.

35 Amos N. Wilson, *Blueprint for Black Power: A Moral, Political and Economic Imperative for the Twenty-First Century* (Brooklyn, NY:Afrikan World InfoSystems, 1998) p.431.

36 Ibid., 443.

37 Eileen Patten, "Racial, Gender Wage Gaps Persist in U.S. Despite Some Progress." (Washington, D.C.: Pew Research Center, 1 July 2016). Retrieved from www.pewresearch.org/fact- tank/2016/07/01/racial-gender-wage-gaps-persist-in-u-s-despite-some-progress/. Accessed 14 Dec. 2017.

38 Ibid.

39 Ibid.

40 Ibid.

41 Ibid.

42 Niall McCarthy, "Income Inequality Between White And Black Americans Is Worse Today Than In 1979 [Infographic]." *Forbes* Magazine, 21 Sept. 2016. Retrieved from www.forbes.com/ sites/niallmccarthy/2016/09/21/income-inequality-between-white-black-americans-i s-worsetoday-than-in-1979-infographic/#aea0a7f37405. Accessed 14 Dec. 2017.

43 Ibid.

44 Welsing, *The Isis Papers*, 5.

45 Michael Krenn, T*he Color of Empire: Race and American Foreign Relations* (Lincoln, NE: Potomac Books, 2006), 63.

46 John Perkins, *Confessions of an Economic Hit Man* (New York, NY:Plume, 2006).

47 Ibid., 212.

48 Ibid., 212 & 213.

49 David Pilling, "Chinese Investment in Africa: Beijing's Testing Ground." Financial Times. Retrieved from www.ft.com/content/0f534aa4-4549-11e7-8519-9f94ee97d996. Accessed 17 Dec. 2017.

50 Ibid.

51 Ibid.

52 Ibid.

53 Ibid.

54 Ibid., 7.

55 Ibid.

56 Ibid.

57 Ibid.

58 Ibid.

59 Pilling, 11

60 Chris Buckley, and Keith Bradsher, "Xi Jinping's Marathon Speech: Five Takeaways." The New York Times. Oct 18, 2017. Retrieved from www.nytimes.com/2017/10/18/world/ asia/china-xi-jinping-party-congress.html. Accessed 22 Dec. 2017.

61 Marimba Ani. *Yurugu: An African-centered Critique of European Cultural Thought and Behavior* (Washington D.C.: Nkonimfo Publications 1994), 418.
62 bid.
63 Ibid.
64 Molefi Asante and Kariamu Welsh-Asante editors. *African Culture: The Rhythms of Unity* (Westport, CT: Greenwood Press, 1985), 210.
65 Garikai Chengu, "Libya- From Africa's Richest State Under Gaddafi, To Failed State After NATO Intervention." *Global Research: Centre for Research on Glob- al ization*. Oct 19, 2014. Retrived from www.globalresearch.ca/libya-from-af-ricas-richest-state-under- gaddafi-to-failed-state-after-nato-intervention/5408740. Accessed Dec 26. 2017.
66 Ibid.
67 Neil Clark, "Slave Markets in 'Liberated' Libya and the Silence of the Human-itarian Hawks." *RT International*. Dec 1, 2017. Retrieved from www.rt.com/op-edge/411562-libya- slave-markets-nato/. Accessed Dec 26, 2017.
68 Michael Bradley, *The Ice Man Inheritance* (New York, NY: Warner Books, 1978), 58.
69 Edward Bruce Bynum, *The African Unconscious: Roots of Ancient Mysticism and Modern Psychology* (Teachers College Press, 1999), .260.
70 Noel Ignatiev, "TOP 7 QUOTES BY NOEL IGNATIEV." *A-Z Quotes*. Retrieved from www. azquotes.com/author/33287-Noel_Ignatiev. Accessed 18 Dec. 2017

Chapter 6

Decoding the Legal Matrix

Pilar Jan Penn

> "The state has been reached in our experience of captivity…wherein we are being challenged to demonstrate a deep self-respect...requiring us to use our whole brain-computers…to analyze critically and decode what is happening daily in front of our eyes and to organize a self- and group-respecting behavioral responses to that which the environment is presenting us. We must have a disciplined, self- and group-respecting response to the specific war being waged against us."
>
> —Dr. Frances Cress Welsing "Justifiable Homicide"[1]

When I was just 14 years old I remember seeing Dr. Welsing on television debating William Shockley on *Tony Brown's Journal*, a show regularly watched in our household. My roots are in Tuskegee Institute, Alabama, a place with a history filled with solid examples of academic excellence and community activism, so I was mesmerized by the Black woman who was a psychiatrist debating the official representative of white supremacy. I was eager to hear what Dr. Welsing had to say. I learned early that the fight against white supremacy was on *all* levels, and I fought it daily in my life at the predominantly white Catholic school I attended. A reminder of her influence on my life path over those many years was Dr. Welsing's visit during my second year of law school. Her talk served as an impetus to confront the challenges of racism and to overcome white supremacy's oppressive grip on non-white people.

Dr. Welsing helped us see that it takes mentally unstable individuals to deny people their rights to freedom under laws created by the system of white supremacy (SOWS), while claiming their own natural right to freedom. Welsing described White Supremacy as an illegitimate director of what is considered order, balance, truth, or justice because its first orders of business are self-preservation, manifest destiny, and maintaining its position of power.

Brushes with the Law

When I was a child, I enjoyed watching episodes of *Perry Mason*.[2] I was a child who loved order, and it appeared to me that Mason and his counterparts were intent on creating a perfect world where truth was foremost in the quest for justice, order, and balance. The bad guys always got what they deserved, and Mr. Mason was always successful. I lived in this bubble of a dream for most of my young life. Little did I know that the truth was far from the fairy tale woven on the television screen.

As a law student, I believed that I was following in the footsteps of such greats as Constance Baker Motley, Thurgood Marshall, Adam Clayton Powell, Walter White, Fred Gray, and others. What I did not know in 1993 was that the mold for the civil rights era had been broken and a new die cast. The struggles of those that came before us were being turned backward. The Supreme Court was becoming more conservative, and our claims to the rights secured by those strivings under the Constitution faced new challenges. Beginning with the Nixon administration, a quiet nationalism turning into fascism has emerged across the nation. We carried on as before, fighting the old battles, not realizing that new battles were marching straight toward us.

It was during this time I went to college in Lawrence, Kansas, 30 minutes away from my parents' home in Topeka. My first interaction with the Law happened one windy Kansas day, awakening me to how things really worked. I became involved in a confrontation between two of my friends and three white female students while driving through campus. We emerged from our cars and exchanged words, and because I was with my girls, somebody ended up getting slapped. I don't know who threw the first punch, but I was told it was me. I pled the fifth. Because cars were involved, the two drivers, I and one of the white students, were made to appear before the court. Nobody was arrested, but later I realized it was in deference to the other group of students involved. We were both in the wrong, but she was handled much differently than I. The white student, of course, had the good sense to be prepared and came to court with a lawyer, and she was given the opportunity to tell her side of the story. However, my witnesses were treated with suspicion and my testimony was questioned. Her testimony on the other hand, was accepted with no need for substantiation from any witnesses. After that, I figured out that the law was not on my side... and something deep down inside told me that it never had been. I walked away from that experience with a bad taste in my mouth and awakened to the fact that truth was not the focus of the law or the courts.

Years later, no longer fooled by the image of Perry Mason's winning ways and caring manner about truth and justice, I found myself captivated by an interview with Bryan Stevenson conducted by Robin McNeil and Jim Lehrer on PBS. During this time, I was in graduate school at Emory University, deciding on my next steps as graduation approached. I had not really thought about going to law school, but when I heard Bryan Stevenson speak about the death penalty work he was doing, the passion with which he spoke caused me to think about the law in a new way, and I fervently started applying to law schools.

I found law school a stimulating environment, giving my mind room to expand and experience the intellectual freedom of expression. My mentors were two Black law faculty and a few of the allied legal professionals at the school. My first year taught me about criminal law's love of Huey P. Newton and the Black Panther Party. It taught me a well-kept secret about how the 13th Amendment's preservation of slavery was lying in wait for Bill Clinton's tacit implementation of the loophole during his administration. This included mandatory sentencing and "Three Strikes You're Out" laws enacted across the nation.

Our presence (Black students) and earned right to be members of the law school were continuously under discussion inside and outside of the classroom. It was assumed, by some, that we were beneficiaries of "affirmative action" admissions policies and did not gain admission based upon solid academic credentials. In receiving such "handouts," or so the logic went, we had denied "more qualified" white applicants their rightful place. In fact, all Black students, regardless of academic transcripts to the contrary, were enrolled in remedial writing workshops. I thought this was because the university assumed we, in contrast to our non-Black counterparts, were unprepared for the rigors of legal writing, even though I, along with several of my peers, attended law school after having earned a master's degree. It was as if our being there was still under scrutiny and every day we had to prove that our acceptances were based on merit.

We [Black students] made it abundantly clear that none of us were given our placements in the class based upon measures different than those used to determine admission for our white classmates. Further, discussions analyzing Affirmative Action ensued, as data supported the fact that white women were the largest group benefiting from such policies.[3] Still, the beliefs of some of our peers persisted and we had to simply move on.

This challenge to our intellectual capabilities and earned right to be part of the legal community was my second realization of how the system of white supremacy works within the legal system. Because my very presence in the *classroom* was being challenged, what did this predict about my future in the courtroom? I did not know it, but my third year of law school was going to provide a preview.

During my tenure at school, I witnessed a transition in the legal community with the retirement of Thurgood Marshall and the investiture of Clarence Thomas on the U.S. Supreme Court.[4] I witnessed the brutal beating of Rodney King on the streets of Los Angeles, and the decimation of the War Powers Act by George H.W. Bush. Through all these events, there were many changes in the way white supremacy functioned under the cover of a "system of justice." That the true purpose and power of law was to maintain an imbalance in society favoring whites and disfavoring everyone else, became more apparent to me. An interview with Thurgood Marshall validated my sense of this when, during an interview, he was asked about his efforts to advance the goals of freedom while serving on the Supreme Court. What caught my attention was his response to the question. Mr. Marshall exclaimed "We ain't free! We ain't nowhere's near free!" as though he was sounding an alarm. No doubt, my first year of law school had given me a lot to think about.

My first-year criminal law professor impressed me deeply during a discussion of the case *People v. Newton.*[5] Being a young Black girl during the '60s and living in a household of community activists, it was hard for me to not love the Black Panthers, and so I studied that material and listened intently to the relevant discussions in class. At the end of the discussion, the professor said that the law had much to thank the Panthers for and that we should appreciate the contributions their efforts made on the development of laws in our country. After class, I asked him to explain his last statement. He stated that without the Panthers and Newton challenging the system of laws in California, the laws would not have evolved to respond to social and political dissent from classes of people that would challenge the rule of law. This is not what I thought he had meant, so his response pained me and I began to see the application of the law from a different perspective. Consequently, my knowledge of the Black Panthers and what transpired with them would later give proof that the system of laws created by white supremacists morphs and develops new "laws," justifications, and restraints depending on how victims of the system of white supremacy (SOWS) respond to it.

These discussions helped me to realize that the law is not about order, balance, truth, and justice. As hard as it was for me to accept, I realized that the system of white supremacy manages the legal system for the purpose of information gathering and neutralizing those it seeks to control. Rather than a system of "law and order," or the much touted "rule of law," when it comes to the disenfranchised, the underclass, the poor, the "colored," the alien, the young, or those considered unworthy of care, the system is one of force and control. The oft-spoken mantra for the victims of white supremacy has been "No Justice, No Peace." But, unfortunately, the beliefs of the white supremacists regarding our calls for justice are best expressed by the infamous head of the FBI, J. Edgar Hoover, when he said that "The answer is vigorous law enforcement. Justice is merely incidental to law and order."[6] In other words, the quest for justice be damned. The first order of the day is to maintain the status quo and uphold the system of White Supremacy.

In 1991, I took constitutional law classes at Vanderbilt University, and our discussions often escalated into arguments around race and the presumptions of race that most, if not all, of our white counterparts expressed. Civil rights law is a key component to any discussion of constitutional law, and, of course, Affirmative Action is dependent on civil rights assertions and constitutional interpretations. One student in class, in an attempt to defend the treatment of Blacks prior to the passage of civil rights laws, stated that because whites did not "know" that Blacks were human, their treatment of Blacks and others should be excused. It was clear to me that in 1991, whites still struggled with the notion of Black people being human. This was just another example of ignorance, and such beliefs feed into the continuation of SOWS.

In reference to the 13th Amendment, which states: "*Neither slavery nor involuntary servitude, except as a punishment for crime whereof the party shall have been duly convicted, shall exist within the United States, or any place subject to their jurisdiction*," my law professor made a concerted effort to avoid discussing the exception *allowing* slavery. When I raised the question, the professor abruptly adjourned the class. This action, of course, raised other questions in my mind and in the minds of the other nine Black students present that day. If the law was straightforward, and was supposed to seek the heights of truth, justice, balance, and order, then why, when it came to the question of slavery, was the American Constitution proclaiming to give freedom to all citizens when in reality it did not?

Dr. Welsing speaks of the psychopathic nature of the white supremacy system within all of the nine Areas of People Activity (Neely Fuller, Jr.). I agree with Dr. Welsing's position and have concluded that our system of laws is in predatory hands, as it exists as a tool to expand white supremacy. European men and women were firmly and unfairly in control of the creation and enforcement of laws developed from bogus "theories" that arose out of their insecurity of being a white minority on a planet overwhelmingly populated by people of color. This led them to justify the brutality and treatment of Africans during the transatlantic slave trade. History is replete with the stories of the victims of the system of laws that have allowed the murder, exploitation, and enslavement of millions of people whose only "crime" was that they were non-white. White supremacy requires victims.

The law under the rule of white supremacists allows law enforcement agents to commit wrongs that are sanctioned under a web of justifications. The victims of white supremacy are in a war with a system of laws developed with the sole purpose of ensuring the survival of a melanin-deficient global racial minority.

White supremacy has built a system of laws that has yet to be successfully challenged by its victims because perhaps, its victims are under the impression that "Perry Mason" is real, that truth will triumph, and that justice will prevail. Justice is not possible in a system of laws perpetrated by white supremacists for their survival. Like the fictional Perry Mason, this is a myth. Its believers are mesmerized by statues of liberties, blind justices, and national pledges that end with "liberty and justice for all." Nevertheless, victims of racism/white supremacy persist in trying to break the spell—they are fooled into thinking they can change the system. Until these victims understand that laws are not established for *their* benefit, they will continue to be subjected to unjust treatment by the very ones who establish and maintain an imbalanced system.

Prior to my second year of law school, I had the blessing of meeting Professor W. Haywood Burns,[7] Dean of the City University of New York School of Law at Queens College. I was in New York on an internship and on a quest to learn the history of lawyers supporting the Civil Rights and Black Power movements. Not only was Professor Burns a historically important figure—he had represented Angela Davis and the Attica inmates—but he was also incredibly interested in the young lives he encountered as dean of a law school. I felt fortunate for Dean Burns to mentor me through the first few years of my professional life because he valued my potential contribution and influenced my first choices in the practice of law. His pedagogy of law and his worldview were liberating forces for me, reinforcing the idea that justice would always be elusive in the SOWS. His untimely death on April 2, 1996 in Cape Town, South Africa, was felt by many. I thank him for opening my eyes to the possibilities and to the truth of the system of law's structure and function under white supremacy's rule.

My third-year curriculum included a clinical course allowing students, under the guidance and direction of an attorney, to take on cases and appear in court on their clients' behalf. As I approached the podium to make my initial statement on my client's matter, the white judge looked up at me, grinned slyly and said, "Oh, so are you getting ready for the Supremes?" Now, in my mind, I thought he was trying to make a racial joke at my expense. I looked at him in shock. I heard other people gasp and several others giggle, but all I could do was look at him in disbelief. The look on his face was bizarre. I had no idea how to deal with the suggestion that I was there to sing. I felt my mentor's hand on my back as he took my arm and whispered something to me as he led me away from the podium, preventing me from saying something offensive in return. The judge looked quite satisfied. My client's matter being unheard, I resisted in protest, but my clinical professor said it would be all right, and that we should just go.

This was the second time I entered a courtroom unprepared for the outcome. Years had passed between the first time and this particular day. I had no guard to put up as I had made my own assumptions about my standing before the court. I was now, instead of a debtor or defendant, a pre-lawyer, someone who would become a member of the bar and a card-carrying member of "The Club" of lawyers. I had forgotten one thing that preceded my presence in the courtroom and that was that the legal profession is a profession of mainly white men. The feeling of being violated, in a figurative sense, had come as the result of my encounters with the law and the analogy seemed fitting.

As Dr. Cress Welsing wrote in "The Symbolism and Meaning of Rape,"[8] "...there is no behavior that can be adequately understood and decoded outside the context of power relationships that exist amongst non-white people. In today's world, the most fundamental of all power relationships is that of White power versus non-white (black, brown, red and yellow) powerlessness." The courtroom, and the legal apparatus that supports it, are built upon the idea of power vs. powerlessness. The imbalance in power and influence between those given the authority to execute laws and to craft those laws and those upon whom laws are executed is extreme. When one steps into a courtroom, he is either in possession of power or at the mercy of those in possession of power. There are no other positions and there is nothing in-between.

In Welsing's chapter on "Learning to Look at Symbols," she refers to guns as phallic symbols and the use of guns in law enforcement as "equalizers." This often equates to a scenario where a Black person is standing before a judge, surrounded by officers with guns, who are prepared to use them to enforce the ruling handed down by the judge. Lynching can be thought of as prelude to the use of guns as an action of terror historically used against Black men; it was a form of "justice" in America, ignored by the law, and condoned. Often, the genitalia of the Black victims were "removed and taken away by white males."[9] Such collective memories do not simply fade away but become part of the cultural meme that is passed down through generations. These generations of white men become judges, legislators, law enforcers, and lawyers. White women are not excluded from this collective memory, as they have become desirous of standing where white men have always stood.

Had I understood this dynamic playing out in the collective consciousness within the system of white supremacy as theorized by Dr. Welsing, I might have been prepared to respond intelligently to the white supremacists that populate the legal system at all levels. Black people take for granted that we will be dealt with fairly and justly within a system that both envies and hates us. This is an assumption that can be detrimental and/or deadly to us. If I am truly honest, looking back at my personal brushes with the law, I felt raped in each instance. This feeling ended when I learned how to deal with the symbolic rapist.

Patterns and Codes... the Badges of Enslavement

Dr. Welsing instructed us in "Learning to Look at Symbols"[10] :

> The process of decoding a power system and its culture is a necessary

> first step to achieve behavioral mastery over that system/culture. The attainment of such mastery is an essential step in the process of total liberation for the victims who wish to end that oppression and regain their self-respect and mental health. Without this process of decoding, the oppressed fail to fully understand what they are dealing with; they have minimal levels of consciousness and self/group-respect, and they are, functionally speaking, mentally ill.

There are numerous symbols that exist and are continuously developed for the legal system's authority over white and non-white citizens. One material symbol is the blindfolded white woman holding a set of scales and named "Justice." Another symbol of the legal system's promise to treat all people from wherever they originate is the crowned white woman in New York harbor holding a torch, named "Liberty." The fact that these powerful symbols exist and have become rooted in our conscious and subconscious minds to represent the promises of freedom, justice, and equality, are no accidents. In my opinion, most people, especially Americans, see these symbols and do not question the birthright of the nation they represent. Once decoded however, these lofty principles they are intended to espouse are merely aspirational concepts.

As Dr. Welsing notes, in the "brain products issu[ing] forth from those who are white and who presently control the power balance in the global system of white supremacy," the legal standards represented by Ladies Justice and Liberty are available to all equally and with malice toward none. Unfortunately for the non-white, justice and liberty are not inalienable rights as promised. These symbols are deeply embedded in the psyche of all Americans, white and non-white, and are reinforced into every generation and every group of immigrants who have come to call America home. For us Blacks in America, the 13th and 14th Amendments to the Constitution are the principal "symbols" of our freedom and liberty. However, these Amendments also represent the loss of property, the Civil War and its aftermath, and the terrorism by whites against the refugees created by the Emancipation Proclamation.

Dr. Welsing suggested that, "once the symbol is formed, it is capable of acting upon the brain-computer, which receives it as an energy or data message...[effecting] the end-product of behavior as carried forth in [law and law enforcement]. The symbol...acts upon the external environment. These "single-picture-sentences" or "single-picture-paragraphs" commence in the brain-computer and act as powerful undetected persuaders, and thus, as powerful determinants of behavioral patterns."

"Incidents of slavery" are "aspects of law that [are] inherently tied to or flow directly from the institution of slavery"[11] or are remnants of memory passed down through the generations of whites who were part of the slavocracy which still exists in the structure and function of the legal system in America. They make the pursuit of justice, equality, and liberty a zero-sum game for victims of white supremacy.

In "Defining the Badges and Incidents of Slavery," Jennifer Mason McAward defines the term "badges of slavery" as a colloquialism used during the antebellum period, which migrated into legal use in the post-bellum south, and refers to indicators, physical or otherwise, of slave or subordinate status imposed upon Black people, whether they were enslaved or free. This badge and its influences in American society and courts did not disappear with emancipation. Discussion of its importance moved from social circles to legal and academic ones as legal concerns and challenges moved through politics and the courts. In her analysis of the term, McAward suggests that it "could obtain new layers of meaning over time."

There are documented links between racial profiling, police brutality, lynching (which never stopped), racial animus and enmity, segregation, mass incarceration, and the workings of the court system (criminal *and* civil), as well as the institution of slavery, and its historical aftermath. McAward concludes that "the best understanding of the 'badges and incidents of slavery' refers to public or widespread private action, based on race or the previous condition of servitude, that mimics the law of slavery and that has significant potential to lead to the de facto re-enslavement or legal subjugation of the targeted group."[12] These terms are represented by the racism within the system of law and function in ways that assure that white supremacist thoughts and goals are served.

An example of an incident of slavery was "the requirement that enslaved people obey the master's commands or be subject to "beating, imprisonment, and every species of chastisement." Today we see it in the beatings of Blacks by police who ask us to "comply" while physically assaulting us. Rodney King fleeing from law enforcement was disobedience, much like our enslaved forebears whose oppositional behavior could legally get them killed. Free Blacks were tried under the same criminal codes as enslaved Blacks but had no right to vote. Today, citizens who are tried under the "law," sentenced, incarcerated, and have served their time, are still routinely denied the right to vote in many states. The irony is that previously incarcerated citizens are counted in congressional districts to facilitate the practice of gerrymandering, which creates a political advantage, particularly for white politicians.

While the Civil Rights Act of 1866 attempted to outlaw such incidents as codified in the law and practice, it did little to remove the symbols from the minds of those in power who would continue to enforce the authority established in the white majority under Jim Crow and the system of white supremacy. In *The New Jim Crow*,[13] Michelle Alexander gives a detailed explanation of how the Black Codes were established to revive many of the legal restrictions existing under slavery. The book reveals that generations were influenced by what happened more than 150 years ago, and that the symbols of oppression through the legal system are alive and well and still function today. To say that "judicial interpretation" has been influenced by these symbols passed down through time to the inheritors of the system of white supremacy is an understatement. Judicial "interpretation" is central to the maintenance of the system, and to the injustices non-whites experience at the hands of the courts and the executioners of contemporary "laws."

"Badges of slavery" attach to a group of people and remain attached to that group so long as the beliefs and preferences giving rise to such badges are transmitted generationally. Noting that Americans are tied together by "common historical and cultural heritage" in which racism plays a prominent role, Prof. Charles R. Lawrence asserts in "The Id, the Ego, and Equal Protection: Reckoning with Unconscious Racism," that:

> Because these beliefs are so much a part of the culture, they are not experienced as explicit lessons. Instead, they seem part of the individual's rational ordering of her perceptions of the world. The individual is unaware, for example, that the ubiquitous presence of a cultural stereotype has influenced her perception that [Blacks] are lazy or unintelligent. Because racism is so deeply ingrained in our culture, it is likely to be transmitted by tacit understandings: Even if a child is not told that [Blacks] are inferior, he learns that lesson by observing the behavior of others. These tacit understandings, because they have never been articulated, are less likely to be experienced at a conscious level.[14]

The primary badge of slavery, servitude, or subordinate status in America was and remains skin color.

Conclusion

To be unconstitutional, racial discrimination by the government must contain two elements: a discriminatory purpose and a discriminatory impact.[1516] Both are the burden of the plaintiff. In other words, the system is "innocent" of any wrongdoing under the constitution and is not designed to protect victims of white supremacy.

One of the most important cases in this country was the Dred Scott case. Dred Scott brought a suit against the United States regarding his rights to citizenship, but he could not plead to the court himself. The resultant opinion of Justice Taney, was based on the system of white supremacy where Blacks were seen as property and had no rights. Taney's dictum that "Blacks have no rights which a white man is bound to respect" are words that continue to reverberate as symbols of white hegemony, and by design, often tries to discourage Black persons from seeking legal recourse.

There was no empathy in the strict reading of Taney's decision for Dred Scott as a human being. On finally reaching the high tribunal, the majority held that since Scott was a slave, he lacked standing to sue.

Taney wrote, that Blacks were "beings of an inferior order, and altogether unfit to associate with the white race, either in social or political relations, and so far inferior that they had no rights which the white man was bound to respect."[17]

While the Dred Scott case was eventually nullified by the 13th and 14th Amendments to the U.S. Constitution, the symbolism of Taney's words did not disappear, but have instead become part of the central tenets of the system of white supremacy. Though the law of citizenship and rights has been argued, analyzed, and decided upon, the themes and trends in the culture and traditions of white supremacy continue to be attached to the question of the rights of Blacks in America. This is demonstrated through the application of laws and their enforcement. In the eyes of the law, symbolically, we are Dred Scott's children.

The time has come for Black people to see the system of Law for what it is. For the majority of Black people, it is in our best interest to understand the law as it has evolved and is being applied from the white supremacist perspective. Once the victims of white supremacy make the decision to seek a path to freedom, we must learn how our minds are being used to ensure the continued propagation of the system that oppresses us. When we do, we as a collective will be able to begin utilizing the law and its loopholes to our advantage and eventually, stem the tide of judicial oppression.

Endnotes

1 Frances Cress Welsing, *The Isis (Yssis) Papers: The Keys to the Colors* (Washington, DC: C.W. Publishing, 2004).
2 Perry Mason (TV Series). Produced by Gail Patrick Jackson. CBS Network, September 21, 1957.
3 Tim Wise, "Is Sisterhood Conditional? White Women and the Rollback of Affirmative Action." N*WSA Journal*, 10, no. 3 (1998): 1-26. doi:10.2979/nws.1998.10.3.1
4 "Retirement of Justice Marshall". Retrieved from https://www.c-span.org/video/?18624-1/retirement-justice-marshall.
5 People v. Newton, 8 Cal. App. 3d 359 (Ct. App. 1970)
6 John Edgar Hoover (January 1, 1895 – May 2, 1972), better known as J. Edgar Hoover, was the first Director of the Federal Bureau of Investigation (FBI) of the United States. He was appointed as the sixth director of the Bureau of Investigation—the FBI's predecessor—in 1924 and was instrumental in founding the FBI in 1935, where he remained director until his death in 1972 at the age of 77. (Source: Wikipedia)
7 After graduating with honors from Harvard College and receiving a law degree from Yale University, Burns served as the first law clerk for District Court Judge Constance Baker Motley. In 1968, he served as general counsel to Martin Luther King's Poor People's Campaign. He was one of the founders of the National Conference of Black Lawyers. He worked on the defense of the Attica prisoners and many other people struggling for self-determination. Burns was also the founding dean of the City College Urban Legal Studies Program, serving from 1977-1987. Burns went on to serve as dean of the Law School at the City University of New York (CUNY). He was a visiting scholar at Yale Law School and returned to New York to establish a Harlem-based law firm. Talent, passion, and zest for life were his signatures. He was tragically killed in an automobile accident while attending the International Association of Democratic Lawyers conference in Cape Town, South Africa. (Source: http:// www.burnsinstitute.org/our-work/w-haywood-burns/)
8 Frances Cress Welsing, *The Isis (Yssis) Papers: The Keys to the Colors* (Washington, DC: C.W. Publishing, 2004), 177.
9 Ibid
10 Welsing, "Learning to Look at Symbols," (Feb. 1979), The Isis Papers, 54.
11 Jennifer Mason McAward, "Defining the Badges and Incidents of Slavery," *University of Pennsylvania Law School Journal of Constitutional Law,* Volume 14, Issue 3 (2012); *Notre Dame Law School Legal Studies Research Paper* No. 10-22. Available at SSRN: https://ssrn.com/abstract=1666967
12 Ibid.
13 Michelle Alexander, *The New Jim Crow: Mass Incarceration in the Age of Colorblindness* (New York, NY: The New Press, 2011).

14 C. Lawrence, "The Id, the Ego, and Equal Protection: Reckoning with Unconscious Racism,". *Stanford Law Review*, 39 (2): 17-388. doi:10.2307/1228797.
15 Washington v. Davis, 426 U.S. 229 (1976).
16 Dred Scott v. Sandford, 60 U.S. 393 (1857).
17 Ibid

CHAPTER 7

We Charge Genocide
The Isis Papers: The Keys to the Colors Revisited

Ife Williams

> "The dynamics that motivate the conquered and the conquerors are never the same."
>
> *The Isis Papers,* 141

> "There is not a Black problem...which is not related to the reality of white domination of Black people."
>
> *The Isis Papers, 29*0

Dr. Welsing's prediction of the elimination of non-white populations is manifested through ever-increasing police executions, expansive poverty, health disparities, mass incarceration, civil wars, and pandemics. This is what people of African descent are exposed to globally, and it is an example of the destruction of Black bodies through state-sanctioned violence, or the charge of genocide.

This chapter, therefore, will focus on Dr. Welsing's views regarding issues of politics as she saw them, whereby they were defined as "all human relations," which are enshrouded within the realm of white supremacy. In other words, Black people have become participants in their own demise through the process of self-negation, which leads to self-annihilation resulting from the internalization of the tenets of white supremacy. The inability to maximize the genetic potential of Black children is "Black Genocide" and the fundamental alienation of the Black race "has grown to the point of Black racial suicide." Black people are in a "crisis" state and will perish unless they take up the struggle against white supremacy.

The *Cress Theory of Color-Confrontation and Racism* is a psychogenetic analysis that offers the most insightful evidence to explain the underlying impetus of white supremacy affecting non-whites, who now comprise three-fourths of the world's global population. It has been predicted that, by the year 2073, people who identify as white will only total roughly 3% of the people inhabiting this planet (254).

The diminishing genetic viability of whites, as Welsing describes, has produced a "...profound sense of numerical inadequacy and color inferiority which results in a psychological defense [of] repression or 'reaction formation'" (4). These types of behaviors include the processes of attributing negative qualities to people of color, discrediting and despising them, and manifesting a "neurotic drive for superiority" (5). In order to compensate for their inability to produce melanin and their numerical minority, whites created a "compensatory logic system": white supremacy. The myth of inferiority is ingrained and maintained in non-whites through the social and political-economic infrastructures controlled by whites.

Dr. Welsing refers to the "open destruction of non-white people" as a holocaust that occurs when:

> There is a sufficient level of insecurity or anxiety in the white population relative to white genetic annihilation;
>
> There is no longer a plan; or
>
> It is considered too expensive to keep non-whites confined in "ghettos," "prisons," "barrios," "Bantustans," "concentration camps," "on reservations" or "on welfare" (228).

Black people are "slaves living in a highly refined state of psychological oppression, which is no less a death than direct physical destruction" (288). Journalist and author Samuel Yette distinguished direct genocide, lynching, or being shot, from more "indirect forms," such as faulty health care, minimal education, and scant employment. These indirect attacks are seen as being justified based on the "deservedness" of a group. The denial of adequate access to resources occurs over a period of time and is legitimated by a "fault psychology" that dehumanizes and blames the victims.

This ideology emerged from puritanical and protestant ethics, thus providing an adequate rationale for (guiltless) black extinction. In *The*

Isis Papers, instances of genocide are evidenced on three specific levels: at the core/self that is defined by its relationship to society; the intra-social relations that constitute the "Black collective"; and "… (t)he global system of white supremacy, (where) oppression functions through all areas of peoples activit[ies]" (166).

The politics of genocide through the spectrum of white supremacy was enshrined in the Constitution as the "founding fathers" upheld the status of Africans in America as chattel, relegated to less-than-animal status and robbed of their native cultures. An upgrade to personhood does not occur until the Thirteenth Amendment, as it was penned that no one will be subjected to the "badges" of slavery (except from punishment for a crime); yet through de facto practices, Blacks people still carry the badge.

Fear was the primary tactic used to enslave African people during the "seasoning process" and has been strategically used through various laws applied throughout history to keep Black people in "their place." Presently, post-enslavement trauma persists through repeated displays of Black bodies which have been abused or murdered via the media, reminiscent of lynched bodies remaining on trees days after the carnage.

"Justifiable" homicide has evolved since slavery. Dr. Welsing referred to justifiable homicide as a "particular form of murder and slaughter" by "…white males in uniforms who have been authorized to carry guns" (184). White supremacy has been supported through law(s) and Supreme Court rulings that have given tacit approval to murder Blacks, and which have set the precedent for the lower courts regarding law enforcement's uses of excessive force. For example, in 1945, Robert Hall, a Black resident of Georgia, was roused from his sleep by Sheriff Screws and his deputies. In a previous encounter between Screws and Hall, the former swore, in front of witnesses, that he was going to "get" Hall. That night, Hall was beaten and died shortly thereafter. Sheriff Screws was found guilty, not of murder, but of violating Hall's right to due process. Upon appeal, the Supreme Court exonerated Sheriff Screws' acts by employing the standard of "willful intent" to deprive individuals of their rights. This same line of reasoning used by Screws permeates cases today as the police apply the defense that they were acting in the line of duty, and that the suspects were ultimately killed because they were trying to escape or resist arrest.

Since then, the Monell case of 1978 took place (and was viewed by many as a victory), when those victimized by officials of the state filed lawsuits under Section 42 U. S. C. §1983; I argue that compensation for loss of life is reminiscent of property status. Further, this action did little to curtail the police, as it was the municipality that was sued and not the officers involved. Even after said cities had paid out millions of dollars in settlements and legal fees, officers were rarely reprimanded, and instead received paid leave.

During the last decade, the Supreme Court has expanded the powers of the police and eroded one's ability to receive compensation for blatant civil rights violations. An illustration is the case of John Thompson who served eighteen years in prison (fourteen on death row) for a crime he did not commit. During the trial, the prosecution intentionally withheld evidence. DNA evidence later proved that Thompson was innocent of the crime and his conviction was overturned. Thompson brought a civil suit against the Prosecutor's Office and was awarded 14 million dollars in damages by a Louisiana jury. However, Thompson never received the money as the case was appealed to the Supreme Court, and the judgement was overturned. The ruling, written by Justice Clarence Thomas, held that the city of New Orleans could not be held liable because it could not be proved that its own policies had violated the Constitution. The fact that its prosecutor(s) blatantly violated the Constitution and Thompson's civil rights was apparently still not enough to make the city liable.

Another ongoing civil rights violation is the subversion of voting rights. From Reconstruction to the present, barriers have been erected to limit the voting power of non-whites, including the Grandfather Clause, literacy tests, felon disenfranchisement, and voter identification, all to ensure white domination over policy and politics. One out of every thirteen Blacks has lost voting rights due to felony disenfranchisement versus one in every 56 whites. In the 2000 U.S. presidential election, 90,000 suspected felons were removed from the voter rolls in Florida without verification; 97% were innocent and George W. Bush won by 537 votes. According to the American Civil Liberties Union (ACLU), 21 million Americans do not have government-issued identification—25% of Blacks of voting age compared to 8% of whites. Presently, 70% of the states in the US now have laws that promote some form of voter suppression.

In the words of Dr. Welsing, "Black people are afraid, but Black people are going to have to get over their fear." It is this mantra we [as Black people] must use in order to assert our rights under a Constitution that was predicated on the tenets of white Supremacy. Although the power of the vote, legislation, and enforcement has been utilized to assert the continuation of mental and physical genocide of people of African descent, as a collective, we must understand the systemic nature of the intent. Black people must not participate in our own annihilation by continuing to internalize the tenets of white supremacy. Dr. Welsing gave us the words and roadmap to understand the politics of a genocidal system created for non-whites. We must begin to minimize the impact for our progeny and our future. In the court of the People…we charge genocide.

Chapter 8

Religion and White Supremacy

Reverend Dr. Jeremiah A. Wright Jr.

A Liberating Black People's Pray For Justice & Peace

(To say and envision when in prayer)

Thou who are Blacker
Than a trillion midnights;
Whose eyes shine brighter
Than a billion suns.

Thou whose hair doth
Coil tighter than a
Million springs, radiating
All energies throughout the Universe.

We beseech Thee, One
And Only One,

To give us total
Strength, to carry out
Thy will for the universe!

To establish justice on
Planet Earth and live in peace.

~Dr. Frances Cress Welsing

Dr. Frances Cress Welsing's "liberating" prayer, with which she concludes her 1996 edition of *The Isis Papers,* summarizes her published perspective on white supremacy and "Christianity." I emphasize liberating, as Dr. Welsing's use of the word in the prayer's title demonstrates her positive approach to combat and undo the damaging and dehumanizing effects of white supremacy on the African mind; effects often caused by an ideology that is not, but claims to be, Christianity. Dr. Welsing's prayer suggests that the liberating—or freeing— of Black People's minds from the chains of white supremacist teachings about both the Creator and the Biblical Christ will give them the strength to establish a world whose foundations are truth, justice, and peace.

Before discussing Dr. Welsing's brilliant critique of the racist distortions of Christianity, some additional reflections on her powerful prayer are in order. Welsing skillfully starts her prayer with a combination of the imagery of John Henrik Clarke's "The Boy Who Painted Christ Black"[1] and the description of the risen Christ found in the Book of Revelation.[2] That imagery of a Black Christ frees Black people of the iconographical distortions of Jesus which have dominated Western Christian thought since the European Renaissance.

A blond-haired, blue-eyed conception and depiction of Jesus (whom Welsing refers to and calls "a black man" several times)[3] has dominated the paintings in Christian literature, from the days of Michelangelo's Sistine Chapel rendition down through the funeral home fans still passed out in Black churches all over America. I am sure Dr. Welsing was familiar with Countee Cullen's poem "The Black Christ," written during the Harlem Renaissance,[4] and Albert Cleage's *The Black Messiah,*[5] given her immersion in African-centered studies, scholarship, and literature. Whatever the inspiration, she starts off her prayer by addressing God as "THOU who art blacker than a trillion midnights," and her use of this imagery frees the Black mind from white supremacist images of God and by implication, negative or deficient self-images.

To underscore her point, Dr. Welsing gives instructions to the readers of her prayer as a superscription right under the title of the prayer and before its first line. She tells the reader "To say and envision when in prayer" a God who is blacker than a trillion midnights. In the first two verses of her prayer, she paraphrases the description of Jesus found in Revelation 1:14-16; in verse three she shows us to Whom we ought to be praying and for what we ought to be praying.[6] The verse corrects what she describes in her essay on Black male passivity, where she describes a "Black female, who periodically drops down on her knees to pray to a white Jesus whose miracles save the situation."[7] Where a white Jesus is powerless to address our black struggle for justice or peace, the God who is blacker than a trillion midnights is the "ONE and only one" who can give us the strength to carry out God's will for the universe. In my estimation, Welsing's prayer poetically summarizes her perspective and position on white supremacy and its distorted propagation of the Christian faith.

I emphasized *Christianity* in the opening of this essay because what Dr. Welsing critiques so accurately, thoroughly, and incisively has nothing to do with Christianity or the religion of Jesus of Nazareth and his followers. It has nothing to do with the Christianity that developed during the first four centuries of the Common Era while it was still an African religion.[8] It has nothing to do with pre-Constantine Christianity. In fact, L.H. Whelchel says, when Constantine took Christianity out of Africa into Europe, Christianity was taken away from its founder.[9]

Kemetic Religion, Welsing cites,[10] is the foundation on which the religion of Moses was built. The descendants of Abraham lived among the Kamites for four hundred years, according to their sacred texts. The faith of Abraham and Moses was the faith (or religion) into which Jesus was born and in which he was raised.

For the first four centuries of its development, the religion of Jesus was an African religion. The church "fathers" (*patristics*) who crafted the different doctrines of the early Christian church—Athanasius, Augustine (whom Welsing misidentifies as European), Tertullian, and others, were all Africans. It was not until Constantine converted to Christianity and moved the capital of Christianity from Jerusalem in Africa to Rome in Europe, that the religion known to the world as Christianity was changed drastically, some would say diametrically, from what its African founders taught.

Dr. Welsing critiques white supremacy which calls itself Christianity, as demonstrated by theologians Charles Mills,[11] Willie Jennings,[12] J. Kameron Carter,[13] and others; and that white supremacy has not only infected Christianity but has also become synonymous with white western Christendom. This "white supremacist" version of Christianity has also produced the "Doctrine of Discovery,"[14] the "civilizing" of the New World, and the scientific racist lens through which miseducation, colonialism, the slave trade, and eugenics are viewed.

Dr. Welsing's essay, "The Symbolism of Christ, the Cross, the Crucifix, the Communion: Christian holidays,"[15] deconstructs the racism and white supremacy as she sees it in these aspects of Christianity. The only flaws I find in this essay on the cross are Dr. Welsing's discussion of the Roman Cross as a "peculiar invention of the Roman (white) psyche," "A symbol of death"; however, she does not mention the Egyptian (Kemetic) cross, the ankh, as the symbol of *life*. I would have welcomed her analysis of the "white" cross as a symbol of death and the black cross as a symbol of life; but Dr. Welsing never mentions the ankh.

Closely related to the Black (Kemetic) cross is the Black Ethiopian cross. Before the white supremacy and white Western European distortions of Christianity, there had been four centuries of Ethiopian Christianity. *Aethiop* — "black face" or "burnt face" in Greek — was the name given to the Nubians or Cushite people by the Greeks when they colonized those countries, and those people had been Christians for more than 300 years before Constantine converted to Christianity, however, Dr. Welsing does not mention them.

In fact, using the same Christian scriptures as Dr. Welsing, the story of the first Ethiopian's conversion to Christianity (found in the Book of Acts)[16] opens an entirely different discussion about the religion of the descendants of Abraham — whom Dr. Welsing consistently calls "Semites" or "half white." In Acts 8, that first Ethiopian was in Jerusalem (the capital of Judaism), worshipping in Solomon's temple and was a Jew.

Today, Westerners would call him a Falasha. He would self-identify as a member of the family of Beta Israel. They had been Jewish since the "marriage" of Solomon and Makeda (900 years before the birth of Jesus) according to their sacred text, the *Kebra Negast.*[17] From Ethiopian (Cushite or Nubian) Judaism, Ethiopian Christianity is born, yet Dr. Welsing does not discuss any of the possible meanings of this black side of Christianity when it comes to the system of white racism. Another flaw I refer to in Welsing's essay may be related to her being baptized in the Baptist Church, christened in the African Methodist Episcopal Church, and matriculating at Antioch College, a conservative Christian Connection school (Arminian).

In this essay[18] and in other places in *The Isis Papers,* Dr. Welsing says that "original sin" was the act of sexual intercourse. That is a forgivable flaw in that many Baptist churches, AME churches, and Dutch Reform (Arminian) theology teach that doctrine. The Hebrew bible does not, however, and to repeat that inaccuracy, in my opinion, weakens Dr. Welsing's argument. Her primary point, however,[19] remains intact: white supremacy is the basis upon which most of Christendom's premises are based.

In the essay, "The Concept and the Color of God,"[20] Welsing continues her skillful analysis and deconstruction of what she calls "The Christian (white supremacy) Religion."[21] Her generalizations may lead some to an incomplete or distorted perspective of Christianity. She makes some sweeping generalizations which, from my perspective as an historian of religions, are inaccurate. One such generalization:

> ...**All** black and other non-white people who professed to be members of the Christian (white supremacy) religion, whether they are conscious of it or not, worship the white man as God (not as "a god," but as "The God"). (emphasis added)

The previous statement follows immediately on the heels of her assertions (#1) that it was,

> The necessary duty of the vast array of white supremacy (Christian) missionaries sent out around the world, following the guns of white supremacy conquest, is to implant — deep within the unconscious logic networks of non-white brain computers the critical image and concept of God as a **white man**.

She then asserts that (#2)

> This unconscious implantation has been successful to the extent that many non-white people on the planet conceive of themselves as members of the Christian (white supremacy) religion. In the U.S., the overwhelming majority of Black people, as well as a large portion of non-white people, consider themselves Christian.[22]

I call these assertions inaccurate for several reasons. First, Dr. Welsing does not consider the various contexts of the millions of Black Christians living in the United States, the Caribbean, the three Americas, and the Black Atlantic. They are too numerous to name (or describe) in one essay. They range from the "Shouting Baptists" or Ethiopian Baptists of Jamaica, through the "ring shout" Methodists (The Gullah people) of the low country; to the *Maroonage* Black Christians. They range from Gabriel Prosser and Nat Turner in Dismal Swamp, Virginia, through Denmark Vesey and the Stono Rebellion. They also include Black Christians in South Carolina, the Christian Maroon communities in Trelawny Parish (also in Jamaica), the Christian Maroon communities in the *Quilombos* of Bahia, and Maranhão in Brazil.

The contexts include (in the three Americas) Christian practitioners of *vodun* in Haiti (and Newark) and Black radical (nationalist) Christians who are members of the Shrine of the Black Madonna. None of the Black Christians in those examples would fit into Dr. Welsing's generalizations of worshipping the white man as "The God." Many of those communities also embrace the images of God and Jesus as Black.

Further, Dr. Welsing's assertions fail to acknowledge the complex history and development of the Black Church either in the three Americas or on the African continent. In the Americas, the gamut runs from the secret African Christian worship services held in the brush arbors, or "hush arbors" away from the eyes and ears of the white slaveholders, through the code songs and the work songs sung by Africans during the period of chattel slavery, to the .44-caliber pistol-toting African Methodist Episcopal Zion minister, Reverend Harriet Tubman, who was a conductor on the Underground Railroad.

In the Americas, the gamut of Black Belief and the complex development of the Black Church runs from David Walker's *Appeal* (1830) and Robert Young's "The Ethiopian Manifesto" (1829) to African Methodist Episcopal Bishop, Henry McNeal Turner's powerful sermon, "God is a Negro." Dr. Welsing's christening in the African Methodist Episcopal church and her powerful prayer which introduces this essay, "A Liberating Black People's Prayer," penned in 1996, demonstrates to me her familiarity with Turner's work or his powerful message to the National Baptist Convention in 1898 where he said:

> We have as much right biblically and other wise to believe God is a Negroe (sic) as you **bukra** or white people have to believe that God is a fine looking symmetrical and ornamented white man. For the bulk of you and all the fool Negroes of the country believe that God is white-skinned, blue eyed, straight hair, projected nose, compressed lips and finely robed white gentleman sitting upon a throne somewhere in the Heavens. Every race of people who has attempted to describe their God by words, or by paintings, or by carvings, or any other form or figures have conveyed the idea that the God who made them and shaped their destinies were symbolized in themselves, and why should not the Negroe (sic) believe that he resembles God.
>
> *Voice of Missions,* February, 1898[23]

Welsing's sweeping generalization, therefore, that all Black Christians worship the white man as "The God" is overstated. In addition, Dr. Welsing's publication of *The Isis Papers* in its final edition does not include any essays which engage The Black Theology of the Americas Project of the 1980s and 1990s, the writings of the Black Theologians, or any Womanist Theologians hailing from the United States, the Caribbean, Afro-Brazilian, Afro-British, or in the African Continental contexts.[24] The writings of these scholars undercut Dr. Welsing's assumptions and assertions radically, and should be engaged by any and all students and scholars who take Dr. Welsing seriously—as I do—and who are interested in her work. The work of the Association of Black Psychiatrists and the Association of Black Psychologists deepened and strengthened and also undercut her assumptions. Having said that, let me conclude my reflections by segueing superficially into the work of these scholars in relationship to the published writings of Dr. Welsing.

I was asked to reflect on and comment on Dr. Welsing's work in "religion." She consistently states that racism is:

> The local and global power system structured and maintained by persons who classify themselves as white, whether consciously or subconsciously determined; this system consists of patterns of perception, logic, symbol formation, thought, speech, action and emotional response, as conducted simultaneously in all areas of people activity *(economics, education, entertainment, labor, law, politics,* ***religion****, sex and war).*

Dr. Welsing writes only about "Christianity." She brilliantly analyzes, critiques, deconstructs, and exposes the content and the symbolism of white supremacy Christianity; and she says several negative things about the Black Church (accurately) and *all* Black Christians (inaccurately). She does not, however, address African Religions or Diasporic African Religions.

In her essay "The Concept and Color of God," Welsing describes in only one paragraph her understanding of African spirituality.[25] But she does not talk about the hundreds, if not thousands, of African religions, nor if, or how, white supremacy/racism affects that area of "people activity." There is no mention of African initiated churches (also called "African Indigenous Churches") and how these Christian churches have incorporated elements of African Traditional Religious beliefs and practices into their worship, their theology, and their praxis. There is no mention of African traditional religion, from the Adinkra symbols of the Akan or the *Orixas* of the Yoruba in West Africa, to the belief systems and practices of the *Sangomas* in Southern Africa.

Moreover, Dr. Welsing does not touch the religions of the Black Atlantic or the Black Pacific.[26] The religions of *Santeria*, *Lucume*, *Garifuna*, *Shang*o, *Cumina*, *Obeah*, *Myalism* and *Vodun* are never mentioned in her writings. In my opinion, those religions are too important to be ignored when talking about continental Africans or diasporic Africans. It was Dutty Bookman's prayer at Bwa Kayman that sparked the Haitian

Revolution and changed the course of Western (and U.S.) history! There would have been no Louisiana Purchase had it not been for the religion of the enslaved and marooned African communities in Haiti.

The combinations of different African traditional religions, Christianity, Islam, and African folk beliefs have created religious systems too complex to be confined by white racism. In my opinion, they need to be a part of the discussion on deconstructing the damage done by the globalism of white supremacy.

Also missing from the conversation is The Society for the Study of Black Religion, which has been producing important papers, books, and research since 1972. In a recent post (September 3, 2016), the Society said:

> The Black Religion/Womanist Thought/Social Justice Series produces works engaging any dimension of Black Religion or Womanist Thought as they pertain to Social Justice. Womanist thought is a new approach in the study of African American women's perspectives. The series includes a variety of African American religious expressions; traditions such as Protestant and Catholic Christianity, Islam, Judaism, Humanism, African Diasporic Practices, Religion and Gender, Religion and Black Gays/Lesbians, Ecological Justice Issues, African American Religiosity and its relation to African Religions, New Black Religious Movements or Religious Dimensions in African American 'Secular' Experiences.

Any meaningful discussion of "Religion and white supremacy" needs to engage these scholars and these areas of consideration: the Christianity of Jesus' followers in first-century North Africa, the African Christianity that developed and morphed into a theological system over the first 300 years after Jesus was lynched; or the white supremacy Christianity which Dr. Welsing writes about.

Black Religion, both on the Continent and in the global diaspora, is much more than Christianity, and needs to be taken seriously and on its own terms if we are serious about saying and envisioning Dr. Welsing's Liberating Black People's Prayer and carrying out God's will for the universe (The God who is blacker than a trillion midnights): to establish justice on Planet Earth and to live in peace.

Endnotes

1 http://www.litstudies.org/bilingual_esl/TaskIII/BoyWhoPaintedChrist.htm.
2 Revelations 1:14-16.
3 Frances Cress Welsing, *The Isis Papers,* 68 & 166.
4 Countee Cullen, *The Black Christ and Other Poems* (Manhattan: Harper & brothers, 1929).
5 Albert Cleague, *The Black Messiah*, (Trenton, NJ: Africa World Press, 1989).
6 Ibid.
7 Frances Cress Welsing, *The Isis Papers,* 90.
8 L.H. Whelchel, *The History and Heritage of the African-American Church; A Way Out of No Way* (St. Paul, MN: Paraon House, 2011).
9 Ibid.
10 Frances Cress Welsing, *The Isis Papers,* VII.
11 Charles Mills, *The Racial Contract*, (Ithaca, NY: Cornell University Press, 1997).
12 Willie Jennings, *The Christian Imagination: Theology and the Origins of Race* (New Haven, CT: Yale University Press, 2010*).*
13 J. Kameron Carter, *Race: A Theological Account* (Oxford: Oxford University Press, 2008).
14 *The Doctrine of Discovery* is a series of Papal Bulls which gave the "conquerors" of the New World the church's authority to convert all in the Indigenous persons to Christianity and seize their land. If they refused to convert, the church ordered the conquerors to kill them. Genocide, baptized by the church!
15 Frances Cress Welsing, *The Isis Papers,* 61-69.
16 16 *Acts* 8:26-39.
17 William Leo Hansberry, *Pillars in Ethiopian History*, Edited by Joseph Harris, (Baltimore, MD: Black Classics Press, 2019).
18 Frances Cress Welsing, *The Isis Papers,* 74.
19 Ibid.
20 Ibid., 163-173.
21 Ibid.,168.
22 Ibid., 108.
23 *Henry McNeal Turner*, "This Far By Faith," PBS, 2003. Retrieved https://www.pbs.org/thisfarbyfaith/people/henry_mcneal_turner.html.
24 See for example James Cone's *Black Theology and Black Power* and *The Cross and The Lynching Tree*; Dwight Hopkins' *Black Liberation Theology: A Historical Perspective, Introducing Black Theology of Liberation, Black Theology and Womanist Theology in Conversation*; George Cummings' *Cut Loose Your Stammering Tongue: Black Theology in The Slave Narratives*; Eboni Marshall-Turman's *Toward A Woman- ist Ethic of Incarnation: Black Bodies, The Black Church, The Council of Chalcedon*; Musa Dube's *Post Colonial Feminist Interpretation of the Bible*; Mercy Odouyoye's *Introducing African*

Women's Theology and *Beads and Strains: Reflections of an Af- rican Woman on Christianity in Africa*; or, Anthony Reddie's *Working Against the Grain: Re-Imaging Black Theology in the 21st Century.*

25 Frances Cress Welsing, *The Isis Papers*, 171.

26 See Robbie Shilliam's *The Black Pacific: Anti-Colonial Struggles and Oceanic Connections* and Kiran Asher's *Black and Green: Afro-Columbians, Development and Nature in The Pacific Low Lands*.

CHAPTER 9

The Isis Papers Revisited: The Politics Behind Black Male Sexuality

Denise Wright, Ph.D.

> In the spirit of Dr. Frances Cress-Welsing, this chapter is dedicated to Jack Johnson, James Baldwin, Dick Gregory, Marcus Garvey, the Maroons, and countless others who were luminaries in history and who personified the essence of our Ancestors in resisting white supremacy. This chapter is also dedicated to those men who withstood the winds of adversity, such as my father, a veteran, who was one of the first licensed Master Plumbers in the state of Ohio and, although legitimately licensed, was not eligible for city contracts. And, Mr. K., who would routinely hold quiet vigils in his master bedroom, looking out an open window, watching his children playing, while holding a shotgun in one hand and a cigarette in the other, after threats from the KKK. This is also a dedication to those Black men (past and present): fathers, brothers, sons and husbands who, under enduring, humiliating circumstances, worked every day to provide for their families and give them a sense of security. To the brothers, who have succumbed to the pathology of racism with their minds and their hearts, as well as those who hold their pants up with one hand while exposing their backsides to the world. Finally, to the young Black male children in kindergarten or first grade, whose fresh faces are filled with expressions of innocence and wonder, holding their parent(s) hands as they are escorted to school; may they grow to become men in a better world…

On the continent of Africa, where humankind began and advanced civilizations thrived, there was a sense of culture and humanity. Africans circumnavigated the globe, routinely traded with China, Europe, and other lands, and consequently, fostered great, prosperous societies. Both men and women oversaw the advancement and expansion of kingdoms throughout the African continent. Encounters with Europeans were frequent, as they were trading partners, and resultantly, the exchange of goods and cultural nuances was common. As the Europeans transitioned to a more materialistic lifestyle, they were exposed to the wealth of Africa and the global balance of power began to shift. Chaos ensued as the Continent's economic, religious, and social systems were dismantled through interior and exterior forces. The Africans had invited the Europeans to sit at the table of prosperity, and when the former were not looking, the legs of their table were literally stolen from under them, and they had nowhere to sit. This is the genesis of white supremacy.

Ancient Greeks and Romans viewed the Earth or Nature as female, hence the terms "Mother Earth" and "Mother Nature." This female personification of the Earth also framed it as territory to be explored, exploited, and controlled. Newly discovered lands were also routinely identified as female, and therefore subjugation was the only recourse for reformation.[1] Rape is a violent sexual act, utilized primarily to exercise power over another person. Rape is also an apropos concept to describe what was done to Africa, as it not only entailed the rape of persons, but also rape in the mental and spiritual realms. The 1884 carving of Africa in Berlin was a plan for massive colonization and, once carved, imperialism in all its glory was born—this, after millions of our Ancestors had been trafficked into toxic servitude. Africa was raped of its honor, its rich gene pool, and its varied and complex culture. This rape forever changed the ecosystem of the planet and established what we now define as white supremacy.

Dr. Frances Cress Welsing, one in a line of master academicians and historians, asked the why and how of white supremacy[2]. Nearly thirty years later, her writings are still relevant and prophetic, and aid in crystallizing the perspective of the global nature of white supremacy.

In *The Isis Papers*, Welsing opens the chapter on *The Politics Behind Black Male Passivity, Effeminization, Bisexuality and Homosexuality* with a description of the growing epidemic of Black male patients in her practice who were grappling with issues around masculinity and sexuality within the context of white supremacy. Welsing contends that due to the persistent and consistent aggression against non-white males on planet Earth, Europeans employed calculated and systemic methods, tactics, and strategies to bring non-whites into submission (p.43). According to Dr. Welsing, the persistent acts of aggression by those people who classify themselves as 'white' are carried out to ensure the genetic survival of 'white' people, which undergirds the practice of white supremacy. Her theory is predicated on the work of Neely Fuller, Jr., who states that "White Supremacy is a global system of domination against people of color." This system of injustice, white supremacy, attacks people of color, particularly those of African descent, in the nine major areas of people activity: *economics, education, entertainment, labor, law, politics, religion, sex, and war.*[3]

This chapter concerns the people activity of sex. The issue of sex or sexuality is extremely important as sex is the means by which species procreate and ensure their survival. A working definition, although broad, helps to guide the discussion. The World Health Organization defines sexuality as:

> ...a central aspect of being human throughout life [which] encompasses sex, gender identities and roles, sexual orientation, eroticism, pleasure, intimacy and reproduction. Sexuality is experienced and expressed in thoughts, fantasies, desires, beliefs, attitudes, values, behaviours, practices, roles and relationships. While sexuality can include all of these dimensions, not all of them are always experienced or expressed. Sexuality is influenced by the interaction of biological, psychological, social, economic, political, cultural, legal, historical, religious and spiritual factors.[4]

This definition, although broad, can be used as a guide to navigate the varied terrain of our Ancestors' past for the purpose of examining the interrelationships of culture, politics, and history in defining the sexuality of the Black male, in particular.

References regarding the sexuality of the African/African American male have often been described by terms such as hypersexual, hyper-masculine, and hyper-heterosexual[5]. Other descriptions have been lacking, as the sexuality of African/African American males has characteristically been more reactive than proactive. Studies often do not examine the cultural, contextual, and personal factors that inform the construction of its meaning, which was often afforded to white males alone.[6]

Further, it is not my intention to *negate* the unending contributions of our female African ancestors or African American women in our crucial history. It is, however, an endeavor to focus on the other half ofthe eternal link of the Black woman…the Black man.

The subject of sexuality is very broad in scope; therefore, the writer will focus on the people activity of sex or sexuality and its *miscegenation* with economics, education, law, and entertainment. It is essential to examine the multi-level nature of the assault on Black male sexuality/masculinity, and its enduring presence in the establishmentof contemporary societies. The first section of this essay, *The Makings of a White Hegemonic World*, focuses on the roots of hegemony; how it grew through the propagation of pseudo-scientific inquiry and propaganda, which dominated in Europe's "Enlightenment Period" and coincided with the height of the slave trade. The second section, *His-story is History*, is a discussion on how race, as a hegemonic construct, has been effectively instrumental in the continued capitulation to and testing of the masculinity of the African American male.

The third section entitled, *The Blood-Stained Gate*, highlights slave narratives, which refer to some of the "unspeakable acts" perpetrated by enslaver(s). Slave narratives not only document first-person accounts of the spectrum of abuses, but also provide an image of complicity and passivity to an unwilling servitude. Slave narratives are instructive in that they hold the original template of how Black male sexuality has evolved to exist in the 21st century, in the telling of the not-too-often told history of rapes, incest, and pedophilia. The sexual violence incurred during this period cannot be underestimated, nor can its transgenerational impact on African Americans' standing in society, the welfare of their families, and their perspectives on morality be denied.

Will That Be One Ball or Two? is the fourth section of this chapter, and addresses the science of submission and the continuity of trauma from mental, physical, and spiritual rape for the past 500 years. The fifth section, *A Traumatized Society*, covers one of the main concepts of this paper: Welsing's position that the Black male and his social choice of sexual orientation and behaviors, were *cultured* by a white male patriarchal society. This section attempts to deconstruct Dr. Welsing's views regarding homosexuality, bi-sexuality and passivity of the Black male, and transport those perspectives into the current political and social climate around gay rights.

The last section, *Aliens and Superheroes Don't Like Black Boys*, is an examination of one of the most powerful influences of contemporary thought regarding Black male sexuality: imagery and marketing. Imagery of the African/African American male conveyed through various forms of media and language has been underestimated as one of the most consistent, damaging or redeeming aspects of how the global society not only views Black male sexuality, but also, how it values the welfare of Black people in the Diaspora. Imagery is an effective vessel for the revisionist narrative of the European (whites/Western) culture, and reinforces the correctness both of their worldview(s) and how the world should function. Globally, people *en masse* have been exposed to distorted views through media and propaganda, resulting in complacency within the millions of African people and their descendants in the Diaspora, encouraging them not to question the institutions of white supremacy. However, it is through these same means that we can begin to restore and connect with our lineage and culture and take back what was taken away from us: our celebrated identity.

The Makings of a White Hegemonic World

> Most persons have accepted the tacit but clear modern philosophy which assigns to the white race alone the hegemony of the world.
>
> — W.E.B. Du Bois

Before the first millennium A.D., Africans lived in Europe as well as many other places. In fact, from about 711 to 1492 A.D., most of Spain was under Moorish control. Racial categories as we now know them, were not used to justify the denial of basic rights. European colonizers knew Africa to be a wealthy, advanced continent in many areas of development and education. Like the Arabs before them, Europeans began participating in what became known as the Atlantic slave trade by targeting well-established kingdoms weakened by internal strife. These empires were built by citizens who had the skills required to develop colonial enterprises—including advanced agricultural practices, metallurgy, navigation, and shipbuilding—and to effectively employ the resources from the lands themselves[7].

The architects of our white hegemonic world were and continue to be constructivists, who have built an argument of superiority atop a foundation of non-truths. White constructivism emerges from philosophy based on European views *constructed* to negate any origins of non-white philosophies and applications in all disciplines.

Hegemony involves persuasion of the greater part of the population, particularly through the media and the organization of social institutions in ways that appear "natural," "ordinary," and "normal." This norm is reasserted through displays of institutional and economic power, as well as institutional and individual violence. It is the combination of these elements that makes complete power and control possible. In the United States, the norm is male, white, heterosexual, Christian, able-bodied, and youthful, with access to wealth and resources. An established norm does not necessarily represent a majority in terms of number; it represents those who have the ability to exert power and control over others.[8] While hegemony, in this sense, is connected with institutions of male dominance, the concept often excludes Black and working-class men.[9] To provide additional context, the paradigm of what we call "race" must be addressed. Part of the construction of white hegemony is the illusion that race exists. As one anthropologist cited, "race is supposed to be strictly a biological category, equivalent to an animal subspecies… the problem is [that] humans use it as a cultural category, and it is difficult, if not impossible, to separate those two things from each other."[10]

Although the concept of race was initially used as a method for classifying human and animal species, Europeans evolved it into a way of delineating humankind into inferior and superior groups. The word "race" was introduced into the lexicon of Western interpretation initially by the Swedish scientist Carl Linnaeus in the early 18th century. Linnaeus divided *Homo Sapiens* into four basic varieties: *Americanus, Europaeus, Asiaticus,* and *Afer* (African). His initial classical taxonomy was not necessarily linear or hierarchical, but geographically based.[11]

However, when said classifications transitioned away from the functions of descriptive geography and towards those of a prescriptive hierarchy, the concept of white supremacy was *legitimized* through the annals of science.

The "Age of Enlightenment" provided the backdrop for 18th-century European theories about human differences. European exploration of Africa, Asia, and the Americas brought them into contact with people whom they found quite different. Prominent Enlightenment thinkers[12] greatly influenced European ideas about economics, government and science. Johann Blumenbach, a German and a student of Linnaeus, revised the initial classifications (taxonomy) for humans from four to five, with his final version published in 1795. Blumenbach, who had a medical degree, was hailed as one of the greatest and most honored scientists of the Enlightenment period and established the most influential of all racial classifications. He was the first to utilize and coin the term Caucasian, which is still used today. The label of Caucasian came about through Blumenbach's observations of the people who lived in the Caucasus mountains—the mountain range that straddles Russia and Georgia. Based on his *belief* that the people from this region were the most beautiful, he theorized that humans were first created there. Blumenbach makes the following rationale for the hierarchy:

> Caucasian variety: I have taken the name of this variety from Mount Caucasus, both because its neighborhood, and especially its southern slope, produces the most beautiful race of men, I mean the Georgian; and because....in that region, if anywhere, it seems we ought with the greatest probability to place the autochthones (original forms) of mankind.[13, 14]

In essence, Blumenbach chose his own European variety as closest to the created ideal and then searched for the subset of Europeans he deemed to have the greatest perfection of the European.[15] Despite being pseudoscience, Blumenbach's taxonomy would continue to be utilized as a guide for all disciplines with wide acceptance and myriad interpretations. This hierarchal version of taxonomy would lay the groundwork for all the major disciplines supporting scientific racism and would serve as the foundation for "scholars" to provide "proof" that the Western view of subjugation was morally and "scientifically" justified. Consequently, the term *race* as envisioned in the 16th century would become the official rationalization for the enslavement and oppression of people of color for the next 400 years.

In the midst of the emerging sciences of anthropology and eventually psychology, the African became the focal point for experimentation and observation; the terms and meanings that we now give to *race* in the US were concretized in 1790, when the first US Census established race as an official category.[16]

The suppositions regarding the sexuality of Black people as well as the obsession with color or darkness of the skin by Europeans is well documented. There were a number of hypotheses about why Africans were dark or black, and how this blackness characterized everything from sexual prowess to intellect. Utilization of instruments was an exercise in taming curiosities, and anthropometric classifications were aids in explaining the differences. In 1904, the Smithsonian spearheaded an effort to increase data collection of human characteristics and commissioned Aleš Hrdlička to publish a manual, which would standardize the measurement and observation of human characteristics.[17] In an effort to "standardize" phenotypes, a number of inventions were designed to determine how much African blood ran through the subjects' veins. The Broca technique (1879) was a collection of color swatches to match the skin hue of subjects. The *tintometer* was created and designed to measure the degree of pigmentation in the hair and eyes (Gray, 1908). The Color Top, which was made by the Milton Bradley Company,[18] was marketed as a device designed for expressing color quantitatively. This device had four color disks, one of which was labeled N for Nigrum (Shapiro, 1928). Along with measuring melanin in the skin, there were also several instruments designed to measure hair texture (Bey, 1863),[19] hair color, as well as the classifications for the thickness of one's lips. Europeans displayed a lot of anxiety around racial identification; it was of paramount importance not only to understand how melanin functioned, but to also provide—through pseudoscience—the tools for assuring identity.[20]

Hair texture, skin hue, and lip thickness continue to be barometers of beauty among African Americans as well as other people of color for the purpose of sexual selection. The issues around the lightness or darkness of the skin still plague parts of the globe today, and have resulted in the practice of skin bleaching in Africa and the West Indies, as well as some regions of the United States. This white hegemonic *construct* of beauty is evident by the repeated placement of lighter-skinned women in the music videos of Black male artists, globally.[21] Other trends of note linked to the issues of skin tone are the increasing numbers of Black men bleaching their skin, and the rising availability of anal and vaginal bleaching agents for purchase on the Internet.[22]

As Welsing references in the global system of white supremacy, it is important to incorporate a contextual perspective by which we see ourselves within this superficial and subjective system. Although there is no scientific or biological foundation for such classifications, race, as a superficial construct, continues to be applied as a measure of who is superior or inferior.

His-Story is History

Prior to the 1980s, historians of Africa did not incorporate or document the culture of sexuality, as such topics were presumed to be in the realm of psychology and anthropology. Moreover, there was a dearth of information about Africa in global sexuality studies, and any references or discussions of ethnography and sexual practices were ill-represented or offered little substance.[23] As history has shown us, many of the leading researchers in the field are non-African so, consequently, there are limitations with research and observations due to language, epistemology, and the understanding of the vast array of culture(s) from an African historical context.[24]

For males, references in the lexicon to *sexuality* are often interchanged with *masculinity*. Further, sexuality is defined and characterized through the lens of Europeans. Historically, Black male sexuality has been objectified, based on observations of a not-too-learned class of slave traders and missionaries, who conveyed stories as seen through their naïve eyes and ethnocentric perceptions.[25] Their stories became fodder for those who self-proclaimed "enlightenment" and emboldened scholars and academicians, who laid the foundation for the architects of white supremacy. Siobhan Somerville cites the following: "The prevailing Western concept of sexuality…already contains racism. Historically, the European construction of sexuality coincides with the epoch of imperialism and the two inter-connect…"[26]

References in writings about sexuality south of the Sahara first appeared in observations by a Muslim traveler, Ibn Battuta, in 1352.[27] As mentioned above, other accounts by non-Africans in the roles of slavers, explorers, missionaries, and colonial officials were given much veracity by their readers. Throughout the mid-twentieth century, the writings of nearly all white male authors tended to characterize Africans as heterosexual and promiscuous, and characterized their sexual behaviors as pathological and dangerous.[28] Alleged issues of sexuality, miscegenation and danger were all sensationalized and *marketed* to promote the aura of the omnipresent threat of the Black man. It was extremely important for promoters to continuously conflate a link between animals and the "bestial" nature of Black men. Robert Shufeldt writes:

> *Observing that the Negro domain is also the habitat of the most an-* thropoid apes-gorilla and chimpanzee... Sometimes the external genital organs are enormously developed in the negro, especially the penis in the man, and the clitoris in the female. The hair on the pubis is coarse and kinky as it is on the head. It may be quite abundant. Many years ago, I dissected an old negro man in Washington, D.C., at the National Medical College. [The] subject …was particularly simian in his organization, and one thing I noticed about him more than anything else, in addition to his immense copulatory organ, was the structure of his toe-nails.[29]

Welsing stated that *"the global behavior patterns of racism are a survival necessity for the white collective."*[30] Applying the concept of Welsing's assertion(s) of a global system, the term *Black Peril* was widely interpreted in the US as a debate about protecting the sanctity of white women from the rapacious sexual proclivities of the Black man. Black men were typecast as animalistic abusers and rapists, and characterized as wanting to steal and sully the belongings of white men—the white woman— this has been a dominant and consistent theme in white supremacy culture.[31]

For example, in a study on the colonization of different regions of Africa, the term *Black Peril* was used liberally during the late-nineteenth and early-twentieth centuries to create hysteria over the white women's alleged risk of sexual attack by Black men. This type of rhetoric was not only used in the US, but also (though not limited to) the settler colonies of southern Africa, Papua New Guinea, Zimbabwe, and post-World War I Germany.[32, 33] The study also cites that the racial and gender politic. of the "Black Peril" were a means through which colonial communities "shored up their interests and created racial unity (among Europeans), during crises of control, whether real or perceived," using the mask of protecting the white woman's alleged sexual and racial purity.[34]

John Pape describes the reactions to the *Black Peril* in colonial Zimbabwe as a hysterical obsession amongst the white population. During the early 20th century, a wide range of legislation spawned, including the prohibition of sexual relations between white women and Black men. In European colonies, as well as the US, the ultimate victim was the Black man who was lynched, castrated, jailed, or killed due to false accusations, amid no evidence of sexual crimes.[35]

Lynching is a form of violence used to primarily suffocate and *kill* the masculinity of the Black male.[36] It personified the white man's obsession with subjugation of the Black male and was used to exalt his own masculinity. The execution of a lynching also epitomizes "the behavior energy equation of white over non-white (white power or non-white powerlessness).[37] Lynching of Black males (and females), included eye gouging, burning, and dismembering genitalia; penises or other appendages which were sometimes kept as souvenirs.[38, 39]

The following provides a framework of a lynching, first chronicled in the *Tampa Bay Times.* It captures the case of 23-year-old, Claude Neal. He was described as short and scrawny, could not read or write, and picked peas and cotton or performed menial jobs to provide for his wife and three-year-old daughter during the Great Depression in Jackson County, Florida. In 1934, he was accused of raping and killing his white boss's 20-year-old daughter, Lola Cannidy. He was moved from jail to jail so that white lynch mobs would not find him before the trial. Eventually, they tracked him down in Alabama, held the jailer at gunpoint and absconded with Neal.

Neal was first killed by six white men who felt the need to send a message. They took him to a location near Greenwood, Florida, lashed him to a tree with tractor chains, cut him with knives and burned his flesh. When he was dead, his body was then dragged back to town attached to the back of an automobile. It was there that a mob of as many as 3000 people had their way: people skinned the lifeless body of Claude Neal, his fingers were cut off (and eventually put in a jar), he was set on fire, and they drove their cars over his corpse. Neal was then strung up in an oak tree that still stands in front of the courthouse, 80 years later. In 2011, Ben Montgomery re-reported Neal's murder for the *Tampa Bay Times*. His article contains a passage in which one of those first six assailants recalls what happened that day:

> Well, I guess we was pretty liquored up, and I ain't like that no more, but we cut off his balls and made him eat them and say they was good. Then we cut off his pecker and made him eat it and say it was good. Excerpt, Tampa Bay Times[40].

Despite the confession of the perpetrator, no one was ever brought to justice, no killer was ever named. After 77 years of ignoring one of the most brutal lynchings in history, Neal's nephew, after repeated requests to the US Justice Department, finally met with the FBI in 2011. In 2016, he received a letter from the Justice Department's Cold Case Initiative stating they could not solve the case.

Like those who were lynched or killed, the specter of the Black Peril still exists in the 21st century. The other end of the spectrum, called

"White Peril," was defined as the sexual abuse of Black women by white men. The incidents of abuse were far more frequent than others, yet were never interpreted as a sexual threat. There was never any law passed to specifically prohibit white men from sexually abusing Black women. In the article *Decrying the White Peril*, Ray notes the perception that African women, unlike their white counterparts, did not possess a form of sexuality that could be violated and, therefore, such actions taken by white men were not deemed to be criminal.[41] In essence, Black women were *masculinized* by virtue of their back-breaking labor alongside Black men, and were denied protection and provision, which ironically, was in the hands of the enslaver.[42]

For the most part, Black men have been socialized, and their presentation regulated, to minimize any potential conflict with whites and to avoid appearing threatening. In the tenets of white supremacy, the white woman's value was directly tied to their supposed purity, and it became the duty of white men to make sure they remained pristine. White women were considered objects whose only duty was to propagate the white race. Romano states, "Whiteness was easily corruptible and blackness was all-consuming... the survival of the white race depended upon its women, who were designated as the guardians of white racial purity."[43] This discussion is relevant to Welsing's position regarding white genetic annihilation. The white male's ultimate fear is to be genetically dominated by non-whites and resultantly, to fade out of existence. It was therefore of paramount importance that "race-mixing" with Black men was prevented to avoid producing offspring that would theoretically be genetically dominant to the white male.[44]

Black Peril terminology has been extended to include Latino men, Asian men, men of the Muslim faith, and men of color in general, all of whom are asserted to be potential threats to the piety and sacredness of white women.[45] Just like the Black woman, the Black man's sexuality was objectified, reflecting the general obsession among Europeans and Euro-Americans around sex and race.

The Blood-Stained Gate

During the past 400 years, Black men in the US have been forced into passive and cooperative submission to white men. The major strategy has been the installation of an overwhelming fear. Specific tactics range from actual physical castration and lynching, to other overt and more subtle forms of abuse, violence and cruelty. We should not be ashamed to recognize these tactics used to oppress Black men. It is the truth. It is reality. Ultimately, this is the meaning of Black oppression.[46]

In the early 1500s in the Port of São, the Portuguese pillaged the African Continent for its primary source of capital, African males. Other groups soon followed. Hundreds of thousands of men were captured initially to work in the sugar cane fields in Brazil and parts of the Caribbean, and eventually the plantations in the US This devastated the stability of Africa, leaving many regions bereft of men, and consequently, leaving many women without mates, and children without fathers. Here we begin to see the cyclical nature of the absent fathers, sons, and brothers from generation to generation in the Western world.[47] The circumstances which produce the absent Black male continue to persist from one millennium to the next, asserting the continued deconstruction of the Black family.

The words of slave narratives provide a vivid rendering of the process of emasculation of the Black male and defeminization of the Black woman through the institutionalization of sexual violence. The narratives describe what Welsing refers to as *passive and cooperative submission.* Documentation of these heinous sexual acts was seldom spoken of in African American families, and the trauma that it engendered was transgenerational. The narratives opened and exposed what Africans saw and what they experienced in lieu of what was reported by Europeans.[48] Within these narratives are references to not only creative ways of cruelty, but also to the sexual nuances and proclivities of the enslaver. Seen as a defense mechanism from a clinical perspective, boundaries that were established under the tenets of a moral and Christian existence were continuously violated as white enslavers acted out their own sexual aberrations. Frantz Fanon notes in *Black Skin, White Masks*:

"[We] know how much sexuality there is in all cruelties, torture, [and] beatings."[49]

The narratives that follow describe instances of these aberrations beginning with Frederick Douglass, who aptly and poetically describing the blood-stained gate as the entry to hell:

> The louder she screamed, the harder he whipped, and where the blood ran fastest, there he whipped longest. He would whip her to make her scream, and whip her to make her hush, and not until overcome by fatigue, would he cease to swing the blood-clotted cow-skin. I remember the first time I ever witnessed this horrible exhibition. I was quite a child, but I remember it. I never shall forget it whilst I remember anything. It was the first in a long series of such outrages, of which I was doomed to be a witness and a participant. It struck me with awful force. It was the blood-stained gate, the entrance to the hell of slavery, through which I was about to pass.[50]

Dr. Welsing writes, "Under [the]white supremacy slavery system, the identity of "sex machines" was imposed upon Black males, especially as many hands were needed in the fields for toil and labor."[51] This is aptly described in the following narrative:

> [Interviewer's summary] On this plantation were more than 100 slaves who were mated indiscriminately and without any regard for family unions. If their master thought that a certain man and woman might have strong, healthy offspring, he forced them to have sexual relation, even though they were married to other slaves. If there seemed to be any slight reluctance on the part of either of the unfortunate ones, "Big Jim" would make them consummate this relationship in his presence. He used the same procedure if he thought a certain couple was not producing children fast enough. He enjoyed these orgies very much and often entertained his friends in this manner; quite often he and his guests would engage in these debaucheries, choosing for themselves the prettiest of the young women.[52]

These formulas of abuse were enacted to paralyze the spirit and reflect the depravities of the enslavers. Abdur-Rahman writes, "representations of sexual perversity under conditions of enslavement have contributed to notions of sexual alterity and to the ideologies by which aberrant sexual practices were named, domesticated, and policed in the first decades of the twentieth century.[53] The following account reflects the descriptions of torture rampantly and routinely inflicted:

> …James was sold again to a wealthy slaveholder, noted for his cruelty. With this man he grew up to manhood, receiving the treatment of a dog. After a severe whipping, to save himself from further infliction of the lash, with which he was threatened, he took to the woods. He was in a most miserable condition—cut by the cowskin, half naked, half starved, and without the means of procuring a crust of bread.
>
> Some weeks after his escape, he was captured, tied, and carried back to his master's plantation. This man considered punishment in his jail, on bread and water, after receiving hundreds of lashes, too mild for the poor slave's offence. Therefore, he decided, after the overseer should have whipped him to his satisfaction, to have him placed between the screws of the cotton gin, to stay as long as he had been in the woods. This wretched creature was cut with the whip from his head to his foot, then washed with strong brine, to prevent the flesh from mortifying, and make it heal sooner than it otherwise would. He was thenput into the cotton gin, which was screwed down, only allowing him room to turn on his side when he could not lie on his back. Every morning a slave was sent with a piece of bread and bowl of water, which were placed within reach of the poor fellow. The slave was charged, under penalty of severe punishment, not to speak to him. Four days passed, and the slave continued to carry the bread and water. On the second morning, he found the bread gone, but the water untouched.
>
> When he had been in the press four days and five nights, the slave informed his master that the water had not been used for four mornings, and that a horrible stench came from the gin house. The overseer was sent to examine into it. When the press was unscrewed, the dead body was found partly eaten by rats and vermin. Perhaps the rats that devoured his bread had gnawed him before life was extinct.[54]

Part of the doctrine of white hegemony is to tame and dominate, and the humiliation of Black males was cultivated and commonplace. In addition, it was extremely important for others to witness the cruelties so that they too could vicariously experience the pain and humiliation.

The residual effects of the trauma(s) manifesting themselves generation after generation continue to beleaguer the quality of life for those of

African descent in the US, and in the Diaspora more broadly. As Franz Fanon notes, "Colonialism is not a thinking machine, nor a body endowed with reasoning faculties. It is violence in its natural state…". The transgenerational damage to the psyche is well articulated by Jean- Paul Satre in the forward of Fanon's work, *The Wretched of the Earth*:

> Colonial violence not only aims at keeping these enslaved men at a respectful distance, it also seeks to dehumanize them. No effort is spared to demolish their traditions, to substitute our language for theirs, and to destroy their culture without giving them ours. We exhaust them into a mindless state. Ill fed and sick, if they resist, fear will finish the job: guns are pointed at peasants; civilians come and settle on their land and force them to work for them under the whip. If they resist, the soldiers fire, and they are dead men; if they give in and degrade themselves, they are no longer men . Shame and fear warp their character and dislocate their personality.[55]

Would That Be One Ball or Two? Is There No end?

Submission strategies have been formulated and exercised through governance and policy through the institutions of laws (courts), the prison industrial complex, and education. Law and education have been essential in harnessing the masculinity of the African American male. The imposition of power through injustice is enacted through what Welsing cites as the "social and political apparatus." The following account, cited from a slave narrative, could be inserted into practically any contemporary news story regarding police brutality towards African American men, which has historically been used to neuter their masculinity:

> The Baltimore American of March 17, 1845, relates a similar case of atrocity, perpetuated with similar impunity, as follows: "Shooting a slave. We learn upon the authority of a letter from Charles County, Maryland received by a gentleman of this city, that a young man named Matthews, a nephew of General Matthews, and whose father, it is believed, holds an office at Washington, killed one of the slaves upon his father's farm by shooting him. The letter states that young Matthews had been left in charge of the farm; that he gave an order to the servant, which was disobeyed, when he proceeded to the house,

> obtained a gun, and returning, shot the servant. He immediately, the letter continues, fled to his father's residence, where he still remains unmolested. [56]

The aforementioned scenario is not unlike the case of Amadou Diallo, an unarmed black man shot 41 times by four white New York City Police officers (all of whom were acquitted). Philando Castile, Alton Sterling, Walter Scott, and Michael Brown are just a few of the cases that illustrate the extent to which the Black man is still denied legal protections, as he has been historically.

Since all the riots and protests from the Stono Revolt in 1739 to 2018, whites have continued to shoot and kill a disproportionately large number of Black people, particularly males. In 2017, Black males accounted for 22 percent of all people shot and killed, yet they are 6 percent of the total population. While the number of unarmed Black males killed by police has declined, they continue to be shot and killed at higher rates than other races, ethnicities, and gender groups.[57]

In December 2016, a judge declared a mistrial in the case of Michael Slager, the former officer who killed Walter Scott, shooting him multiples times in the back as he ran away.[58] There have been scores of unarmed Black men killed over the past century that have never been reported or known to the general public and, like the slave holder or overseer, the rate of officer indictments and convictions has been extremely low.[59] The structure of the prison industrial complex, is another component of the social and political apparatus that has, over the decades, insidiously taken Black males out of the community into confinement. The ever-increasing population of Black males (and women) in prison has, and will, have unforeseen collateral damage to African American communities.[60]

In a study published in *Demography*, it is estimated that one-third of African American men have a felony conviction as of 2010, a significant increase over the past 30 years (since 1980). This study is one of the first of its kind to provide state-level demographic information on the adult male population with felony convictions in the US, which provides a comparative analysis of the frequency of felony convictions and incarcerations of African American males and non-African American males, from 1948 to 2010.[61] To put the numbers in perspective, estimates show that 3% of the total adult population in the U.S has been to prison compared to 15% of the African American adult male population. Persons with felony convictions account for 8% of all adults compared to 33% of the African American adult male population.[62] Researchers found that the percentage of African American men with a felony conviction increased from 13% in 1980 to 33% in 2010 (compared to 5% and 13% for all adult men during these periods, respectively). Further, the percentage of African American men who had experienced imprisonment increased from 6% in 1980 to 15% in 2010 (compared to 2% and 6% for all adult men during these periods, respectively); these estimates are thus a reflection of a rising punishment rate, although actual crime ratings have declined. In essence, the numbers *are not representative of criminal behavior by race, but rather differential rates of punishment by race.*[63] The creation of a *"criminal class"* has as its foundation, young African American males who have a 49 percent likelihood of experiencing arrest prior to the age of 23.[64] In the historic context of the prison boom of young African American males, incarceration has reshaped adulthood and has contributed to a change in life trajectories for millions of these youth.[65] A recent finding by the Sentencing Project, determined that despite long-term declines in youth incarceration, the disparity between Black and white youth who are held in juvenile facilities has grown; as of 2015, African American youth were five times as likely as white youth to be detained or committed to youth facilities. Nationally, the youth rate of incarceration was 152 per 100,000. Black youth placement rate was 433 per 100,000, compared to a white youth placement rate of 86 per 100,000. Overall, the racial disparity between black and white youth in custody increased 22 percent since 2001.[66]

With the expectation that one out of every three Black boys born today will go to prison during his lifetime, the destabilization and destruction of Black families and communities will continue to be affected for generations.

*****

The hallmark and legacy of white supremacy is the US educational system, in that it lays the foundation for the stratification and bifurcation of society. The institutionalization of supremacist views is exercised at the beginning of the Black child's educational experience. During this time of development, the brain begins to encode experiences and begins to learn the culture of the environment; this occurs in the context of an established social system that has assigned social roles for every child born into the system.[67] Under these conditions many urban Black children are taught at a very young age that they are somehow different, subject to admonishments, lack of nurturance, and a flaccid curriculum; a curriculum that portrays whites as heroes and Blacks as having an inferior or secondary status. It is at the early stages of the Black child's educational experience that they are placed in a role that Welsing calls "*functional inferiors*" or exposed to the process of *inferiorization.*[68] In this sense, the educational system effectively serves as a portal for social stratification, asserting a road to prison or power. Kozol writes, "those of us who have those benefits have to live with the uncomfortable knowledge that all our victories in life will be contaminated by the fact that we were winners in a game that was never played on a level playing field."[69]

For the Black male child, in particular, the American educational system has been a land mine, as Black male children are often labeled at pre-K and kindergarten ages as students with behavioral problems. Black boys account for 20% of US students labeled as "mentally retarded", even though they represent just 9% of the population. On the other end of the spectrum, Black boys are 2.5 times less likely to be classified as "gifted and talented," even if their academic record shows that potential.[70, 71]

A recent study indicates that more Black boys are put into special education classes when they do not have a disability than children who actually have learning disabilities. If all things were weighed equally, these statistics would indicate that there is something genetically wrong, that there is a higher incidence of disabilities and smaller percentage of gifted individuals in the Black population. Black boys are the most likely to receive special education services and the least likely to be enrolled in honors classes.[72] In a study this writer conducted nearly 25 years ago, there was, literally, a 50 percent reduction of Black male students from ninth to twelfth grade; further, out of the three schools studied there were no Black males in honors classes. This data was consistent for all three schools located in urban and suburban areas.[73] As stated previously, one of this writer's former positions was as a psychologist for a school system and I have witnessed first-hand the inordinate number of African American male students placed in special education without being given the proper supports within the classroom environment.

Consider the possibility that it is statistically impossible for so many Black male students to be labeled and placed in these classes with no visible disability. This comes down to *subjective* placement in classrooms across the country where these young male students are drugged and exposed to a curriculum that offers little or no support for allowing the child to return to mainstream classrooms. Many are not reassessed and oftentimes parents are not given the tools to understand that their child[ren] do not have to be labeled forever. Even if the child reaches twelfth grade with the special education program, what type of diploma would they receive? This is, in part, how the school-to-prison pipeline functions. There has been an aggressive movement for over three decades to socialize and program many young African American males (as well as parents) to passively accept their status as unteachable. More importantly, the system of education has done little to rectify this problem and, from this writer's experience, has been complicit in not grooming young Black males for leadership.

In addition to being assigned to special education classes, the discipline of Black male students, even first-time offenders, is more frequent and punitive compared to other demographics. Black students comprise 18% of children in US preschools, but make up half of those students who are suspended. Black boys receive two-thirds of all school suspensions nationwide—even when gender was considered.[74] Increasingly, school-assigned law enforcement officers are shepherding students out of schools for minor offenses such as class disruption, tardiness, and non-violent arguments with other students.[75, 76] For example, NBC News found that Black students have been charged with crimes like assault for getting frustrated and pushing past a teacher, or battery for getting in a schoolyard fight.[77]

Take the case of 15-year-old Ryan Turk, who was charged with theft for taking a 65-cent carton of milk from the cafeteria. When Ryan, who went to Graham Park Middle School in Prince William County, Virginia, was in the eighth grade, he forgot to grab milk when going through the lunch line. Ryan's mother says he was enrolled in the free lunch program and he went back to get it. Watching Ryan, the police officer assigned to the school thought he had stolen the milk. The officer confronted Ryan and asked him to go to the principal's office. When the middle-schooler resisted, the officer handcuffed him and later charged him with petit larceny and disorderly conduct. Ryan, who is Black, was suspended and forced to go to court. In January 2017, the prosecutor ultimately declined to press charges, but retained the right to bring back charges for one year. "I think the whole situation was handled wrong," Ryan's mother commented. She says her son now has trouble trusting authority figures and adds, "The principal, she should've been the one addressing the situation, not the officer.[78]

Ivory Toldson cites that suspension is reserved for only the most deviant white male students; however, suspensions appear to be interwoven into the normal fabric of the Black male's school experiences. Research suggests that Black boys' transition to and through the ninth grade shapes their future odds of graduating from high school.[79, 80]

Welsing, in the chapter *Black Children and the Process of Inferiorization*, poses the following questions: 1) Will Black children in the US ever develop to their maximum genetic potential? 2) If so, who will assume ultimate responsibility for bringing about the maximal development—Black people themselves or white people? 3) If Black children are not to be maximally developed, what do Black people really think is going to happen to this large, underdeveloped mass of Black human beings? 4) Are white people in any way looking to Black people for the maximal development of white children?[81] The answers to these questions are meant to serve as a guide for parents and Black educators to realistically address how to guide Black children toward their maximum potential, and serves as a foundation from which Black children can be groomed to be productive, confident leaders.

The process of inferiorization affects the young in increasing numbers to deleterious effects. For example, the incidence of suicide among young Black children and particularly among males under the age of twelve, has increased. Bridge, et al., conducted a period trend analysis of suicide rates among children between five to eleven years of age. The significant finding was that analyses by race and subgroups indicated young Black males had an increase of suicide rates between 1993-1997 and 2008 to 2012. There was a significant difference in the rate of increase in comparison with young white males. Researchers observed this was the first time that they have seen a higher rate of suicide among Black individuals compared with whites in the US The primary modes of suicide were hanging, suffocation, and use of a firearm, which accounted for 96 percent of the deaths. Hanging and suffocation were the most frequent modes of suicide among young Black boys under the age of twelve.[82] Welsing writes, "All Black children should be protected by Black people from being alienated [from] against any of their genes." This comment was prophetic, in that there has to be a deep feeling of alienation and a mental and spiritual castration of the soul when a young child feels that their only option is death. As Jawanza Kunjufu writes: "Black men kill themselves with their futures ahead of them and white men when their futures are behind them."[83]

The systematic process of *emasculation* is fluent yet compartmentalized; there are many Black males that have similar experiences, but the system is not designed to address them. The need to address these issues from a holistic perspective is explained by Welsing: "..[B]ecause there is the failure on the part of most investigators (people) to perceive the total outline of the Western culture dynamic; it is difficult, if not impossible, for them (behavioral scientists), to make sense of the isolated behavior patterns (in this case the function of institutions) within the total behavioral system framework."[84]

The mental and spiritual castration caused by persistent exposure to institutions that are designed for oppression, has caused a subtle, yet persistent psychic pain, causing depression amongst many African American males. This factor is relevant because it parallels what has happened continuously since the 1500s — the absence of the Black man in the home. Throughout the centuries, Black women have had to raise their children alone, without the economic, physical, emotional, and spiritual support of the father, a fact which has merely continued to reinforce the type of pattern that is still evident in Black families in the 21st century. The syndrome of the "missing father(s)," which started hundreds of years ago, has had transgenerational effects that cannot be measured.

Traumatized Society

One of the more contentious parts of Dr Welsing's writings is her discussion on homosexuality. Welsing's essays were not popular in the gay community and were the source of much-heated discussion and debate. As referenced in the forward of this chapter, it is not this writer's intention to contextualize this discussion around the nature vs. nurture question nor to take an antagonist or protagonist position about homosexuality. But whether the reader feels one way or the other about this debate, there is no doubt that the sexuality of the Black male, regardless of orientation, has been distorted and biased through the lens of white supremacy.

The Isis Papers were released less than twenty years after the American Psychological Association (APA) removed the diagnosis of "homosexuality" from the second edition of its Diagnostic and Statistical Manual (DSM) in 1973. The decision to change and remove the designation of adult homosexuality from being a mental disorder or pathology, did not come without conflict and protests at the annual meeting. When Welsing published her book in the early 90's, the US was still in the middle of an HIV/AIDS epidemic and African American males in the gay community were disproportionately exposed to the virus with exceedingly high mortality rates.[85] In the midst of all this Dr. Welsing's essays fostered controversy, and were negatively received due to her views on the genesis and occurrence of homosexuality. Although the discourse has been intense and oftentimes critical, there are aspects of her work that have not been completely examined. A socio-historical context will hopefully shed light on where we were 25 years ago, when the essays were published, and how it has evolved to the current political and social climate.

The terrors homosexuals go through in this society would not be so great if the society itself did not go through so many terrors which it does not want to admit. The discovery of one's sexual preference doesn't have to be trauma. It's a trauma because it's such a traumatized society. I think white gay people feel cheated because they were born, in principle, into a society in which they were suppose[d] to be safe.... cheated of the advantages which accrue to white people in a white society. [86]

In the quote above, James Baldwin refers to a traumatized society within Western society where there have always been issues around one's sexual orientation or preferences. This issue of sexuality is one which has served as a focal point of debate and a locus for confusion. Homosexuality, in particular, has been designated as a taboo subject, particularly in Western societies where the issue of sex is one that has been mired in the Puritan ethic and the foundation of America's values and moral compass: filled with contradictions, non-truths and shame. "When entering the realms of gender and sexuality, it is notunusual to encounter another form of binary thinking: "morality tales" about whether certain kinds of thoughts, feelings, or behaviors are "good or bad" or, in some cases, whether they are "good or evil". The good/bad binary is not confined to religion alone, as the language of morality is inevitably found, for example, in theories about the "causes" of homosexuality. For in the absence of certitude about homosexuality's "etiology," binary gender beliefs and their associated moral underpinnings frequently play a role in theories about the causes and/or meanings of homosexuality. When one recognizes the narrative forms of these theories, some of the moral judgments and beliefs embedded in each of them become clearer." [87]

In the 1930s, the Committee for the Study of Sex Variants scrutinized homosexuals' bodies in an effort to document the atypical traits of their genitals and secondary sex characteristics.[88, 89] Homosexual brains and nervous systems were assumed to have some cross-gendered characteristics. In the 1950s and 1960s, some therapists employed aversion therapy of the kind featured in the film, *A Clockwork Orange,* to "cure" male homosexuality through a behavioral conditioning process involving electric shock therapy or drugs.[90] Just 30 years ago, in 1991, Simon LeVay conducted neuroanatomical research to determine sexual orientation, arguing that the homosexual man's hypothalamus was closer in size to that of women's than to that of heterosexual men.[91]

As the aforementioned demonstrates, Europeans/Western culture displayed an obsession with sex and sexual parts, and this is all too-evident in the telling of the slave narratives and literature that describes aberrations of the colonizers. Despite de facto oppressive violent practices by colonizers, the Black penis is still "weaponized" and its owner assigned to a class of sexual deviants. The Black male heterosexual is classified as hyper-masculine and possibly even a rapist, and the Black homosexual is classified as a rapist, a pedophile and weak. "All societies invent classes of outlaws…history has a virtual parade of social types who have at one time or another been viewed as threats to the prevailing social order…. One function of the deviant is to help define for others that which is not deviant."[92] This is the yardstick by which others are measured and judged: white, male, heterosexual, Christian, with access to wealth and resources.; It is rare that a child is teased because they are white and wealthy. In order to reinforce that foundation of the supremacist position, it is necessary to determine and define what is right and just, and what is bad and deviant.[93]

There have been many suppositions regarding homosexuality among Africans/African Americans. The foundational discourse on Black male sexuality is often traced back to the sexual practices on the slave plantation. "The sexual violence was understood as a sexual deviance … and established whiteness as the requisite category for heteronormative qualification."[94] As referenced in the previous section of this chapter, some of the slave narratives refer to sexual experiences of homosexual contact with the enslaver as "unspeakable acts." Other references in early literature and essays generated among white observers of African culture refer to "peculiar ways," referring to same sex engagements. If we utilize the lens of white supremacy on the issue of homosexuality, there are similar ways in which the sexuality of African and African-American males were/are perceived, regardless of their sexual status.

Scholars such as Siobhan Somerville, who have written extensively on the evolution of labeling sexual practices, trace the development of discrete sexual categories under the pathos of enslavement. These ideologies of sexual behavior, which emanated under conditions of enslavement, gave birth to the ideologies where aberrant sexual practices were named, domesticated, and policed, by the end of the twentieth century.[95]

Utilizing a historical context of enslavement as a backdrop to Welsing's position on homosexuality, her views highlight how the progenitors of white supremacy have been successful in compromising the sexuality of the Black male through systemic racism and targeted violence. In essence, the residual effects of violence and oppression have caused the Black man to modify the expression of his sexuality/masculinity in more passive ways, which may present as effeminization, and/or engaging in bisexual and homosexual acts. Welsing writes:

> ...the Black male arrives at this position secondarily (engaging in homosexual or effeminate acts) as a result of the imposed power and [the] cruelty of the white male and the totality of white supremacy social political apparatus that has forced [over] 20 generations of Black males into submission.[96]

Moreover, the effeminate stance of the Black male, to which Welsing refers could be interpreted as those who are passive and reticent due to the experience of seeing "masculine" and assertive Black men silenced through incarceration or assassination. History has shown us the mortality of men such as Malcolm X, Martin Luther King, Jr., Medgar Evers, and other community leaders who have stood up to white supremacy, and were often murdered and removed from an active state of influence for their troubles. Welsing describes this as the ultimate frustration of Black manhood—the position of passivity—which is a response to a *deep-seated fear of death.*[97] Morrison writes, "For many black men, so much of their self-worth can be wrapped up in "being a real man." Often, parents play a major role in these early tests of a boy's 'manhood,' going to great lengths to prod their sons into masculinity. They are often doing so out of a fear that, in addition to racism, their son may be seen as 'too feminine.'"[98] Whatever position a parent takes towards raising their Black male child, it is oftentimes a position of fear for their survival.

Welsing references her clinical experiences in therapeutic sessions with young Black male children to demonstrate that they learn early on to modify their behavior(s) to minimize the experience of alienation.[99] This observation undergirds Welsing's nurturist position on effemization, homosexuality, and bisexuality, in that part of the Black man's socialization has been the experience of being consistently challenged when flexing or presenting his "masculinity."

In her essays, Welsing expresses profound concern about how the realities of prison have affected hundreds of thousands of African American males spiritually, and clouded their perceptions of their own sexuality. Without jobs in order to generate income and power to protect and care for their families, Welsing asserts, there is no proof of sexual functioning. In illustration, she [Welsing] relays a discussion with a Black man who was an ex-prisoner: "[I]t is easier to endure life on the inside than to try to put up with the pressures of being a man, a husband, and a father in the street." She refers to prisons as the milieu that feeds on the Black man's masculinity, "...but the fate and the dynamics of racism again play a vicious trick because the young males only become more alienated from their manhood and more feminized in such settings. They are given orders by men to whom they must submit; they wait passively to be fed three meals a day by men; and finally they have sexual intercourse with men."[100, 101] Welsing observed that even after a person is released from prison, the experiences, the trauma, and the submission endured still haunt his psyche, while on the outside, the man's confinement still exists under the auspices of cultural and social dominance.[102]

Welsing gleaned these positions during the course of her clinical practice and acknowledged that Western psychiatry's inability to identify the interrelationships between racism, homosexuality, and sexism is due to an inadequate conceptual and theoretical base. She cites, "Black psychiatrists must understand that whites may condone homosexuality for themselves, but we as Blacks, must see it as a strategy for destroying Black people that must be countered." Welsing further asserts that Black male bisexuality and homosexuality "should neither be condemned or degraded, as they did not decide that they would be so programmed in childhood. The racist system should be held accountable... Black male bisexuality and homosexuality has been used by the white collective in its effort to survive genetically in a world dominated by colored people…"[103]

This dovetails into what Welsing writes about in *The Theory of Color Confrontation*: "[W]hites are vulnerable to their sense of numerical inadequacy. This inadequacy is apparent in their drive to divide the vast majority of non-whites into fractional, as well as frictional minorities. This is viewed as a fundamental behavioral response to their own minority status."[104] Another aspect of Welsing's views that caused debate was the issue of homosexuality juxtaposed with the tenets of Black nationalism. In the offering of Welsing's revolutionary treatise, some critics of her work have problems with her assertions measuring the Black man's masculinity by how he defends himself against the system and ultimately, the denial of the Black gay male's role as a revolutionary in the fight against white supremacy.[105] Dwight McBride discusses Welsing at length and argues how Welsing implies that "to be a representative race man, one must be heterosexual."[106] McBride adds, "still another of the vexatious implications of this [Welsing's] logic is that in a world devoid of racism or white supremacy, there would be no Black male homosexuality."[107]

In reality, the experiences of Black gay males is one in which discrimination presents as the proverbial double edged sword, being Black and gay. It is this writer's contention that the juxtaposition of race and sexual orientation becomes conflated due to the visceral reaction to skin color. In essence, a man of African descent is the primary assessment; whether he is gay or straight is secondary. As James Baldwin writes:

> A Black gay person who is a sexual conundrum to society is already, long before the question of sexuality comes into it, menaced and marked because he's Black or she's Black. The sexual question comes after the question of color; it is simply one more aspect of the danger in which all Black people live (1961).[108]

In essence, although a Black person is a member of the gay community, they still have to contend with the vestiges of discrimination that have been historic and prevalent within the community,[109] and that often mirror similar issues that all Black people experience within the realm of racist institutions.

Politically, the wave of the gay right's movement afforded such forays and primarily benefited the white LGBTQ community. Two of the overarching issues in the Black gay community are acceptance and belonging as an integral part of the policy and politics (gay rights) in the greater gay community. There is a plethora of anecdotal accounts and posts regarding the issue, as well as published literature. As one writer put it with regard to white gay males:

> Gay white men were born gay, but they were also raised and socialized as white men—the social group vested with the most privilege in America. Here's the brutal truth: The social privilege of whiteness still affords them a disproportionate amount of power in the gay community.
>
> That privilege elevates white, gay men above men of color. They cover both gay and mainstream magazines. They lead primetime shows about gay men. White, gay men set the standard against which other gay men's attractiveness is measured. If we hope to eradicate racism within the gay community, white gay men must acknowledge their privilege — and the way it's used, in ways subtle and not, to denigrate minorities.[110]

For the most part, a culturally relevant discussion, bereft of the usual exotic and taboo perspective around the sexuality of Black gay or straight men, has been virtually non-existent. These attitudes and beliefs about sexuality have only recently been addressed with a sense of scholarship by non-white researchers. African scholars have begun to take the mantel to provide more insight into the different regions of Africa, and

African American scholars have entered into the discussion with content and gravity. There has been a growing amount of gay-positive or homonormative imagery on a global scale.

The politics of the West have foisted an acculturation to liberal ideas regarding homosexuality. During the Obama years, the US distributed funding globally, with $41 million going to Africa. However, the applications of policies and laws in Western culture are not always applicable in non-Western countries. The funding, and the regulations attached to it, has brought about resentment by African governments and private organizations accusing the US of cultural imperialism. The overall perspective is that "pressing gay rights on an unwilling Continent, is the latest attempt by Western nations to impose their values on Africa and has consequently caused more violence against those in gay community(ies)."[111]

To get a better understanding of the understudied LGBTQ community, increasing numbers of population-based surveys in the United States and across the world include questions designed to measure sexual orientation and gender identity.[112, 113] A Gallup tracking poll indicates that there is an increase in those who identify as LGBT. 3.5% in 2012 to 4.1. in 2016, which translates into 1.75 million more Americans who have identified since the count in 2012; or, a total of 10 million American adults who identify as LGBTQ.[114] Demographers theorize that the increase in numbers is attributed to people feeling more comfortable and willing to identify themselves. Millennials are responsible for "virtually all of the increases observed in overall LGBT self-identification" which, according to Gary Gates, is unsurprising because they are "the first generation in the US to grow up in an environment where social acceptance of the LGBTQ community markedly increased."[115]

The landscape of LGBTQ communities of color has largely been ignored, and it is important to put into perspective this stratum of the population whose demographics are understudied, giving way to the usual stereotypes leveraged against the gay community. A recent Gallup survey shows that "non-whites" are more likely than white segments of the US population to identify as LGBTQ.[116] LGBTQ families are more racially and ethnically diverse than families headed by married heterosexual couples; 41% of same-sex couples with children identify as people of color compared to 34% of married different-sex couples with children. Both Black and Latino same-sex couples are more likely to raise children than white same-sex couples. Children raised in LGBTQ families of color are more likely to be living in poverty than children raised in white LGBTQ families or children raised by married, heterosexual parents. For example, 32% of children raised by Black male gay couples live in poverty, compared with 13% of children raised by married heterosexual Black parents and 7% of children raised by married heterosexual white parents. Gates commented on the outcomes of the study stating, "If you spend a lot of time watching network television, you would think most LGBT people are rich White men who live in big cities. These data suggest [that] the LGBT community reflects more of the diversity of the US population than is commonly perceived."[117]

On one last note, it is virtually impossible to view one oppression, such as sexism or homophobia, in isolation because they are all connected: sexism, racism, homophobia, classism, ableism, anti-Semitism, ageism. They are linked by a common origin—economic power and control—and there is no hierarchy of oppressions. In the world of white supremacy, these "isms" are the lingua franca used to divide and conquer.

Aliens and Superheroes Do Not Like Black Boys

> Most persons have accepted the tacit but clear modern philosophy which assigns to the white race alone the hegemony of the world.
>
> — W.E.B. Du Bois

In the realm of media, journalists, advertisers, politicians, psychiatrists, designers, playwrights, film-makers, actors, novelists, musicians, activists, academics, coaches, and professional sportsmen are considered to be some of the most influential agents. They are, as Antonio Gramsci cites, the "weavers of the fabric of hegemony," its "organizing intellectuals." These people regulate and manage gender regimes; articulate experiences, fantasies, and perspectives; and reflect on and interpret gender relations.[118] But, the one thing that these organizing intellects have not been able to manage is the Black penis, the dominant gene pusher, and our superhero.

Wesley Morris an at-large critic for the *New York Times*, wrote an illuminating and astute discourse on the intersection of sexuality and race in the media and explains why the Black penis cannot be shown:

> A vast majority of these penises [shown] are funny, casual, unserious. Their unceremonious appearance—as naturalism, comedy, symbolism, provocation—is new, and maybe progressive. But that progress is exclusive, because these penises almost always belong to white men. As commonplace as it has recently become to see black men on television and at the heart of films, and as normal as it's becoming to see male nudity in general, it has been a lot more difficult to see those two changes expressed in the same body. A black penis, even the idea of one, is still too disturbingly bound up in how America sees—or refuses to see—itself.

Morris goes on to reflect how the few Black actors were portrayed in the movies and how we see the evolution of the neutering of Sidney Poitier:

> By the end of the 1960s, some black people were wondering that about Sidney Poitier: How much longer would a 40-year-old man have to stay a movie virgin? How many more times could he be made a mannequin of palatable innocuousness? In 1967, after black neighborhoods across the country burned in race riots, Poitier slapped the face of a haughty racist at the emotional apex of "In the Heat of the Night," when he was just about the biggest star in Hollywood and at the peak of his talent. By the end of the year, though, in "Guess Who's Coming to Dinner," he was back to his serene, tolerable self, playing the only kind of Negro a liberal white family could imagine as worthy of its young daughter: Johns Hopkins and Yale-educated, excruciatingly well-mannered, neutered.[119]

Irrespective of whatever role Sidney Poitier played after that, it was that slap across the face that Black folks would remember, a sense of redemption. It is characteristic in blockbuster films that the Black male character plays a secondary or supportive role, as it is invariably disruptive for the Black male character to interfere with the algorithm of established order. On the other hand, it is incumbent upon the white male character to restore [narrative] order. Whatever the conflict, the Black male protagonist is inevitably punished, whether it is Gus in *Birth of a Nation* or Apollo Creed in *Rocky II*, the Black man's defeat is necessary to establish the white male character, [like] Rocky, as the "hero."[120] And, what about Morpheus, from *The Matrix*, why is he *not* "The One?" Morpheus not only protects and assists Neo through the Matrix, but Morpheus is harassed by nasty Sentinels, all of whom are white.

Western programming is *global*. Many foreign markets have picked up programming that portrays the white ideal, an Americanized version of a type of utopia, reserved only for those of European persuasion. When I traveled to South Africa after the disaster of Katrina, the Black South Africans articulated their steadfast observations from the images on television that all white people were rich, and Blacks were poor.

In the utopia of a white supremacist world, literature and imagery of non-whites are used as the pillars of dehumanization and promote the bestiality of Black men. Over the centuries, simianization of the African/Black man has evolved to uphold the specter of the Black Peril, crystallized in the image of King Kong. There have been many iterations since the original film was shown in 1933. Kong Kong has been re-released several times over the past 90 years, most recently in 2016.[121] At the time of the original film production of *King Kong*, the US was consumed by a rape trial. The Scottsboro Boys were nine Black teenagers accused of raping two young white women. In an excellent historical analysis in *Simianization: Apes, Gender, Class, and Race*, the authors refer to 1935, when a picture story by Japanese artist Lin Shi Khan and the lithographer, Toni Perez was published. Their book, *Scottsboro Alabama* carried a foreword by Michael Gold, editor of the communist journal *New Masses*. One of the 56 images showed the accused young men, labeled as "The Fiends," beside a newspaper with the headline "Guilty Rape." The rest of the picture is filled with a monstrous black simian figure baring its teeth and dragging off a helpless white girl.[122] This is another example of the techniques employed to characterize the

Black man as having a bestial nature.

It is ironic that the only person in the world that King Kong would admire and perceive as a love interest would be a white woman. Highlighted throughout the iterations of Kong is the piety and purity of the white woman; Kong could only admire her longingly and put her on a pedestal. The white man always conquered Kong, and the white women's purity is saved, along with the rest of the world.

Research shows how the image of Kong has become enduring and omnipresent, stoking thoughts of danger and the "bestial" nature of the Black man. Phillip Goff, et al., demonstrated how US citizens implicitly associate Blacks and apes through a series of laboratory studies. Their research indicates that this association influenced the study participants' basic cognitive processes and significantly altered their judgments in criminal justice contexts. The researchers found that "...this Black-ape association alters visual perception and attention, and it increases endorsement of violence against Black suspects".[123] Further, in an archival study of actual criminal cases, the research showed that news articles written about Blacks who are convicted of capital crimes are more likely to contain ape-relevant language than news articles written about white convicts. Analysis showed that those who are implicitly portrayed as more apelike in these articles are more likely to be executed by the state than those who are not. This research is valuable in that it underscores the often-anecdotal evidence of the persistent and malingering historical representations that are routinely utilized in contemporary literature and imagery for the purpose of dehumanization and stereotyping those of African and African American descent.[124]

*****

In the marketing and advertising world, sex/sexuality is conflated with certain standards of beauty, masculinity, and desirability, and has remained profitable for centuries. Some of the earliest ventures in marketing with wide distribution were produced via print media. During the slave trade, under the guise of "commodity racism,"[125] marketing strategies were used to ease the consciousness of the Europeans about the "takeover" of the African continent. Corporations that exist today (such as Unilever), are the same companies that assisted in marketing the idea to Europeans and Africans that certain commodities would deliver them from their darkness and hedonism.

The concept of commodity racism is epitomized in an ad that emerged in the 1890s and 1900s, depicting one African/Black man on his knees and the others scantily clad, paying homage to a bar of Pears Soap. At the top of advert, it reads, "the formula for British conquest." A more familiar advertisement was called the "white man's burden"[126]; the advert reads, "The first step towards lightening is through teaching the virtues of cleanliness. Pears [S]oap is a potent factor in brightening the dark corners of the earth as civilization advances, while amongst the cultured of all nations it holds the highest place–it is the ideal toilet soap." On the side of the ad is an African or Black male kneeling before the white man with his hands up to receive the soap. The image of the Black man kneeling before his oppressor, apparently abdicating his masculinity to the "savior" asking to be cleansed, was ludicrous but, effective.[127]

Interestingly, Europeans had an aversion to bathing. Queen Elizabeth I was distinguished as bathing "regularly every month whether she needed it or not"[128]; ergo, the regularity with which the European commoner bathed was assuredly even less frequent.[129] Soap was not routinely used, although it was the cheapest of all toiletries (in Europe) sold at the time.[130] However, with the rise of colonialism (imperialism) and the spread of European/white nationalism, European culture became obsessed with cleanliness in the context of European/white nationalism—the cleanliness associated with whiteness relied upon the projection of dirtiness as inherent to Blackness.[131] However, according to many early accounts of European explorations into Africa, its inhabitants were very concerned with cleanliness in everyday personal hygiene, using "native soaps" to clean the body, and palm oil, lard or shea butter "to anoint" it, at least twice daily.[132] Ironically, it is white (not Black) skin, that makes the presence of dirt unmistakably apparent.[133]

During the colonial period, [Black] people's culture and body images were constructed as pathological, backward and ugly. Corporeal blackness was associated with moral darkness, unrestrained sexuality, pollution, and disease.[134] While teaching at a University in West Africa, I asked the class if had they had ever heard comments about how Africans stink or were dirty, the majority of a class of 30 raised their hands. The aforementioned is important in that something as innocuous as soap can be utilized as a branding tool to make the subjugation of another civilization's whole population appear to be hygienic. It is worth mentioning that soaps, deodorants and fragrances, and bleaching creams, are now a multi-billion-dollar business in Africa.[135]

Like in Africa, African Americans were, and are still, exposed to marketing techniques to teach them to be "civilized" and "respectable," by disengaging themselves from their native color, language, and culture. The vernacular of white supremacy becomes common and bleeds into the psyche; the same themes emerge, irrespective of the timeline. The social and political climate of the '70s gave birth to the Blaxploitation movies that presented images of strong, powerful Black characters. With bell bottoms and leather and packing a gun to take out the "man," Shaft was a big hit. Morris, from the *New York Times* writes: "The ingenuity of the Blaxploitation era, with all its flamboyant, do-it-yourself carnality, was its belief in black women and men and its conflation of danger and desire." The movies—self-consciously, hyperkinetically black—were at full strength from the very end of the 1960s through the first half of the 1970s, and more or less kicked off with a literal bang: Melvin Van Peebles directing himself doing the nasty in "Sweet Sweetback's Baadasssss Song." If the movies are ridiculous, they're ridiculous in the way that bell-bottoms, platforms, and hair the circumference of a disco ball can now seem like camp. But back then, that was simply the way things were: baad. You went to "Slaves," "Super Fly," "Dolemite" and "Blacula" because you wanted to see yourself, but also because these movies were the political repossession of toxic myths. "Shaft" named a detective while winking at his anatomy. Black men were swinging their dicks for black audiences. The films wanted not just to master the myth but also to throw it headfirst out the window.[136]

In the '80s there was a shift in imagery from the strong and decisive

Black male, to little Black boys being taken care of by white families because every member of their nuclear and extended family seemed to have disappeared. Remember *Different Strokes* and *Webster*? Recurring stereotypical themes, such as the configuration of the Black family, have been distilled within the conscious mind through the science of advertising.

I propose that the utilization of the tenets of classical conditioning in advertising and other media has raised the bar by morphing the cute and adorable little Black boy of the '80s, into a future version of himself that is a violent citizen and a menace to society. In this case, a neutral stimulus, such as the little Black child, is paired with a gun and, through repeated exposure, the Black child and the gun become one and the same. There have been a number of experiments conducted, particularly after the "in broad daylight" murder of 11-year-old Tamir Rice, to determine the reason behind the mindset of people, particularly the police, who shoot when there is no real threat.

According to reports, the subsequent homicide started with a caller who states: "...there is a young Black boy—'probably a juvenile'—brandishing a gun around in the park near him". Reportedly, the man said, "It's probably fake, but it's scaring the shit out of me." The officer who responded, fatally shot the subject within seconds of arriving. The *subject*, a child named Tamir Rice, only had a toy gun. The officer was not indicted and the murder was described as a "perfect storm of human error, mistakes, and miscommunications." A video shows that Tamir, who was Black, was drawing the pellet gun from his waistband when he was shot, either to hand it over to the officers or to show them that it was not a real firearm. The officer who fired stated he had a reason to *fear for his life*.[137]

There are certain patterns and behaviors here, as quoted from court documents, that contain practically the exact same wording and responses to a plethora of other shootings of young Black males. In other words, the police and the caller perceived an 11-year old Black boy with a toy gun as an existential threat.

In classical conditioning, the pairing of adult Black men with stereotypes of violence has been extended to Black boys—even those as young as five years old. Researchers at the Association for Psychological Science found that, "although young children are typically viewed as harmless and innocent, seeing faces of five-year-old Black boys appear to trigger thoughts of guns and violence."[138] For the study, a series of experiences, similar to the implicit bias detection test were used. In the first trial, 64 white college students were shown two images in quick succession. The first image, which the participants were told to ignore, showed the face of a Black or white child; the second showed either a gun or a toy (like a rattle). The participants were then asked to identify the object in the second image. The findings indicate that study participants were quicker in correctly identifying the second image as a gun, after being flashed the image of a young Black boy. The findings also indicate that there was an inherent bias to wrongly label the image of the toy as a gun more frequently, after looking at a picture of a young Black boy. However, participants were more likely to wrongly categorize the second image of a gun as a toy after being shown a young white boy.[139] In two subsequent tests of the same study, researchers made small, but significant, modifications. The first image presented was either that of a Black or white adult or a child; the second showed a gun or a non-threatening object, like a tool. The results of the first trial with 63 white college participants and a second trial with 88, showed that participants associated Black faces with guns and white ones with non-threatening objects, regardless of age. In a fourth and final experiment, the researchers found that 82 study participants connected words like "violent," "dangerous," "hostile," and "aggressive" more strongly with images of Black boys than white ones.[140]

The researchers concluded that the four experiments provided converging evidence that brief presentations of Black male faces—whether of adults or children—primed the detection of threatening objects (that is, guns) and increased accessibility of threat-related words. Furthermore, these racial biases were driven entirely by differences in automatic processing. The collective findings, therefore, support the hypothesis that youth sustains, rather than attenuates, race-based threat associations. In other words, negative attitudes towards certain races are deeply ingrained in the way our minds process the world and inform split-second judgments. In essence, the science of human behavior confirms that in the mind of whites, their violent actions toward young Black men are justified.[141]

Prophecy

At the beginning of *The Isis Papers*, Welsing states "Just as the problem of the color line (racism) has controlled events in the 20th century (and prior centuries), the solution to the problem will regulate events in the 21st century and beyond as we enter the era of justice." (p 1).

The words of Dr Welsing are prophetic, as we are in the era of justice. Against the backdrop of the political melee accompanying the current Administration and its treatment of those of African descent, we must begin to shift the energy of how we comport ourselves in this white hegemonic world. The presence of justice is something that we must elevate every day to achieve a sense of balance, not in relation to whites but for ourselves. We of African descent can determine the narrative of our prophecy. We are currently following a fictional script of white supremacy, which has influenced how we see ourselves and the future of our progeny. There is no race, there is no inferior vs. superior; supremacy is manufactured to benefit a small group of people who are overwhelmingly responsible for setting the global agenda, although whites represent only 17% of the world's population.[142, 143] As this chapter is being written, a larger narrative is being told. Any clarity around the challenges of masculinity/sexuality are now in abeyance. The concepts of genderless babies, being gender-neutral, and non-binary gender identit(ies) are taking center-stage. Gender identity now trends as an issue that reflects the societal changes in the concept of gender and sexuality. Expressions of gender and sexuality are increasingly moving from the margins to the center. Facebook, with more than one billion users, now has at least 60 options for a users' gender identity.[144]

The Black man's worth cannot be measured in the context of white supremacy, nor can his masculinity be defined through the lens of white supremacy, for he has already been defined. The paradigm must be changed because the norm as we have been programmed to experience it is not the standard of rightness or righteousness, where all others are judged in relation to it.

As addressed in this chapter, the institutions of law, education, and the media have served as a "pressure cooker" of sorts, affecting the perception of how Black males see themselves as viable and necessary. These institutions that are based on the perpetuation of myths, and general acceptance of these beliefs often informs policy, law formation, access to information, disciplinary environments in our education systems, racial profiling, deliberate use of force, biases in court-based custody decisions; and many more unknown and unseen implicit ways in which society perceives Black males.[145]

The increasing incidents of suicide among Black male children serves as a "canary in the coal mine," and is a barometer of the mental health of our communities. The state of the young Black male has not been adequately addressed, as there appears to be a persistent malaise and acceptance of the supremacists' narrative of his fate. Once a false claim such as the masculinity of the Black male, constructed by white supremacy, is disseminated and accepted by the public, it becomes established and harder to deconstruct or invalidate.[146]

If we follow the narrative, then we do not "see" in reality that the majority of Black fathers actually live with their children (2.5 million versus 1.7 million). Further, Black fathers are more likely than white or Latino fathers to eat, dress, toilet train, play, and read with their children; in other words, they tend to be more involved as compared to fathers from other races and ethnic groups, whether living in the same home or not.[147, 148] These truths and others are not revealed so readily through the lens that we have been given, as it does not support the narrative that has been written.

We must always remember that we, as the children of great civilizations, had our destinies altered, and we continue to be resilient. We find ourselves in a world that had its foundation erected on the backs of our

Ancestors; without us, white supremacy would not have survived. The seemingly focused sabotage of the Black males' ascendancy through systemic oppression has perhaps only boiled down to being an envisioned sexual rival of the white male. Irrespective of what white people perceive or believe, that focus no longer deserves attention. Our full attention must be devoted to saving our progeny because the culture of the descendants of Africa is worth saving.

Endnotes

1 Anne Fausto-Sterling. *Gender, Race, and Nation: The Comparative Anatomy of "Hottentot" Women in Europe, 1815-1817*, in *Deviant Bodies: Critical Perspectives on Difference in Science and Popular Culture,* ed. Jennifer Terry and Jacqueline Urla. (Bloomington, IN: Indiana University Press, 1995), 19-48.

2 Welsing defines white supremacy as the local and global power system structured and maintained by persons who classify themselves as white, whether consciously or subconsciously determined; this system consists of patterns of perception, logic symbol formation, thought, speech, action and emotional response, as conducted simultaneously in all areas of people activity. The ultimate purpose of the system is to prevent white genetic annihilation on Earth, a planet in which white-skinned people (The Isis Papers, p 2) classify the overwhelming majority of people as non-white (Black, Brown, Red and Yellow).

3 Neely Fuller, *The United-Independent Compensatory Code/System/Concept* 1984.

4 World Health Organization, *Sexual and Reproductive Health*, 2006.

5 CL Ford, *et al.,* "Black sexuality, social construction, and research targeting 'the down low'." *Annals ofEpidemiology*. Vol 17, (2007), 209–216.

6 WP Hammond and JS Mattis. "Being a man about it: Manhood meaning amongAfrican-American men". *Psychology of Men & Masculinity.* Vol6, (2005),114–126.

7 Anjana Cruz, "Europeans invented the concept of race as we know it." *Timeline* (Jul 2017), Retrieved from https://timeline.com.

8 Suzanne Pharr. *Common Elements of Oppression In Homophobia: A Weapon of Sexism.* (Inverness,CA: Chardon Press, 1988).

9 Q. Hoare and G. Smith, *Selections from the Prison Notebooks of Antonio Gramsci.* (New York, N.Y.: International Publishers, 1932).

10 James Shreeve. "Terms of Estrangement." *Discover Magazine*, Nov, 1994.

11 Carl Linnaeus 1707-1778

12 Jean-Jacques Rousseau, Immanuel Kant and David Hume

13 F. Blumenbach, *The Natural Variety of Mankind.* (London: n.p.,1865).

14 Despite the varieties being on a hierarchical scale, Blumenbach was convinced of the superficiality of racial variation and defended the mental and moral unity of all people. Despite his assertions that the Caucasian variety was superior to others, he had strong opinions about the equal status of BlackAfricans and white Europeans and campaigned for the abolition of slavery.

15 Stephen J. Gould, "The Geometer of Race in The Science of Race," *Discover Magazine*, 1994.

16 Anjana Cruz, 2017.

17 Robert V. Guthrie, *Even the rat was white: A historical view of psychology* (New York: Harper Row Publishers, 1976).

18 Milton Bradley was a major game board manufacturer in the US, which produced games like Yahtzee, Battleship and Twister. Hasbro, Inc. bought them out in the 1980s.

19 Robert L. Guthrie, *Even the Rat was White*, 1976.
20 Ibid.
21 Reasons for bleaching are a conundrum of sorts. Ghanian women, for example, cite that bleaching helps to counteract the effects of the sun, to appear clean, to appear beautiful, to attract attention or potential mates, to appear sophisticated or modern, and to gain or maintain economic or social capitol citations, Blay, 2011; Wright, 2014.
22 Denise L. Wright, "The changing face of color: A social and public health dilemma for young populations in Nigeria". J*ournal of Educational and Social Research: Special Issue* Vol 4, 2014.
23 Marc Epprecht, "Sexuality, Africa, History". *The American Historical Review* Volume 114, Issue 5, 1 December 2009, 1258–1272. doi.org/10.1086/ahr.114.5.1258.
24 Ibid.
25 American Anthropological Association.
26 Siobhan B. Somerville, *Queering the Color Line: Race and Invention of Homosexuality in American Culture*, (Durham, NC: Duke University Press, 2000).
27 Ibn Battuta: Travels in Asia and Africa 1325-1354 In Medieval Sourcebook. H. A. R. Gibb, (London: Broadway House, 1929).
28 Ibid.
29 Robert W. Shufeldt, *America's greatest problem: The Negro*, (Philadelphia, F. A. Davis, 1915).
30 Welsing, *The Isis Papers,* 44.
31 Welsing, *The Isis Papers,* p 7.
32 John Pape. "Black and white: the 'perils of sex' in colonial Zimbabwe," *Journal of Southern African Studies* Vol 16, 4, 699-720, 1990.
33 Carina Ray. "Decrying White Peril: Interracial Sex and the Rise of Anticolonial Nationalism in the Gold Coast," *American Historical Review*. 2014.
34 Ibid., 86.
35 Ibid.
36 Not until the 1880s, after the end of Reconstruction, did "lynching" become associated with African Americans; gradually the number of Blacks lynched each year surpassed the number of whites until it became almost exclusively directed at Black people late in the century. (Between 1882 and 1944, Tuskegee University recorded 3,417 lynchings with Black victims— and 1,291 lynchings with white ones.)
37 Welsing, *The Isis Papers*, 44
38 Andrew Sullivan, "Torture in American History. The Daily Dish:" *The Atlantic*. Nov 30 2007. Retrieved from www.theatlantic.com/daily-dish/archive/2007/11/torture-in-american-history/223112/
39 "Waterboarding," a torture technique the majority of GOP candidates cannot bring themselves to condemn and which the new attorney-general refuses to

declare illegal, was used against African-Americans to extract false confessions in the South.

40 Ben Montgomery, "FBI closes book on Claude Neal's lynching without naming killers,". *Tampa Bay Times*, November 23, 2017.

41 Reverend William Henry Moses of Philadelphia's Zion Baptist Church and William Garrott Brown used White Peril to comment on the racial, political and economic danger that whites posed to Blacks in the United States and beyond. Moses published *The White Peril* in 1919 to raise awareness among "the darker races in general, and the Black race in particular" of the "danger of political, industrial, social, and economic slavery or extermination by the white Christian nations of the world. (Excerpt from "Decrying White Peril," Ray, 87).

42 Allaayh Abdur-Rahman, "The Strangest Freaks of Despotism: Queer Sexuality in Antebellum African American Slave Narratives," *African American Review* (2006), 40, 2, 223-227.

43 Renee C. Romano, *Race Mixing: Black-White Marriage in Postwar America* (Cambridge, MA: Harvard University Press, 2006).

44 Welsing, *The Isis Papers*, 84.

45 White patriarchy perpetuated the idea that East Asian men wouldsystematically rape and kill white women if they had a chance. In Asian American Dreams: The Emergence of an American People, Helen Zia quotes 1800s orator Horace Greely, who described stereotypes of Asian males: "The Chinese are uncivilized, unclean, and filthy… lustful and sensual in their dispositions." They were also portrayed as men who strategically stole white men's jobs and tricked white women. A recurring stereotype, after 9/11, the idea of the "Muslim Predator" that Muslim men want to destroy Western civilization and at the same time, rape and kidnap white women. Latino men target white women in order to corrupt them (Loubriel, 2016).

46 Welsing, *The Isis Papers*, 83.

47 *Africa's Great Civilizations*. The Atlantic Age, Documentary Film, Public Broadcasting Service, SO1, E05, Henry Louis Gates, Jr., March 2, 2017.

48 Slave narratives were the dominant literary mode in early African American literature. Thousands of accounts, some legitimate and some the fictional creations of white abolitionists, were published in the years between 1820 and the Civil War. These were political as well as literary documents, used to promote the anti-slavery cause and to answer pro-slavery claims that slaves were happy and well treated. Most slave narratives featured graphic descriptions of the violent whippings and severe deprivation inflicted, in an attempt to appeal to the emotions and conscience of white readers.

49 Frantz Fanon, *Black Skin, White Masks* (France: n.p.,1952).

50 Frederick Douglass, *The Narrative of the Life of Frederick Douglass An American Slave*, (Boston: Anti-Slavery Office, Boston, 1845).

51 Welsing. *The Isis Papers*, 87.

52 Sam and Louisa Everett, enslaved in Virginia, interviewed 1936, WPASlave Narrative Project.
53 Ibid.
54 HarrietAnn Jacobs, *Incidents in the Life of a Slave Girl*. Written by Herself: (1813-1897). Edited by L. Maria Child. Boston, 1861. Electronic Edition.
55 Jean-Paul Satre, *The Wretched of the Earth*, p 50.
56 Frederick Douglass, 1845.
57 John Sullivan, Zane Anthony, Julie Tate, Jennifer Jenkins, Nationwide, police shot and killed nearly 1,000 people in 2017. Washington Post, January 6, 2018.
58 Rachael Reversz, US police have already killed more than 100 people this year. February 7, 2017. Retrieved from https://www.independent.co.uk/news/world/americas/us-police-killings-2017-total-deaths-caused-officers-sandra-bland-trayvon-martin-a7568056.html.
59 Ibid.
60 Approximately 42% of incarcerated fathers and 60% of mothers lived with their children prior to incarceration; 40% of nonresident, ever-incarcerated fathers had regular visitation with their children. To a large extent incarcerated parents were parenting, assuming the responsibilities associated with providing for and raising their children (Christopher Uggen, Suzy McElrath, Parents Behind Bars, Criminology, 104, 3, 2014.)
61 Sarah K.S. Shannon, Christopher Uggen, Jason Schnittker, Melissa Thompson, Sara Wakefield, and Michael Massoglia. The Growth, Scope and Spatial Distribution with Felony Records in the United States, 1948-2010. Demography (2017) 54:1795–1818, Population Association of America. Published online: DOI 10.1007/ s13524-017-0611.
62 Sarah Shannon, et al., 2017
63 Christopher Uggen and Suzy McElrath, "Parents Behind Bars, What We Know and Where we Need to Go," *The Journal of Criminal Law & Criminology* 104, 3, 2014., (Northwestern University School of Law).
64 Robert Brame, Shawn Bushway, Ray Paternoster and Michael Turner, "Demographic Patterns of Cumulative Arrest Prevalence by Ages 18 and 23," *Crime & Delinquency* April, 60, 3: 471-486. doi: 10.1177/001112871351480.
65 Ibid.
66 The Sentencing Project. Black Disparities in Youth Incarceration, September 12, 2017. Washington, DC.
67 Welsing, *The Isis Papers*, 240.
68 Inferiorization is the conscious, deliberate and systematic process utilized specifically by a racist (white supremacy) social system, as conducted through all of its major and minor institutions (including the institution of the family), to mold specific peoples within the system (namely, all the peoples as non-white) into functional inferiors, despite their true genetic potential for functioning. Isis Papers, 241.

69 Jonathan Kozol, *The Shame of a Nation: The Restoration of Apartheid Schooling in America* (New York: Three Rivers Press, Random House, 2005).

70 Ivory A. Toldson, "How Black Boys with Disabilities end up in Honors Classes-while others without disabilities end up in special education," *Journal of Negro Education* v 80 n4. 439-443 Fall 2011.

71 Matthew Lynch, "4 Troubling Truths About Black Boys and the US Educational System," *Education Week* August 26, 2015. Retrieved from http://blogs.edweek.org/edweek/education_futures/2015/08/4.

72 Nick Chiles, "6 Reasons Black Boys Without a Disability End Up in Special Education", March 11, 2015. Retrieved from atlantablackstar.com/2015/03/11/6-reasons-black-boys-without-disability-wind-up-in-special-education.

73 Denise L. Wright, *Concrete and Abstract Attitudes, Mainstream Orientation, and Academic Achievement of African American males. Dissertation Abstracts*. (Washington, DC: Howard University, 1995).

74 Black students are 2.9 times more likely to be arrested while at school than all non-Black students; Black students without a disability are 3.49 times more likely to be arrested at school than white students without a disability; Black students without a disability are 2.25 times more likely to be referred to law enforcement while at school than white students without a disability. Students with disabilities are 2.96 times more likely to be arrested while at school than students without disabilities. Students with disabilities are 2.91 times more likely to be referred to law enforcement while at school than students without disabilities. Black students with disabilities are 2.80 times more likely to be arrested while at school than white students with disabilities. During the 2013-2014 school year, schools reported 65,150 school-based arrests of students. Students were referred to law enforcement more than 200,000 times. The Education Department defines a "referral" as anytime a student is reported to any law enforcement agency or official for a school-based incident, regardless of whether official action is taken. (NBC News, 2017).

75 Toldson, How Black Boys with Disabilities, 2011.

76 Lynch, 4 Troubling Truths About Black Boys, 2015.

77 Hannah Rappleye, Brenda Breaslauer, Stephanie Gosk, & Kenzi Abou-Sabe. Kids in Cuffs: Why Handcuff a Student With a Disability? *NBC News*, February 20, 2017.

78 Ibid.

79 Toldson, How Black Boys with Disabilities, 2011.

80 Robert Cooper and Daniel Liou, "The Structure and Culture of Information Pathways: Rethinking Opportunity to Learn in Urban High Schools during the Ninth Grade Transition," *High School Journal* 91 (1), (2007): 43-56.

81 Welsing, *The Isis Papers*, 140.

82 Jeffrey Bridge, Asti Linsey, Lisa Horowitz, et al. "Suicide Trends Among Elementary School–Aged Children in the United States From 1993 to 2012," *JAMA*

Pediatrics 169 (7) (2015): 673-677.
83 Ibid.
84 Welsing, *The Isis Papers*, 43.
85 HIV and AIDS—United States 1991-2000. Morbidity and Mortality Weekly Report, Centers for Disease Control.
86 James Baldwin, "The Last Interview & Other Conversations". Interview with James Baldwin in1961, Studs Terkel. Published in Conversations with James Baldwin, University Press of Mississippi, 1989. Melville House Publishing, 2014. Brooklyn, New York.
87 Jack Drescher, "Out DSM: Depathologizing Homosexuality," *Behavioral Sciences* 5(4), December, 2015: 565-575
88 Journal of the American Medical Association (JAMA), Sex variants: A Study of homosexual patterns. August, 1941 117(8): 657. doi:10.1001/jama.1941.02820340079029.
89 In the 1940s this committee studied the problem of homosexuality in the American Armed Forces. If found to be a homosexual, you were dishonorable discharged. The main type of discharge involved forfeiture of G.I. benefits, barriers to many forms of civilian employment and it "carried a real social stigma," especially in a small community (Nimmons, 1994).
90 In the 1940s, homosexuals were involuntarily committed to psychiatric facilities by their families, with the hospitals promising that the patient would eventually leave the facility cured of their "sexual illness." Not only were they not allowed to leave, but they were often subjected to cruel and inhumane treatments, including castrations, torture drugs, shock therapy, and lobotomies.
91 David Nimmons, "Sex and the Brain". *Discover Magazine,* March 1, 1994. http://discovermagazine.com/1994/mar/sexandthebrain346
92 Larry Gross and James Woods (Eds), *The Columbia Reader on Lesbians & Gay Men in Media, Society & Politics* (New York: Columbia University Press, 1999). 4,5.
93 Ibid.
94 Abdur-Rahman, Ibid.
95 Siobhan Somerville, *Queering the Color Line: Race and the Invention of Homosexuality in American Culture.* (Durham: Duke UP, 2000).
96 Welsing, *The Isis Papers*, 86.
97 Ibid., 87.
98 Aaron Morrison, "Here's One Brutal Truth Every Black Man Needs to Hear About Masculinity". June 21, 2016. Retrieved from https://mic.com/articles/144618/here-s-one-brutal-truth-every-black-man-needs-to-hear-about- masculinity.
99 Welsing, *The Isis Papers,* 88-89.
100 Ibid.
101 The clothing culture of the sagging pants allegedly emanated from prison cul-

ture, which symbolizes the willingness to have sex with men.

102 Welsing, *The Isis Papers*, 89.

103 Ibid., 91.

104 Welsing, *The Isis Papers*, 10.

105 Matthew Quest, *Afrocentricity vs. Homosexuality: The Isis Papers*. Retrieved from http://www. spunk.org/texts/pubs/lr/sp001715/isispap.html

106 Anthony J. Lemelle, Jr., "Black Masculinity Matters in Attitudes Toward Gay Males," *Journal of Homosexuality* Vol. 47(1) (2004), 47. Retrieved from http:// www.haworthpress. com/web/JH © 2004 by The Haworth Press, Inc. doi 10.1300/ J082v47n01_03

107 In the 1940s this committee studied the problem of homosexuality in the American Armed Forces. If found to be a homosexual, you were dishonorable discharged. The main type of discharge involved forfeiture of G.I. benefits, barriers to many forms of civilian employment and it "carried a real social stigma," especially in a small community (Nimmons, 1994).

108 James Baldwin, "The Last Interview & Other Conversations. Interview with James Baldwin". 1961 Studs Terkel. Published in Conversations with James Bald- win, University Press of Mississippi, 1989. Melville House Publishing, 2014. Brooklyn, New York.

109 *Gay life in 1940's Bronzeville: The Story of Nancy Kelly* Retrieved from http:// outhistory.org/exhibits/show/queer-bronzeville/part-2/nancy-kelly

110 Matthew Rodriguez, "Here is one Brutal Truth Every White Gay Man Needs to Hear," *Mic.*, June 1, 2016. Retrieved from https://mic.com/articles/144985/here-s-one-brutal-truth- every-white-gay-man-needs-to-hear.

111 Normitsu Onishi, "US Support of Gay Rights in Africa May Have Done More Harm Than Good," *New York Times*. Dec 20, 2015. Retrieved from https://www. nytimes.com/2015/12/21/world/africa/us-support-of-gay-rights-in-africa-may-have-done-more-harm-than-good

112 Gary J. Gates, "How many people are lesbian, gay, bisexual, and transgender?" Williams Institute, UCLA School of Law, (2011). Retrieved from https://williamsinstitute.law.ucla. edu/wp-content/uploads/Gates-How-Many-People-LGBT-Apr-2011.pdf

113 Challenges in measuring the LGBT community vary for a variety of reasons. These include differences in the definitions of who is included in the LGBT population, differences in survey methods, and a lack of consistent questions asked in a particular survey over time. In measuring sexual orientation, lesbian, gay, and bisexual individuals may be identified strictly based on their self-identity or it may be possible to consider same-sex sexual behavior or sexual attraction. Identity, behavior, attraction, and relationships all capture related dimensions of sexual orientation but none of these measures completely addresses the concept.

114 Gary Gates, "In US, More Adults Identifying as LGBT". *Gallup News*, January, 2017.

115 Ibid.
116 Gary J. Gates, "How many people are lesbian, 2011.
117 "Gallup Poll Finds People of Color More Likely to Identify as LGBT". *Huffington Post*, Black Voices, Updated. October 19, 2016. Retrieved from https://www.huffingtonpost.com/2012/10/19/black-gays-lgbt-community_n_1989859.html
118 Quentin Hoare and Geoffrey Nowell Smith, *Selections from the prison notebooks of Antonio Gramsci* (New York: International Publishers, 1971).
119 Wesley Morris, "Last Taboo: Why Pop Culture Just Can't Deal With Black Male Sexuality," *New York Times Magazine*, Oct 27, 2016.
120 Flannigan Saint-Aubin, *Callaloo*, Vol. 17. No. 4, Autumn, 1994:1054-1073. DOI: 10.2307/2932171. http://www.jstor.org/sta- ble/2932171.
121 In 1975, King Kong was named one of the 50 best American films by the American Film Institute, and, in 1991, the film was deemed "culturally, historically and aesthetically significant" by the Library of Congress and selected for preservationin the United States National Film Registry.[74] In 1998, the AFI ranked the film #43 on its list of the 100 greatest movies of all time.
122 Silvia Sebastiani, Wulf D. Hund and Charles W. Mills edited a volume of the Racism Analysis Yearbook on Simianization. Apes, Gender, Class, and Race. Zürich, Berlin, Wien, Münster: Lit 2015/16 (ISBN 978-3-643-90716-5).
123 Phillip Atiba Goff. "Not yet human: Implicit knowledge, historical dehumanization, and contemporary consequences," *Journal of Personality and Social Psychology*. 94 (2): 293. doi:10.1037/0022-3514.94.2.292.
124 Ibid.
125 Yaba Blay, "Skin bleaching and global white supremacy: By way of introduction," *The Journal of Pan African Studies* v 4, 4 (June, 2004).
126 See Rudyard Kipling.
127 See Pear Soap Ads, Google Search.
128 Anne McClintock, *Imperial Leather: Race, Gender and Sexuality in the Colonial Contest* (New York: Routledge, 1995), 210.
129 Blay. "Skin bleaching and global white supremacy, 2004.
130 N. Williams, *Powder and Paint: A History of the Englishwoman's Toilet - Elizabeth I-Elizabeth II* (New York: Longmans, Green and Co., 1957).
131 Blay, "Skin bleaching and global white supremacy, 12.
132 W. F. Daniell, "On the Ethnography of Akkrah and Adampe, Gold Coast, Western Africa," *Journal of the Ethnological Society of London (1848-1856)*, 4, 1-32.
133 Blay, "Skin bleaching and global white supremacy, 14.
134 Nicola Hugo, "The Color Conundrum: Understanding skin lightening in Africa," *Polity*, March 16, 2012. Retrieved from http://www.polity.org.za/article/the-colour-conun- drum-understanding-skin-lightening-in-africa-2012-03-26.
135 Blay, "Skin bleaching and global white supremacy, 15.
136 Morris, "Last Taboo".
137 James Queally, "Tamir Rice Report: Cleveland Policeman Who Fired Fatal

Shots Said He Had "No Choice,"" *LA Times*, June 13, 2015. Retrieved from http://www.latimes.com/ nation/nationnow/la-na-nn-tamir-rice-investigation-documents-20150613-story

138 Andrew R. Todd, "Faces of Black Children as Young as Five, Evoke Negative Biases". *Psychological Science*, Feb 8, 2016. Retrieved from www.psychologicalscience.org/news/releases/faces-of-black-children-as-young-as-five-evoke-negative-biases

139 Ibid.

140 Ibid.

141 Ibid.

142 EJ Addington, What is the percentage of white people in the world? Sept 17, 2017. Retrieved from https://www.quora.com/What-is-the-percentage-of-white-people-in-the-world

143 If using the outdated "white-meaning-pale" definition is applied, then only some 500 to 700 million people are white in the entire world, i.e ~7% to 8% of humankind. If you apply the definition of "white" as basically "all light skinned people among the European spectre of skin tones", then that number grows significantly to some 1.3–1.4 billion people in the world, i.e. 17%-19% of humankind (See White People, *Wikipedia*).

144 Katy Steinmetz, "Beyond "He" or "She": The Changing Meaning of Gender & Sexuality," *Time Magazine* v 189, March 27, 2017, 11.

145 Saheed Richardson, "Breaking Myths about Black Fatherhood this Father's Day," *The Chicago Reporter*, June 13, 2019.

146 Dennis, 2014.

147 National Health Statistics Reports, Centers for Disease Control. Fathers' involvement with their Children: United States, 2006-2010. December 20, 2013, No 71.

148 Charles Blow, "Black Dads Are Doing the Best of All". *The New York Times*, June 8, 2015.

CHAPTER 10

PRAISE SONG FOR DR. FRANCES CRESS WELSING: OUR RACE CHAMPION!

Mama Marimba Ani, Ph.D.

In 1974, I experienced Dr. Frances Cress Welsing for the first time as she confronted William Shockley, the white supremacist, physicist, eugenicist, on Tony Brown's Journal, a talk show on PBS. Watching Dr. Welsing shock Shockley as he, no doubt, had never been shocked before, was to have a lasting effect on me and many others, including Shockley himself. As I subsequently studied her and her work, "The Cress Theory of Color-Confrontation," I came to realize that, "Confrontation" was, indeed, her forte, her strength, and her method of healing Afrikan people in preparation for War against those who would destroy us.

Dr. Welsing turned Shockley's world upside down. She challenged his perception of himself. She took the ground from beneath him, robbing him of the confidence he had taken for granted. As a white person he functioned in a system that had been constructed to convince him of his "superiority" and the inferiority of Afrikan/Black people. But Dr. Welsing snatched the rug out from under him by questioning the very things that he assumed. She sat facing him, brilliantly countering his arguments, showing them to be inept. She calmly considered his words, before coolly demolishing his assertions.

He had banked on the defensive posture which most of us took when told that our Intelligence Quotient was lower than that of white people. We sought so desperately to prove that we were "as smart as they." We didn't understand that we were thereby accepting the reality that they had imposed to prove the opposite. By defending ourselves within the context of their definition of reality, we had accepted it as true. We were allowing them to define the terms, putting them "in charge". (We had not learned the most important axiom of cultural warfare; ever let your enemy choose the game or make the rules. He will determine the rules to guarantee that he wins, even if you are the more skilled.)

The idea of the quantitative measurement of human intelligence should be obviously absurd, its cogency a figment of the white imagination. Rather than "defend" against a bogus claim, Dr. Welsing explained why his delusional behavior was necessary. She confronted his propositions head-on and dismantled them. She "flipped the script" and made him the object. His genetic inadequacy became the focus. His rather disjointed and feeble "arguments" were simply manifestations of his fear of genetic annihilation.

Even more than all this, for us as Afrikans, it is her posture that calls us to her and inspires us to be unapologetically and forcefully, Afrikan. From that day, as she continued to disarm white supremacists by exposing their illness and their source of power, her confidence became our confidence, her resolve our resolve. She was brilliant for us, and so we are "brilliant". She was courageous, and so we gain the courage to take on the enemy. She did not run from the enemies of our people. She calls them out! Bolekaja! "Come on down, let's fight."

I was trained as a Pan-Afrikanist by Nana John Henrik Clarke. I later developed as an Afrikan Nationalist in the tradition of The Honorable Marcus Mosiah Garvey. I am now striving to be the best Afrikan Sovereignist-Race Vindicatonist that I can be, as taught by Dr. Anderson Thompson, Dr. Bobby Wright and Baba Djedi Shemsu (Dr. Jacob Carruthers). The combination of these Race-Champions has influenced my style of combat, and my commitment to teach Afrikan students to be unrelenting as warriors for their people. Dr. Welsing's example adds to this composite of trainers. She stood on the solid ground of Race Pride, much as Marcus Garvey had done. She broke the rules of academic ambivalence, detachment and intentional fuzzy-headedness. Her theories and arguments issued from the dire needs of a people under siege – her people. She knew that we couldn't afford to spend another 400 years in captivity, not another decade. But without an understanding of those who have colonized and enslaved us, that would be our fate- for in the minds of the enemy, their survival depends on our demise.

Our healing as a captive and exploited people lies in our ability to acknowledge our fear of the system that has been constructed to imprison us. Acknowledging that fear is the operating principle. Acknowledgment of the fear will take away its power. She knew that confronting our fear would enable us to confront the system itself.

Through confrontation we become confident and therefore powerful. Dr. Welsing went "toe to toe" with white supremacy. That was what she did. She was consistent, unrelenting and unyielding. Her work was the healing of her people, Black People. She spent her entire adult life committed to that work. She, like Nana Marcus Mosiah Garvey and Nana John Henrik Clarke, is a warrior-healer who has helped to heal our trammeled and battered psyche. She understood, as did Bobby Wright and Baba Amos Wilson, that in a white supremacist world order, all human experience is Racial. Everything is political. All reality has racial significance. It is all about Power.

These ideas are threatening to non-Afrikans and to their allies and apologists. But hers was the total warrior posture. To be comfortable in the maafa is cultural, racial and political insanity. Everything she did was in opposition to racism/white supremacy. And she brought home, in clear sharp terms, the significance of Black Power. Dr. Welsing, along with others named here, was among the few who could carry the epithet of Leader of the Race. To truly lead us, one has to be courageous enough to speak always in the interest of Afrika even when it is unpopular and dangerous to do so. She has to have Vision. So Dayi. "The Clear Word."

II

The brilliance of Dr. Welsing's leadership and vision in the development of intellectual weaponry was enhanced by her ability to move beyond the self-serving restrictions of the academy. She, like Nana Clarke, Nana Marcus Garvey, and Bro. Malcolm Omowale X, is not handicapped by the affliction of academeitis. She did not try to impress the white world or confused Afrikans with a feigned "objectivity". She had no need to camouflage or compromise her Race-First ideology. Her systematic analysis is born out her heart-mind (Ib). That is what gave her the courage to confront an entire system of institutions constructed as a defense mechanism by the white collective psyche. Everything she did was toward the end of training us for successful combat. Her teaching, lecturing, writing and actions all took place in the combat zone. She ran interference. She was on the front lines.

In this continual process of confrontation with the enemy, she put forth tenets and configured weapons which we can use to attack what had been perceived as the impenetrable fortress of racism/white supremacy.

She begins by identifying the pathology: "Racism/White Supremacy". She took control of the battlefield. She gave us "spectacles" and a microscope with which to examine the pathogen that she identified. She laid bare the nature of the illness, its etiology (cause) and its various manifestations.

Dr. Welsing proceeded to take the definition of racism out of the hands of the "racist." She tells us that racism is inextricable from power. In this case, power is conferred by a system which gives power to white over Black, white over non-white. So only those in power can be "racist". There is only one racism, and that is the system of white supremacy.

She defied the academy, knowing it as a product of the european world view, and the values and behaviors promulgated by white culture. The academy assumes the "rhetorical ethic" (see Yurugu, Ch. 6, pp. 311 – 336). "Never say what you are really thinking"… "Hypocrisy is the norm"… "Always hide your true agenda."Dr. Welsing broke these "rules" of racism/white supremacy - psychopathology. She was always "in their face". Not the academic establishment, nor any other aspect of the white supremacist order, could intimidate her. They labeled her "essentialist". But that is what she was and that is what we are. We are race-identified. She was clearly centered in her Blackness. Everything she said and did was for us and in the interest of her race. Her word was bond; what she told us to do, she did. She thereby alienated the liberals, leftists, academics, and the other whites as well as all cowards, apologists, assimilationist and integrationists. We consider this a great Afrikan Sovereignist achievement!

Knowing that the white supremacist academy prevents the level of authentic and effective confrontation in which our people need to be engaged, Dr. Welsing provided a space in which we could "think" with Afrikan minds, through her Cress-Welsing Institute. There she continued the tradition of the Communiversity, so prominent in Chicago under the leadership and inspiration of Bobby Wright. The Cress-Welsing institute is a space in which Afrikan/Black people can "be real". Dr. Welsing needed to take us beyond the rules of the academy which disallow the connection of heart and mind because she felt the urgency of reaching out to the Black Community with her healing work.

Her definition of "Black Mental Health" is "patterns of thought, logic, speech, action, and emotional response in all areas of people activity that simultaneously reflect self and group respect and respect for harmony in the universe."(p.164) Since white supremacy does not allow for Black self- respect, within it, we, the Black Collective, have "negative impact" on our environment. This renders us powerless. The white supremacy system shapes us, molds us into functional inferiors. This is the process of inferiorization. Clearly, there can be no Black mental health within the context of white supremacy. Thus, as long as we allow the system of white supremacy to stand, Black Manhood must be understood to mean warrior/soldier. To be a Black man is to fight against the system of white supremacy "embracing everything that the words warrior or soldier imply". (p.192)

Dr. Welsing rejects the Marxist explanation of white racist behavior. Instead, she understands capitalism to be firmly imbedded within the European, yurugu world view; the thought and behavior which issue from white fear and result in anti-life ways. While Marx offers a systematic analysis and critique of capitalism, he does not deal with either the european world view or racism/white supremacy. To do so would be especially difficult for Marx since he was himself, afflicted by that pathology.

One of her most important achievements is to have established that "racism white supremacy" is a system. Once we understand that, then it becomes possible to approach racism/white supremacy with a "unified field theory", a perspective which brings seemingly isolated patterns of behavior into an interconnected whole.

She understood that the global system of white supremacy includes but is not coterminous with exploitative, predatory, monopolistic capitalism. Racist white supremacist behavior is a compensatory response (or reaction formation) to an overwhelming minority status numerically when compared with all of the world's people. (The white collective constitutes only 8% of the global population, and even that number is diminishing.) Capitalism, like individualism, intense competitiveness, aggression, greed, narcissism, alienation, and other aspects of sociopathy is symptomatic of white collective fear of genetic annihilation.

Dr. Welsing was able to apply a psycho-historical analysis to white, western culture, by focusing on its "major patterns". She used the symbolic matrix of white collective behavior to "decode" the cultural system." Welsing focused on the particularity and peculiar nature of this smallest and most violently anti-life collective. Joel Kovel, a white psychiatrist, in his book, White Racism: A Psychohistory, also attempted to apply psychohistorical methodology to a study of the same phenomenon, but, as we would expect, reached very different conclusions.

Dr. Welsing correctly particularized the white collective psyche, identifying it feelings of inferiority and self-loathing. That is what makes her so formidable and threatening to the white world and to academia, as she focuses on their uniqueness. Their illness is not shared by other racial collectives. Kovel, on the other hand, assumes Freudian "stages" of development to be universally applicable. His conclusions are, in the most important respects, the reverse of Dr. Welsing's. She maintains that racism white supremacy is the result of white self-hatred. He argues that in the psyche of all human beings, whiteness is a desirable trait because in the anal stage of development, blackness is associated with feces, and whiteness with "purity". White skin, he argues, enabled the white collective to "discover" and use this symbolic "purity" to structure and exercise their power over other populations. Whites have used this kind of elaboration of anal fantasies" systematically…in the generation of power. No other culture has so drawn upon these primitive beliefs to superordinate itself to others" (Kovel, p.95). Welsing forces white people to look at themselves as aberrations (mutations). No white theoretician, no matter how "liberal", no matter how "radical," is going to approach the analysis of white racist behavior from that perspective. Dr. Welsing takes the ball out of their court. She examines racism/white supremacy in terms of white genetic inferiority and its attendant defensive behavioral construct.

Frances Cress Welsing raises the question of the psycho-biological implications of Melanin in the human body. She argues that melanin is a neurotransmitter, and, as such, has the ability to enhance human communication, development and functioning. She postulated that Melanin is a "superior absorber of all energy" (p. 231), and suggests that it accounts for "soul" or connectedness. She related Melanin to the "affirmation of life" in contrast with "evil" as the destruction of life (p. 233). Speaking directly and forcefully to her people, Dr. Welsing tells us that it is our role to confront and fight evil, and that to ignore evil is to participate in evil (p. 234). In her view, psychiatry needs to deal with the proliferation of "evil" in the world. Her analysis has spiritual implications.

Her ideas demand the serious scientific study of Melanin/melatonin (See T. Owens Moore, The Science of Melanin, 1995). Melanin is a subject conventionally avoided by the mainstream white supremacist controlled scientific hierarchy. They always avoid the subject publicly, often studying it intensely in hard to find places (see: the Journal of Pineal Research) No one wants to talk about Melanin. The findings might imply that there is indeed a special role played by "blackness" in Afrikan human functioning, especially since the first humans were, indeed, hued and quite Black. Whiteness, on the other hand, is caused by the absence of proper Melanin functioning in a way that supercedes the perfunctory role that it plays in the "albino mutant" body. Whiteness is caused by the absence of melanin, the absence of "hue", resulting, as it did, from a mutated adaptation to the conditions of the ice age. (see Cheikh Anta Diop, The Cultural Unity of Black Africa, 1989; Civilization or Barbarism, 1981; The African Origin of Civilization, 1974 , and Vulindlela Wobogo, Cold Wind From The North, 2011).

Dr. Welsing used her healing skills to address the "inferiorization of the Black Child". While there is a plethora of studies, articles and books addressing the poor and "negative" self-image of our children, almost none of them (with the exception of Bro. Amos Wilson) place this tragic circumstance in the context of the need to confront racism/white supremacy. Sister Frances was concerned with "enabling patients to neutralize the impact of white supremacy on their lives" (p.258). She told us that our "Black children can achieve a development of their Black genetic and constitutional potential second to none." For Dr. Welsing the objective of healing and nurturing the potential of Black children is much more than getting better grades, or even admission into colleges, professional schools and "good jobs". She was concerned that the Black child become a Black Warrior, capable of "destroying destruction" (Ayi Kwei Armah, Two Thousand Seasons). This can only happen if their parents are mature enough and have the "space" to train, support, and love them. It is because of her vigilant Afrikan warrior posture and commitment that for over 4 decades she advised us to have fewer children, later in life. We have misunderstood her meaning. She was concerned with preparation for parenting, in order to prepare our children (our people) for war. She is not trying to show us how to be "successful" within the confines of the white supremacist "social" order, She was preparing us to confront it and to neutralize its power over us, which is the necessary prelude to war. This was her work. This was her intent.

We have touched lightly on some of the salient themes that make Dr. Welsing's work so impactful and so extraordinary. She helped to change the way we see the enemy, the way we see ourselves and the way we reason about reality. This discussion is admittedly only the tip of the iceberg with regard to her impact on our thinking. As a racial collective, we have barely scratched the surface of her brilliance and her warrior-scholar-practitioner import for the Afrikan/Black political agenda. We must listen to her voice much more carefully now, lest we miss what should be its continued ideological and organizational impact on our political thought and behavior.

Let us now turn to, a critical issue that is a major feature of racism/white supremacy, yet has not been analyzed deeply by the Afrikan

Sovereignty Movement. This discussion will help to demonstrate the timeliness, contemporary relevance, and the urgent need the analytical framework that Frances Cress Welsing has given us. We have focused on her argument that white fear of genetic annihilation is the cause of their racist, white supremacist behavior, but we have dealt far less with the implications of her analysis as it relates to the real threat of total Black annihilation.

Sister Frances argues that "people who classify themselves as white" operate from a "kill or be killed" imperative. Let us suppose that is accurate and not merely a rhetorical exaggeration (which most "Black leaders" need to believe it is). Dr. Welsing is absolutely correct in her assessment of the motivation and objective of the white supremacy, global system of domination and control. If she is correct, if this overwhelming fear drives them, causing them to be psychopathically and compulsively destructive of Black people, then what would they be doing? What would they be saying? What would their geo-political policies be? Indeed, what is the "logic" of white fear?

In 1798, Thomas Robert Malthus, a yurugu Briton, published the book, *Principles of Population*. In it, he argued that the human population was increasing in geometrical ratio, while their subsistence (food resource, agricultural production) was increasing only arithmetically. He warned of the danger of too many people, not enough food. He suggested that human reproduction be limited to the amount of food they needed to survive. Malthus was expressing his white fear of genetic annihilation and giving it "scientific" rationalization. Frances Cress Welsing has alerted us to this syndrome. Malthus was responding to his own observation and instinctual grasping of the fact that nonwhite populations, Afrikans in particular, outnumbered the white population, and were reproducing at, what for Malthus and other whites, was an alarming rate. The white population, on the otherhand, was small and getting smaller. Scary? You bet. So Malthus constructed a "white lie" (the "biggest" kind), which has become the argument for Black extermination in particular, and the destruction of first world melanated populations in general. White "scientists" certainly did not want non-whites to realize their power potential, nor could they consciously face the implications of their own extreme minority status in the world.

So they made up a story, and made it sound "real". "If we don't get rid of the majority of the earth's people," they reasoned, "we will starve." So now in 2016, children are learning in school that "there are too many people on earth, and something must be done about it" (says the Gates Foundation). "The food supply is shrinking, so we must manipulate it and patent seeds for the good of mankind" (says Monsanto). Malthus sublimated the real fear with this new invention – the proliferation of Black life, and exchanged it for the fear of inadequate food supply, but it didn't work. White genetic inadequacy still terrifies them. What Malthus did achieve, however, was the "rhetorical ethic". The diversionary lie floats, and too many of us go for it.

That is the real deal with agriculture and food supply? There are 30,000 species of edible plants on earth at this time. Less than 100 are being cultivated. The yurugu (white) collective controls the cash food market. They create scarcity for profit. (Global, monopolistic capitalism). About 90% of what the world eats comes from only 20 species of grains and vegetables. This group cultivates the foods that they choose, that suit their taste, and that make them money. (This information comes from Dr. James Conyers, and Sturtevant's, Edible Plants of the World, also Dr. Vandana Shiva, Five Pants that Changed the World.) So the claim of "inadequate food supply" due to inordinate population growth is a "Big white lie," a cover for the extermination of what the white racist capitalists, call "useless eaters".

Dr. Welsing has given us the only explanation for the perpetration of genocide by the white population against the Afrikan/Black race. A further elaboration of the Malthusian doctrine is seen in "eugenics" a white "social movement" of the 19th, 20th, and 21st centuries in which white fear of genetic annihilation takes the form of the promulgation of non-white (Afrikan/Black) genocide. "Eugenics", is literally "good genes" – "science" which becomes the ideology of white dominance. The stated objective of this "anti" social movement is to "improve the human gene-pool". This is done through selective breeding, sterilization of those who carry "inferior" genes, and other mechanisms of genocide. Eugenicists , like Galton (Darwin's cousin), in 1869, said that what was needed were higher rates of sexual reproduction for people with "desired traits," while simultaneously destroying "bad genes".

Sound like "The Cress Theory of Color Confrontation"? It should! White people are subconsciously aware of the fact that they have always been genetically and numerically "minor". So they label everyone else as "minorities". ("Hypocrisy as a way of life." Yurugu, p.312f) The truth is that their fertility index is dangerously low. "Improving the gene-pool" means many more whites, and fewer Afrikan/Black people. Black people should be discouraged from reproducing, whites need to be encouraged. But Dr. Welsing explained that white self- reproduction is problematic because they despise themselves and so do not want to reproduce. However, for some decades now, several European countries (including South Africa), monetary and work relief incentives have been used to encourage pregnancy among the white population. The U.S. magazine industry is inundating the public with images of Hollywood personalities being pregnant and having babies.

Who are these eugenicists? Are they merely the "lunatic-fringe", without financial means or influence in the world, figments of an active "conspiratorial" imagination? Think again. All of the players on the chessboard of global white supremacy are eugenicists. John

D. Rockefeller, Carnegie, Vanderbilt, J.P. Morgan and now Bill and Melinda Gates, Ted Turner are some of the names that supply the funds that not only keep this "movement" alive and well, but also provide the ideology out of which the power institutions (schools, hospitals,agencies, foundations, corporations, etc.) are molded.

"The Rockefellers and other East Coast elites including Prescott Bush, the father of George H.W. Bush, funded and supported the pseudoscience known as eugenics" (Nancy Turner Banks, AIDS, Opium, Diamonds, and Empire: The Deadly Virus of International Greed, 2010, p. 223). These powerful eugenicists have put systems in place that will guarantee their power for generations to come. (See Nancy Turner Banks, AIDS, Opium, Diamonds and Empire, 2010).

The term "eugenics" is no longer "politically correct", it is too obvious- racism white supremacy laid bare. So a new, more seemingly benign term is in use; "population control". This is the same Malthusian doctrine in a somewhat new package. Eugenics now goes by the name of "population control." The 2016 eugenicists claim to "love humanity", especially Afrikan/Black people and other "underdeveloped "First World people. Their weapons of choice are: vaccines (2.3 million women and girls in Kenya sterilized through tetanus vaccines), GMO's (controlling the food supply), HAARP (High Frequency Active Auroral Research Program) using the environment (weather) to create unnatural disasters (for more information, go to: geoengineeringwatch.org), chemicals polluting water, and forced vaccinations in Afrika. All of these are forms of race-based genocide. The Rockefellers have always been eugenicists; the World Health Organization is a vehicle for Afrikan extermination; The Center for Disease Control helps to spread disease among Black people, and promotes unnecessary and harmful vaccinations. In the 1950's and 60's only three vaccinations were recommended for children; now there are 60-70! "The Vaccine Inquiry Compensation Program is a federal project that began in 1986. It relieves vaccine manufacturers, doctors, and hospitals from liability for vaccine damage. VICP has paid over $500 million taxpayer dollars to compensate families for damage and death caused by vaccines that was also paid for by your tax dollars." (Banks, AIDS, Opium, Diamonds, and Empire, p.36, n.49)

The work of the Bill and Melinda Gates Foundation is to stop the expansion of the world's non- white population. According to Melinda Gates, she "loves" the people whose destruction she finances, and when asked what she considered the greatest gift to humankind in recent times, she quickly answered, "Vaccines". The Gates couple believes in "population control".

What population? Who controls? Ted Turner says that the total population of the world should ideally be 250-300 million, a fraction of what it is now. The present population is approximately 7 billion, 280 million. Do the math. Who are the "extraneous" people? Who decides? Who does the killing? One guess. Ted Turner says that the world would be better off if almost 7 billion people no longer existed!

Dr. Welsing is the only one who explains such psychopathic behavior. These are the strategies of racism white supremacy that threaten our existence. The Honorable Marcus Mosiah Garvey warned us. Nana John Henrik Clarke warned us. It's simple. The whites are thinking "there are too many of them and not enough of us". Yurugu with money are funding projects guided by policies that attempt to balance the scales, no matter what it takes; "kill or be killed". Dr. Frances Cress Welsing has told us clearly that "White Supremacy is the greatest evil on earth." Are we listening?

III

To more fully understand the meaning of Dr. Frances Cress Welsing's transition, we must go to Afrikan spiritual philosophy which is rooted in Afrikan "Deep Thought" (Dr. Jacob Carruthers, Baba Djedi Shemsu). An explanation of the Afrikan Life Cycle and Ancestor Communion provides the context for that understanding.

In the Eternal Cycle of Afrikan Life, a human being is acknowledged as having come from the Spirit World (the Ancestors and the Source of Life and Being.) Spiritual reality manifests as "human beingness". Thus, the Afrikan human being (Muntu) comes with a consciousness ('Kra,). His or her "destiny" (Nkrabea) is carried within the 'Kra and contains a "mission", a "message", an "intelligence". We who are Afrikan have chosen to be so. To choose to be Afrikan, is to choose to fight for Afrika, otherwise, why come back? We believe that each of us is an Ancestor Returned. Rebirth into Afrikanness is, then, both a privilege and a duty. We achieve continued connection to the Afrikan Family and we become part of the Race Army. As Afrikans, we have serious work to do. Being Afrikan is not meant to be easy.

The Cycle is maintained through the progression of developmental stages. These stages represent ever increasing levels and degrees of-responsibility, participation and maturity; moving from Birth through Childhood, Adulthood and Eldership. Movement from one stage to the next is a "transition". Understood symbolically, one "dies" from one stage and is "reborn" into the next. Birth, Death, and Rebirth form a Cycle of growth in human beingness, in cultural beingness, and commitment. Life begins at the Source of Being, Energy, Power and Reality, (the Life Force, Odumakroma, Amma, Oludumare) and returns to the Source, to be reformed into new life, or, the alternative which would be ultimate disgrace, pain and failure; that is, to become totally disconnected from the Cycle: Spiritual and cultural "death".

At each stage of our development as Afrikans, we become more knowledgeable. We become "bigger" as we become more spiritually powerful. Perhaps the most important transition that we will make, is that between being an Elder and becoming an Ancestor. The physical "death" of an Afrikan Elder is not the end of the life of a Muntu, an Afrikan human being. If handled properly, it is the beginning of a transition to the next stage in human beingness. Our "muntuness" takes on another more mature, spiritually and culturally powerful form. Physical death for the Afrikan is not the end of human conscious existence. We still are able to act with will and intent and to influence the physically alive world nation of Afrikan people. All cultural growth is focused on the achievement of becoming an Ancestor, who is capable of guiding, protecting and nurturing the Afrikan/Black Race. This achievement is of extreme political importance. It is the warrior Ancestors who tell us where to go and what to do as a people. The Ancestors are in front of us (Dr. Mario Beatty), so if we are culturally and racially connected, they will lead us. Thus Afrikan Ancestor Communion ("worship," but a spiritual joining in reciprocal relationship), is a political, ideological concept, as well as a spiritual and cultural one. It places us within a system of race- accountability.

Dr. Frances Cress Welsing is now transitioning to the Ancestral stage of her existence. She is being "reborn" as one of the most powerful Afrikan Ancestors in "Ourstory". Our relationship with her is one of reciprocity (MAAT). With our help, she will continue to guide us, to teach us and to love us. It is our responsibility to remember her, commune with her warrior spirit, and to elevate her, as she guides, protects, and blesses us with her wisdom and courage.

IV

Although some may take umbrage, the discussion that follows is elevated far beyond what some might consider a "personal attack". It is simply Race, family-business! (and if you can't stand the heat...) I am speaking specifically to those Black people who have chosen this time to attempt to critique Dr. Welsing, those committed to anti-Afrikan ideologies and death-styles, who couldn't take her on when she was "in their faces". They are revealing the same fear that she used her energy to heal: fear of the responsibility of being Black. They are clinging to ideas and elevating anti-life behaviors that do not work for the achievement of global Afrikan sovereign power. Not only are their loyalties misplaced, but they are manifesting intellectual and moral cowardice, and they are at a serious disadvantage. Having separated themselves from Afrikan spiritual deep thought, they have made the serious tactical error of acting as though Dr. Welsing would be easier to attack in what the european world view defines as "death". Based on the Afrikan concept of the eternal cycle of life, we operate from a radically different frame of reference. As the honorable Marcus Mosiah Garvey tells us "In death I shall be a terror to foes of Afrikan liberty!...If death has power then count on me to be the real Marcus Garvey I would like to be!...I shall never desert you and make your enemies triumph over you!"

So if you were afraid to confront Nana Welsing "in the physical", you should be terrified to confront her now! For you have struck a rock in the spirit of Dr. Frances Cress Welsing and you have not only her to deal with, but all the rest of us, race vindicationists, who honor the lessons that she taught us. You were afraid to confront her when you could see her, but she sought you out. You were afraid of her, but she was not afraid of you. In fact, she would have healed you if you had only known that you were Afrikan and ill (Nana Arimenta Harriet Tubman, "I freed hundreds of slaves. I could have freed thousands more, if only they knew they were slaves."). In attacking our Nana Frances, you have compounded your tactical error. Black people will dismiss you as non-entities in our race movement. No one who loves Afrikan/Black people will listen to you, for we are seeking to be healed of "Black fear". We are seeking to claim our power. Those of our people who may have been confused or ambivalent will never again pay attention to anything you have to say! They will gain a new clarity. This is a moment of truth (Bobby Wright). It is time to look the "bull" in the face.

This is indeed a learning/teaching moment. Dr. Welsing's passing separates the Race-warriors from the race-traitors; the sovereignists-vindicationists from the integrationist-assimilationists. She is separating those who are not afraid to be "Race-First", from those who have made an ideology out of sexual behavior. Make no mistake, if it ain't about Race –First, it ain't about nothing.

Dr. Welsing told us, "If we do not have confidence in our ability to make independent Black observations, Black analyses and Black plans for Black actions, why should we talk about or seek Black liberation?" (p.160)

Clearly, no person who "loves black people" (R.L. Stephens' claim, in Black Agenda Report) no matter how often they professed to, would respect the ideas of Karl Marx, who dismisses Afrika, her history and civilization as "primitive". Marx's analysis is limited and cannot be used to construct the guidelines for the "Afrikan World Revolution" called for by Nana John Henrik Clarke. Marx was an avowed white supremacist whether the name was applied to him in the 19th century or not. He very often referred to Afrikans with the "n-word" in his writings and disparaged our physical characteristics and mental abilities.

It is now quite clear to me that, as his cranial structure and hair type prove, Lassalle is descended from the Negroes who joined Moses' flight from Egypt. That is, assuming his mother, or his paternal grandmother, did not cross with a nigger. Now this union of Jewry and Germanism with the negro-like basic substance must necessarily result in a remarkable product. The officiousness of the fellow is also nigger-like. (Karl Marx from a letter to Friedrich Engels, 1862)

Marx was incapable of critiquing the European world view, or of putting racism/white supremacy in its proper context. He was just another yurugu with despiritualized ideas about the acquisition and distribution of material objects to be manipulated.

Dr. Welsing focused on the need for the development of collective self-confidence and self- respect as a prerequisite for overcoming Black fear. Her passing is a critical moment for us. Will we be true to what she has taught us, or will we be intimidated by those who criticize her? This is an opportunity for our people to move forward toward authentic Afrikan sovereignty. Let us remove the nay-sayers from the discussion. We have no time for academic bantering. This is not a "seminar". Dr. Welsing's work was to get us to think clearly in the interest of Black people. The marxists are clearly powerless. They can only "talk". The fact is that the white sexual ideologues are powerful at this time, but only within the system of white supremacy. They have financial backing. They are well-organized and have used mafia-type methods to co-opt entire industries. As an organized collective, they usurp valuable real estate from Afrikan Elders. They intimidate through phobia-labels (perhaps because they are heterophobic). They constitute a powerful lobby within white supremacist electoral politics. The left has aligned itself with this power-base. So do those Black people who identify as part of this political cohort. The Marxists have been parasitic. They need Black power. So they get some of us to refer to ourselves as "the black left," as though it were an authentic movement of Afrikan/Black people. They are being manipulative. (But we outgrew Marxism with our Ancestors, Richard Wright, George Padmore, even W.E.B.Dubois and others.) Why not just "the left"? The answer is "because they need our energy". They have none of their own. No popular movement can be sustained by rationalistic, academic discourse and semantic repartee alone. They construct "fronts" which feed off of our spiritual and cultural energy. There is apparently no "black left" that has not capitulated to the financial and political power of homosexual politics. Their agenda is not Black. It is not Afrikan. And we certainly do not need Marxian analysis in order to critique capitalism. We know that capitalism is anti-Afrikan and bad for Black people. (see Wobogo, ch. 6, and Armah, Remembering the Dismembered Continent, 2010, ch. 3 "On Marx and Masks) The so- called "black left" cannot be trusted. Dr. Welsing knew that. She was clear. She spoke truth (Maat). She stayed the course and so must we.

Everything is political. Every choice has political implications and issues from a political position. To choose one's pattern of sexual behavior over Dr. Frances Cress Welsing is a choice made in fear. To listen to those who tell you that you have to make that choice in order to be "free", is to listen to the cacophony of confusion that she was able to expose as mere noise. Dr. Frances Cress Welsing is already sacred and iconic to the global Afrikan/Black Collective. Her detractors, choosing the time of her passing, to come out of their closets, have effectively removed themselves from the discourse of a truly "black agenda". Dr. Welsing is the quintessential Afrikan, she is the "Brain of Black Power". This is not a "defense" because she needs none. This is an announcement that any would-be critics at this special time, have made her all the more powerful among us and have exposed the opposition. As she would point out, the "left", ironically, gets its power from white supremacy. Within Afrikan Sovereignty, and an Afrikan power system, they have none. She has forced them to expose themselves. They messed with the wrong one. Their critique is an affirmation of her work. According to one critic "1000's will be influenced by her ideas" (R.L. Stephens, published in Black Agenda Report, January 5, 2016) Absolutely! Thousands have been influenced by her ideas and thousands more will be, and your feeble attempts have done nothing so much as increased that number tenfold.

V

The attack at this time in particular has another purpose. These confused Blacks and their yurugu teachers, must seek to anger us. But our Champion taught us how to fight. And we should pay strict attention to the behavior that she modeled. She never seemed to be disoriented by anger, although anger was certainly justified. She always approached her opponents with poise, the queenly posture of confidence. And she always won. We must not be distracted from our ceremonies of praise and honor. We must not be caught off guard or lose our rhythm. Their cowardly behavior cannot detract from our outpouring of love; it should only make the outpouring more profuse. She consistently focused on exposing the only form of racism; that is white supremacy, and on expunging Black Fear. Everything she did and said was a preparation for confrontation with that seeks to destroy us. Let us not lose focus at this time.

We must use our love for this brilliant and fearless Afrikan warrior to keep moving toward race victory. We are blessed because she belongs to us. She intimidated our enemies and those who may be used by our enemies, but she was never intimidated by them. She was never dissuaded. For over four decades she never lost focus and neither should we. She did not waste time shadow- boxing. She taught us that we are in a Race War, and the "Real Game" is the "Power Game." And we love her because she is still teaching us how to win it!

This is a praise song. She is my hero.

Versions of this Praise Song have appeared in The Atlanta Black Star and The Journal of African Studies.

All quotes from Dr. Welsing are taken from *The Isis Papers*.

EPILOGUE

Auset Rising

Jeff Menzise, Ph.D.

> "There is nobody else on the planet like her. She was one of a kind, that's all you deserve. There'll be no more."
>
> – Dick Gregory speaking on Dr. Frances Cress Welsing

Dr. Frances Cress Welsing was among the most profoundly deep thinkers of the 20th century. Her insights, perspectives, and uncanny ability to decode the symbolism contained within the human mind were second to none. She was a true healer; a third-generation physician who unapologetically lived her life on purpose. As a graduation gift, she asked her parents to send her to Germany so that she could better understand the illness that would motivate a nation of people to dehumanize and kill another. Her quest for knowledge led her on a lifelong journey to find the "Keys to the Colors." She remained humble and ever receptive to flashes of insight that often came from unexpected and unsolicited sources. For example, the subtitle to *The Isis Papers* (*The Keys to the Colors*) was actually a phrase repeated by a psychiatric patient in her presence. She took this patient's utterings as a profound insight into her life's purpose. She found value in wisdom regardless of its source and sought to understand and resolve the most pressing problems facing humanity. I have had the good fortune of retrieving and organizing the hand-written manuscripts that Dr. Welsing left behind at herWashington, D.C, home. While in the throes of this process, I came across several versions of her "Preface" to *The Isis Papers*, some of which contained different statements about Isis, and the reasons she named the book after the African Goddess. These renderings ranged from a detailed description of Isis to a brief teaser and a statement that the reader should go forward and do their own research to gain a deeper understanding of the glory of Isis. Interestingly, she chose a version where she gives only a brief statement about Isis, her relationship to Osiris, and a glimpse of the cosmological correlations to Sirius "the Dog Star." She had a special interest in the Sirius star system, in part because of how it phonetically sounds like the word "serious," an attribute she believed was necessary for Black people to resolve their issues with the system of racism/White supremacy. She was so in touch with this notion that she actually used Sirius in one of the versions of the title to The Isis Papers, Vol. 2. On page vii of the Preface she writes:

> Finally, the time has come for unveiling the true nature of white supremacy (racism). For this reason, I have entitled this work, *The Isis (YSSIS) Papers: The Keys to the Colors.* Isis [Auset] was the most important goddess of ancient Africa (especially Egypt). She was the sister/wife of the most important Egyptian god, Osiris [Ausar] ("Lord of the Perfect Black"), and the mother of Horus [Heru]. In the astral interpretation of the Egyptian gods, Isis was equated with the dog star Sirius (Sothis). According to the ancient African story, after the murder and dismemberment of Osiris by his evil brother Set (Seth), Isis discovered the crime, recovered the pieces of the body of Osiris, and put them together again, restoring his existence and his power. According to legend, Isis admired truth and justice and made justice stronger than gold and silver.

In the present era, truth and justice have been crushed by the global power system of white supremacy, making the existence of peace on the planet impossible under this reign of terror. The attempt in this work to reveal some aspects of the in-depth truth about the white supremacy power system for the ultimate purpose of establishing justice and peace in the world is in the tradition of the great African goddess, Isis.

This epilogue contains a deeper exploration of the significance of Dr. Welsing's desire to model Auset's (Isis') bravery and devotion, and her journey to find and establish truth and justice (*Maat*). The correlations between Dr. Welsing's actions, theories, thoughts, statements, and writings, and those found in the various stories of Auset's life, travels, and adventures are profound and will be highlighted and discussed throughout. It is my aim to demonstrate how, in true African fashion, Dr. Frances Cress Welsing was indeed an incarnation of the Auset energy, divinely inspired to live without fear and without apology.

For the sake of context, and to aid in understanding these correlations, I submit the following compilation of stories from various sources,[1] regarding the life of Auset (Isis):

> When he [Ausar] became King of Kamit, the men he came to rule were in a savage state. They were nomadic tribes in constant warfare against each other. They were wholly given over to evil and sinful behavior.
>
> He brought civilization and spirituality to the people, enabling them thus to achieve prosperity. He gave them a body of laws to regulate their conduct, settled their disputes justly, and instructed them in the science of spiritual development. He shared the rulership of the land with the Queen Mother Auset, who domesticated wild barley and wheat. Along with Ausar, who taught men agriculture—tilling of the soil, cultivation of grains, and of fruit trees—they also laid the material foundations for the development and growth of civilization.
>
> Brothers no longer lifted their hands against each other. There was prosperity and peace throughout the land of Kamit. Having civilized Kamit, he turned the government of his native land to Auset, and traveled around the world to spread the same instructions. He induced people to accept his teachings, not by force of arms, but by the use of persuasive lectures, spiritual hymns, and music. Wherever he went, he brought peace and learning to the people.
>
> While he was away, Auset ruled the land so expertly that her brother Set, who was consumed with jealousy over Ausar's success, was unable to realize his main desire. He sought in vain to stir up rebellion in the kingdom, so he plotted to overcome Ausar by deception—his chief characteristic—with the help of a confederacy of 72 followers. When Ausar returned from his mission, he was greeted with a royal feast. Set came with his 72 conspirators, supposedly to honor Ausar, and to make merry.
>
> He brought a funerary chest in the shape of a man which was so beautiful that everyone at the feast desired it for themselves. When everyone was in a joyous state from beer drinking, Set stated that he would give

the chest to anyone whose body fit the chest perfectly. They all tried it for size, but no one could fill it out perfectly. He came last to Ausar and asked him if he would try it, knowing all along that it would fit the king, as he had made the chest to the exact dimensions of his body. Ausar entered the chest and his body fit it in every part. Before he could get up, the followers of Set jumped quickly to close the lid of the chest and nailed it down and soldered it fast with lead. Needless to say, the king died immediately of suffocation.

The feast was broken up in great confusion, as the followers of Set fell upon the people with their weapons to take over the government. Set commanded his followers to take the chest away and dispose of it in a secret place. They hastened through the thick cover of darkness and flung it into the Nile. The Nile's current took it to the open ocean and it was presumed lost forever on the bottom of the ocean.

So ended the world's reign of peace, harmony, and prosperity. When the bad news regarding Ausar's fate was taken to Auset, she was stricken with great sorrow. She wept bitterly and could not be consoled. In her grief she cut off a lock of her hair, put on mourning clothes, and vowed to never rest until she found the body of her beloved king and husband. She searched everywhere, questioned everyone she met, and when it seemed that all was in vain, she met up with some children who told her that they had seen the chest floating down the Nile and entering the sea.

Meanwhile, Set usurped the throne of Ausar and reigned over the land of Kamit. Law and order which followed from the moral upliftment of the people was replaced by the use of force. Everywhere men were robbed of their possessions and land[s], through legal unjust means. Once owners, they were now renters and wage earners. Tyranny and the law of might prevailed as the Divine Law was repealed. Everywhere the followers of Ausar—who lived by Maat—were persecuted.

The good Queen Mother Auset became a fugitive in her own land, and she fled to conceal herself in Set's own stronghold, the swamps and marshes of the Delta of Lower Kamit. She believed that it was the last place he would [ever] dream of looking for her. Seven scorpions followed her and served as her protectors. Ra also came to her aid. Looking down from heaven and seeing her distress, he took pity on her and sent Anpu (Anubis), the son of Ausar and Nebthet, to serve as her guide, and guard dog.

One day Auset requested shelter at the house of a poor woman, but was refused by the woman who was stricken with fear on seeing the scorpions accompanying her. But a scorpion managed to slip in before the woman closed the door and bit her child, causing his immediate death. To repair the damage, Auset uttered words of power which caused the child to come to life again, for which the mother was so grateful that she allowed Auset to stay in her house.

The coffin of Ausar was taken by the waves to Byblos, a port city in southern Syria, and it was cast on to the shore. A tree sprang up and grew around it, enclosing the body of Ausar in [its] trunk. News of this tree [of such beauty], which grew so rapidly, came to the king of this alien land, and he commanded that it should be cut down, and its trunk brought to him. He erected it as a pillar in his house without knowing the great secret it contained within.

A revelation came to Auset in her dreams that she might find Ausar's body in Byblos, so she set off towards Syria by ship. When she arrived, she dressed as a commoner and sat beside a well, weeping bitterly. At the well she befriended the queen's handmaidens, whose hair she braided. Into each lock, she breathed a sweet and unique perfume. They went back to the palace and told their queen of this woman who had the strange power of exhaling and exuding perfume from her breath and body. The queen commanded that she should be brought immediately before her. Auset found favor in the eyes of the queen who made her the nurse to one of her sons.

Auset refused to nurse the child, and to silence his cries for milk, she put her finger into his mouth. Instead of milk, at night she caused him to be enveloped in a sacred fire which would confer immortality to the child. In the meantime, she transformed herself into a swallow and flew to where the pillar containing the body of Ausar was kept, and uttered loud cries of sorrow, while flying around it. While she was thus engaged, the queen came by and saw the babe surrounded by the flame and snatched him from it, denying him thus of immortality.

Auset transformed herself back into human form and confessed to the queen who she was and the purpose of her mission. She then asked the king that the pillar be given to her. The king granted her request, and she cut deep into the trunk and took out the chest, which she wrapped in linen and anointed with myrrh. The empty pillar was returned to the king who erected it as a monument to Auset, and for many centuries it was worshipped by the people of Byblos. Auset returned by ship with the coffin, accompanied by the [boy] Maneros, the king's first born. While at sea, Auset could not wait to see Ausar, so she opened the chest and embraced the corpse and wept bitterly. Meanwhile, the boy Maneros had secretly stolen behind her to see what was in the chest, and what was going on. She turned suddenly and the fire in her eyes caused the boy to die of fright, and he fell into the sea.

When Auset reached the land of Kamit she took the body and according to the Pyramid Texts numbers 632 and 1636, as well as murals at Abydos and Philae, she transformed herself into a swallow and hovered over the dead body. Causing a wind with her wings, she raised the weary phallus of the silent-hearted (dead), and received his seed. Thus, was Heru conceived.

She then hid the body in a secret place and hastened to Buto, in the city of Khemmis to give birth to her son Heru. Her triumph was short-lived. While she was in Buto, Set came hunting the boar at full moon in the marshy swamps of the Delta and by accident found the chest. Recognizing it, he opened it and took the body of Ausar and cut it into fourteen pieces and scattered them in various parts of the country. On hearing about Set's deed, Auset set out again in search of the members of Ausar's body, this time accompanied by her sister Nebthet, who until then was married to Set. At length she recovered all the parts except the phallus which was swallowed by the Lepidotus, Phagrus, and the Oxyrychus fish. She buried an image of each member where it was found and erected a tomb which became a place of worship by the people of the area. The existence of the actual members were kept secret so that Set would not resume his search for the body.

Set continued his tyrannical rulership over the land, unrelenting in his persecution of the followers of Ausar. The people's worship of Ausar strengthened his spirit and caused him to appear in a dream to his son Heru who was now a grown man. He encouraged him to regain the throne to which he was the rightful heir and gave him instruction in battle. Heru gathered his army and went to confront Set. They first met at Edfu, where Set's army slew many of the followers of Heru. But Heru and his followers, although greatly outnumbered, resumed the war. His greatest weapon was his faith in the counsel from Tehuti, whose words were God's Words. They attacked Set again and drove him to the eastern frontier. He sought refuge at Zaru where Heru caught up with him, and the last battle of the war ensued.

In this pitched battle that went on for many days, Set gouged out Heru's eye, which would have cost him the war had not Tehuti healed it. With his [in]sight regained, Heru managed to castrate Set. This was the decisive point in the war. Set was defeated, taken prisoner, and condemned to death. Heru turned him over to the Queen Mother Auset for her to administer the judgement, but she refused to kill him on the grounds that they were all family, and set him loose. Outraged, the impetuous youth cut her head off—some say her royal diadem—which was replaced by a cow's head or crown by Tehuti.

Although Set had been defeated, Auset and Nebthet were still grieving over the death of Ausar. In a chant Auset exclaims:

> *Gods and Men before the face of gods are weeping for thee at the same time when they behold me Aes! I invoke thee with wailing that reaches high as heaven yet you do not hear my voice. I, your sister, loves you more than all the earth and you love none other more than me.*

And NebtHet in her chant exclaims:

> *Overcome your sorrow in the hearts of us, your sisters. Live before us desiring to behold you.*

The lamentations of the goddesses were heard by Ra, and he sent them once again Anpu, who with the assistance of Tehuti and Ra reunited the dismembered body of Ausar, wrapped it in linen bandages, and mummified it. Tehuti, Auset, and Heru performed upon the mummy the Ceremony of Opening the Mouth, and Ausar was brought back to life through the gift of the Eye of Heru, which Set had destroyed, but was healed by Tehuti. Brought back to life, he was declared the Judge and King of the Dead, while Heru was to take his place as king of the living.

Set objected. He publicly complained, according to one account, that Heru was a bastard, and could not thus, be the legitimate heir to the throne. According to another account, he staked his claim to the throne on the basis that he was the strongest in the world. Might, he argued, was the chief virtue of government. He also brought charges contesting the position of Ausar.

Although Set, now emasculated, could have easily been disposed of by Heru through force, righteousness returned to the land with the return of Ausar, and Set was given his day in court. A great tribunal made up of 42 gods with Tem as leader, and Tehuti as judge was assembled. As

> Set's government was based on might and pure deception, where force could not be openly applied his words were found to be untrue. It was shown that in most instances, he contradicted and violated the laws he imposed on others.
>
> On the other side, Ausar and Heru had been shown to have lived by the laws as promulgated, thus they were found to be *Maa Kheru, True of Word.* Thus the "*Great Quarrel*" was settled on the basis of right over might. The night on which this great verdict was awarded is known in the Kamitic spiritual tradition as the *Kerh Utchau Metut, Night of Weighing Words*. Set was sentenced to serve as the wind that propelled the boat of Ausar.

Water, Childbirth, and Children

As a *Neter* (Kemetic word for personified natural energy), one of Auset's main correlations is with the element of water. This association helps to identify the tools, characteristics, and attributes of receptivity, nurturing, reflection, accommodation, emotions, meditation, altered states of consciousness (trance), purposeful dreaming, etc. In the case of Auset, and her many African correlations including *Mami Wata*, *Yemoja/Olokun,* and the *Iyami*, there is always a strong connection to bodies of water, more specifically the oceans and seas. This relationship identifies the powers and vastness of the feminine principle and how it is the source of the world's material wealth and of life itself. Midwives, nursing mothers, and all things associated with pregnancy and gestation come under the jurisdiction of Auset; the fact that human beings develop in a sac of "water" (amniotic fluid) within the mother's womb makes this correlation salient. Although she had no biological children of her own, Dr. Welsing held that the rearing of healthy children, by mature and fully capable adults, was the most valuable counter-strategy against racism/white supremacy. This counter-strategy is based on the theory that racism/white supremacy is a system designed to promote white genetic survival by controlling the genetic procreative potential of all non-white people in the known universe. She devotes chapters 20 through 23 to Black children and Black parenting, sharing insights on both the problem and solutions.

Often, she would repeat that parents should have no more than two children, no closer than three years apart. This was for the purpose of guaranteeing enough "lap time" for each child, in order to meet their emotional and attachment needs while giving them enough nurturance to grow into healthy, well-adjusted adults. The "no more than two" was explained, in part, as a strategy for humans living in war situations (in this case, under racism/white supremacy). She said that with two children, each parent could carry one if it ever became necessary. This would also minimize the economic, emotional, and physiological strain on parents who overtax their systems by repeatedly conceiving and birthing children within short periods of time.

Perhaps the most profound correlation between Auset, water, and Dr. Welsing is the fact that she "conceived" the Cress Theory of Color Confrontation while at home washing dishes. Her hands were literally in water when the flash of insight came to her. That day, she had been questioning and pondering why global racism operates the way that it does and how the victims of such an experience could protect themselves and eventually replace that system with a system of justice. Asking these questions in the serenity afforded by the quiet of that afternoon, combined with the almost oracle-like properties of water,[2] Dr. Welsing emerged from her brief moment of trance with a model that eventually would lead to the construction of the *Isis Papers*, namely, her Theory of Color Confrontation. She often called it the "Two Qs," that is, Questions and Quiet.

Devotion

Devotion plays an integral role in the many stories about Auset. She is portrayed as both a devoted mother and a devoted wife. She goes through great lengths for her family, facing innumerable trials and tribulations along the way. Perhaps the most popular story characterizing the depths of her devotion is the Story of Ausar. Now, many say this story is a later creation in Egypt and that it does not appear, as popularly conveyed, in any Ancient Egyptian texts. However, there are aspects of the story written in stone. Regardless of its antiquity, the embedded truth is timeless and universal. Within this one story, the process for breaking the psychological chains of slavery is laid out metaphorically within the journey of Auset, who is on a quest to recover the body of Ausar. In this case, as described by Amen (1991), Auset represents the human personality, and what it chooses to identify with: the higher divine nature or the lower human nature.

The body of Ausar, Ausar as husband, and Ausar as father represent various aspects of identifying with your Divine self. The body of Ausar represents the body as temple to the divine spirit. When a person truly embraces, understands, and begins to interact with their physical body as if it truly were a holy temple, their body is thought to eventually become "incorruptible," as symbolized by the mummified Ausar. Dr. Welsing addressed this aspect of Ausar by encouraging Black people to love their physical characteristics and to resist the urge to do damage to their physical selves via the multitude of weapons provided by the system of racism/white supremacy (e.g., skin bleaching creams, cosmetic surgery, chemical hair treatments, and illicit, "recreational," and over- the-counter drugs).

As husband, Ausar symbolizes the wedding of your everyday personality to your highest spiritual self. This "marriage" is simply a metaphor for a person committing to their own personal refinement and continued maturation as they experience life; in other words, one's devotion to constantly improving upon their current state of functioning, for the purpose of producing justice in all areas of their life. Auset's marriage to Ausar symbolizes the power brought about by self-refinement, and how this eventually leads one to function optimally and beyond the influence of Set, who represents the destructive element in every society. Dr. Welsing's teachings of Black self-respect, and the prayer she crafted to be recited at least once every day, was designed to rewrite the script of self-hate implanted into the minds of non-white people from the times of their childhood and, thereby, facilitate the refinement process on a mental level.

Ausar as father symbolizes how our higher consciousness participates in birthing insight and wisdom when given the medium of a steady, receptive and well-nurtured mind to speak through. This relates to how the unconscious mind plays the background to our daily conscious experiences. We often ignore its many whispers to "do this," "avoid that," and so forth, because we can be distracted by the external world. For those who have found mental peace, this whisper becomes a very clear and distinct guiding voice. Dr. Welsing often referred to it as our "brain computers" and this whisper as the necessary voice of reason, which will automatically respond once we begin to ask our questions, silently contemplate the possibilities, and await an answer. Auset's "immaculate" conception of Heru (Horus) after remembering Ausar is also symbolic of being pregnant with the possibility to topple the system of injustice.

Just like Auset and against all odds, Dr. Frances Cress Welsing stayed the steadily unpopular path of challenging that which opposed justice and made it her purpose in life (Set/racism/white supremacy). Regardless of negative repercussions, she remained steadfast and devoted to the truth, without apology, seeking to heal the people of the known universe by freeing their minds so that they too could find purpose and function accordingly.

Re-membering

In the story of Auset and Ausar, one of the most profound metaphors is that of Auset recovering the dismantled body of Ausar, which had been scattered by his brother Set. She set out on a journey to find and re-member the individual parts back into a whole. As a psychiatrist and physician, Dr. Welsing's task was similar. She sought to find the missing pieces to the African saga as it was being fragmented and played out as a tragedy on the stage set by racism/white supremacy. Welsing often spoke of how important it is for victims of trauma to resolve the associated traumatic memories by placing them within the context of the whole. This task requires that we, as victims, seek out the fragments of African historical greatness that have been scattered throughout the material, academic, and political worlds, and re-member (reassemble) these parts into a complete narrative that is more reflective of the truth than the deception (indirect violence) promulgated by the system of racism/ white supremacy.

Whereas Auset sought the body parts of Ausar, Dr. Welsing was on a quest for "the keys to the colors." She stood a giant among giants in this regard because she was better equipped than most to understand psychologically the meaning of and motivating forces behind the system of racism/white supremacy. As a psychiatrist, she was well-trained at assisting her ill patients in the process of memory recovery via the various techniques afforded by psychoanalysis. Through free association, dream interpretation, symbolism, and the recognition of ego-defense mechanisms, psychoanalysts delve deeply into the unconscious minds of their patients, unearthing memories of their pasts that, due to repression and or suppression, have led to a maladaptive and mentally unhealthy state and, thus, to suboptimal functioning. Regarding victims of racism/white supremacy, these memories of Black self-love and Black self-respect, are directly associated with trauma and punishment. This is symbolized in the movie *Roots* when Kunta Kinte was beaten while attempting to maintain his African identity, only to eventually be broken and forced to identify himself as Toby. As for the perpetuators of racism/white supremacy, Dr. Welsing helped them to remember and unearth their own traumas related to their whiteness, genetic inadequacy, decreasing birth rate, and the fact that they are a numerical minority on the planet.

As stated by Neely Fuller, Jr., and quoted on page four of *The Isis* Papers:

> Most white people hate Black people. The reason that most white people hate Black people is because whites are not Black people. If you know this about white people, you need know little else. If you do not know this about white people, virtually all else that you know about them will only confuse you.

Exposing the underlying psychological issues related to whiteness, to both whites and non-whites alike, Dr. Welsing began the work of reconciliation within and between the races. Her attempts to establish justice, universally, are akin to restoring balance to the scales of *Maat*, a task that was charged to Auset as well. Naturally, she was met with resistance by both whites and non-whites who were made psychologically uncomfortable by the memories and experiences surfacing as a result of conscious awakening to their apparent illnesses. Just like Auset, Dr. Welsing stayed the course and continued to search for the "keys," fully confident in her ability to re-establish justice for the people of the known universe. It was, as she would say, her cosmic purpose.

The Unconscious and Subconscious Mind

As a psychiatrist, Dr. Welsing operated from the psychoanalytical perspective, meaning that she valued and understood the unconscious mind as both a source of mental illness, as well as the source for the potential resolution of the same. The majority of topics covered in *The Isis Papers* somehow relate back to the unconscious and/or subconscious minds of both the victims and perpetuators of racism/white supremacy. In *The Cress Theory of Color Confrontation*, Dr. Welsing demonstrates the role of the unconscious mind in the behavioral manifestations of white supremacists by detailing the various ego defense mechanisms, many of which operate on the unconscious and subconscious levels of the mind. These ego defense mechanisms, including repression, reaction formation, denial, projection, and displacement, are all employed to protect the conscious mind from what can be considered a painful reality.

This need for protection from reality makes it necessary for organisms to develop systems through which they may feel secure and powerful in an otherwise "hostile" environment. Unfortunately, these systems only serve to mask reality while the truth remains very much alive beneath the surface of observable and dominant expression. For example, a person dealing with the loss of a loved one may smile and attempt to carry on with their day as if the loss is not impacting them deeply. They may occupy themselves with activities in order to distract their thinking from the reality, or they may even deny the reality altogether (one of the known stages of the grieving process). A trained psychologist or psychiatrist is capable of readily identifying subtle cues that indicate the individual's true emotional and/or cognitive state. In other words, they are capable of getting past the ego's defense. In some cases, the people utilizing these defense mechanisms are themselves unaware of the need for and presence of these tools and protective factors; it is totally taking place in the "background," without their permission or knowledge, but always in their best interest. If the need for ego protection is pervasive enough throughout a society, then its expression becomes normalized within the fabric of society, eventually becoming embedded into the culture itself. This is most commonly done through the use of symbols.

Symbols are highly effective representations of reality, designed to convey a message via a streamlined, efficient and effective delivery system. Nine of her 25 chapters in *The Isis Papers*—more than 35%—have some version of the word "symbol" in the title. Upon further exploration, the reader will also realize that every chapter in *The Isis Papers* is about symbolic expression and decoding that expression for the purpose of understanding the behavior which manifests under the system of racism/white supremacy. This is significant because it orients the problem of racism/white supremacy within the jurisdiction of the unconscious mind. This helps us to understand why the police officer who shot Charles Kinsey, an unarmed mental health worker in Miami, stated "I don't know" when Kinsey asked, "Why did you shoot me?" Kinsey was trying to make sense of the confusing situation while the officer could not.

Dr. Welsing dealt deeply with symbolism and the role of symbols in human consciousness generally, and in the system of racism/white supremacy specifically. She would spend hours going through popular media stories, pointing out and decoding the various symbols displayed in ads, news reports, logos, and literature authored by whites. She saw it as "gathering intelligence" around the problem of racism/white supremacy and understood that there was no shortage of data from which to conduct our scientific investigations. In her own words:

> Though symbols are usually visual entities, they also take the form of speech, or can be found in activities—such as games. Symbols are specific to people and their experiences, their evolved cultures and circumstances. As such, symbols are the entities that carry highly compacted messages pertaining to the origin, identity and survival of individuals and collective peoples.
>
> In the form of visual entities, patterns of speech and/or activity, symbols contain complex messages distilled from the conscious levels of the brain-computer. These messages have been reduced to their essence in subconscious functioning; there, these highly coded messages are stored and continuously referenced for existence and survival.

> Once a symbol evolves in a person's subconscious, that person uses the symbol with high frequency and has little or no necessary conscious understanding of its meaning.
>
> A shared symbol speaks volumes, although contained in a relatively small visual or auditory package. A symbol speaks loudly, or even shouts its meaning without uttering a sound. Symbols communicate from one person's subconscious to the subconscious of another who shares the same identity and survival necessity[ies]. Such communication transpires at subconscious levels when the conscious levels of brain-computer functioning cannot bear to address certain issues. White supremacy is a topic that few can or dare discuss in-depth at the conscious level of brain-computer functioning. Few dare to probe or research white supremacy, as this could lead to the dismantling of the system. Therefore, it is not surprising that there are many symbols in the system of white supremacy that reveal its roots in the struggle for white genetic survival.[3]

It is no coincidence that, while stationed in Japan during the Korean War, Mr. Neely Fuller Jr.'s role was to intercept symbolically codified communications for the purpose of decoding and gaining valuable information, nor that he and Dr. Welsing would come to work so closely together. They functioned as two sides of the same coin, with Welsing focusing on the "why" of racism/white supremacy, and Mr. Fuller focusing on the "what" and "how" of racism/white supremacy. In the stories of Auset, this dynamic relationship was expressed through the relationship between Auset and Tehuti, the Neter of wisdom (more on this later).

Welsing's role as Auset (Isis) could not be more evidenced than it is in this capacity. In the story of Ausar and Auset, Ausar is eventually relegated to serving as the active principle of the unconscious/subconscious mind (ruling from the *Duat*). His role is to maintain all the background functions of all creation, meaning that Ausar is responsible for all of the body's automatic and unconscious/subconscious processes. His influence is the reason why you don't have to consciously focus on digesting food (beyond chewing and swallowing), why you don't have to consciously exchange the oxygen from your lungs for the carbon dioxide in your blood, and why you don't have to actively signal and route neural pathways while learning and doing work. It is Ausar that is also responsible for the structuring and activation of unconscious thoughts, be they good or bad, harmful or beneficial. Auset's role in the unconscious mind is to serve as the mechanism through which these unconscious processes are programmed and actually function. In other words, she formulates the framework through which Ausar operates (hence her conception of Heru and his role of governing the conscious aspects of life). She is also simultaneously the vehicle through which the unconscious mind is expressed and decipherable.

Dreams, symbolism, sympathetic magic, trance states, memory, and personality all operate, at least in part, within and from the realm of the unconscious/subconscious mind, and are all considered attributes of Auset. Per psychoanalysis, and the wisdom traditions of many indigenous cultures on the planet, dreams serve as an important tool for understanding the unconscious mind of the dreamer. The personality, or how one identifies as a person, colors the interpretation of events and experiences occurring throughout life and, thus, helps to validate and/or reprogram the operations of the unconscious mind. This is why in many systems of initiation there is a period during which the initiate must learn to identify with the divine aspects of their nature as opposed to the conditioned understandings of being "only human." This shift in identity/personality, serves to expand the individual's conscious understanding of their true potential; as victims of racism/white supremacy, Dr. Welsing taught us to identify with the greatness of our genetic disposition as it relates to the genetic mutation to albinism and the subsequent whitening of the human species. The language she used was "Black self-respect," in contrast to the inferiority and self-hatred projected upon non-whites by the culture and system of racism/white supremacy. The birth, trials, and eventual triumph of Heru is what brings forth the healthy and awakened aspects of human consciousness and, thus, Ausar as the father is symbolic of the unconscious mind expressing itself consciously to the degree that our identities have been shifted towards our greatest and highest potential. Using her tools of psychoanalysis coupled with her knowledge of racism/white supremacy, Dr.

Welsing treated racism/white supremacy as if it were an ill patient who presented certain behavior and cognitive patterns. She analyzed these patterns in order to identify the root cause of this behavior syndrome. Once identified as the drive to survive, it became clear to Dr. Welsing how and why this underlying fear played itself out in all areas of people activity, albeit on sub- or unconscious levels. Thus, she was able to develop counter-strategies designed not only to protect the unconscious minds of non-white people, but to also develop methods for the healthy reprogramming of the same.

Queen Mother, Teacher, Nurturer, Healer

As a Queen Mother, Auset (Isis) was directly responsible for the well-being of Kemet (ancient Egypt). She was in charge of the society and ruled in the absence of Ausar whenever he left for a mission abroad. She was at once a warrior, teacher, nurturer, and healer, serving her people to her fullest capacity in the most selfless, loving way possible. These attributes are highlighted in the earlier story of Auset, for example, when she protected the child in the flames, granting him immortality, and when she secured the kingdom from Set after Ausar's murder. They are also represented in her dealings with conception and ultimately, with raising her son Heru, who was destined to reclaim justice and to reestablish harmony in the known universe. Such was the case with Dr. Frances Cress Welsing. Among other things, Dr. Welsing consistently convened The Cress Welsing Institute at Howard University for more than 30 years, free of charge and open to the public. She would use her own resources to develop a platform from which she could begin the healing work of countering racism/white supremacy's negative impact on the mental and physical health of non-white people. She would take the time to painstakingly break down complex psychological concepts into plain language for all to understand. She would patiently address those that felt extreme discomfort as a result of the reality she was revealing to them. She would point out the snares and traps being laid by the system of racism/white supremacy in the form of biological and chemical warfare, while also addressing the social determinants of health and how popular culture imagery and subtle messaging was negatively impacting outcomes.

She remained very consistent in how she delivered her message, and at all times displayed calm and poise, even when being verbally assaulted by suspected and known racists/white supremacists. She was a true warrior queen in this regard. Never have I seen her, in person or in a taped conversation/lecture/interview, raise her voice, nor become upset, defensive, or disrespectful to anyone she was engaging. As a teacher and nurturer, she understood the need to always maintain her superior status by never engaging at the level of the ignorance she was working to dispel. Dr. Welsing understood the necessity of intentionality, especially in times of war.

As one of our most valuable strategists in this fight to produce justice, Dr. Welsing was beloved by many and, perhaps, feared and targeted by more. Similar to the story of Auset, Dr. Welsing had to call on higher powers to give her guidance and protection, and to order her steps as she navigated this labyrinth of unconsciously derived systemic and individual racism. I recall a conversation between Dr. Welsing and I in Nashville, Tennessee. I was taking her back to the hotel after she delivered a message to an audience at Fisk University. There was a white woman who was interested in following Dr. Welsing around as she traveled, teaching and lecturing on racism/white supremacy. The woman wanted to serve as a validator of what Dr. Welsing was saying, demonstrating as a white woman the truth of Welsing's interpretations and perspectives. I felt uneasy about this offer and Dr. Welsing's consideration of it, so I verbalized my concern. Dr. Welsing appreciated and acknowledged the possibilities that I pointed out but had absolutely no fear of the woman's ability to carry out any ill-conceived plans to harm her. Her certainty and faith in her understanding of God allayed my concerns. She was powerful.

Goddess

Many believe the stories of African deities (*Neteru*, *Orisha*, etc.) to be stories of heavenly beings incarnated in flesh, meaning that these divine principles actually lived as human beings on the earth. This belief is consistent with the African worldview of reality (ontology), and has served to keep the spiritual science found embedded in their "mythologies" tangible and accessible to those who seek to study and practice them, fully intact as left by our ancestors. Viewing Dr. Frances Cress Welsing and her life from this perspective helps to solidify the notion that she was Auset incarnate and that we were, in fact, in the presence of African spiritual greatness.

Mr. Fuller served the role of *Tehuti* (wisdom) and *Anpu* (opener of the way) as mentioned earlier in the story of Auset. His understanding of racism/white supremacy to be a system that operates, simultaneously, in all areas of people activity and for the purpose of maintaining the power equation of white power over non-white powerlessness, gave Dr. Welsing the "Keys to the Colors." Adopting this perspective from Mr. Fuller, Dr. Welsing had the framework that she would use to develop a solid understanding of what racism is and how it functions. She was then able to shift her energies towards deciphering the "why" of racism/white supremacy. To unearth the motive is to reveal its driving force and, thus, the means by which to dismantle it.

She took this insight and applied it to her studies, evidencing mastery via her workshops, lectures, and writings. The strategies outlined by Mr. Fuller, including the wisdom, guidance, and direction he offered via his own conceptualization of racism/white supremacy, and Dr. Welsing's immediate adoption and assimilation of this understanding, is likened to the story of Auset wherein she receives wisdom and protection from *Tehuti*, in the form of *Anubis*, the guard dog and opener of the way. This is exactly what Mr. Fuller's insights did for Dr. Welsing during their "chance" meeting at a Black Power gathering in Washington, DC, where she serendipitously overheard him talking about racism/white supremacy as a system.

The Missing Phallus

One of Dr. Welsing's most memorable lessons is her description of ball games and how the various games reflect the unconscious fixation of white supremacy on the black genetic material contained within the testicles (balls) of non-white men. She would, in a very comical fashion, describe how the game of golf is played, demonstrating the stance and pretending to hold a long golf club between her legs, aiming to "hit the little white ball into big brown mother earth." She often elaborated on how white supremacy culture symbolically acknowledged their genetic inferiority via the presentation of cultural symbols and their functional usage, as evidenced by the two categories of ball games: big brown and little white. She further supported this notion by pointing out how cigarettes, known as "fags," are small, white, phallus-shaped smoking objects through which their white substance is inhaled and ingested into the body. On the flip side, cigars are large, brown, phallus-shaped smoking objects, through which their white substance is inhaled and ingested into the body. This white substance, smoke, is symbolic of the genetic reproductive substance sperm. Cigars are a symbol of male virility and are often given to men who recently had a son and are smoked by those deemed powerful, while cigarettes are constantly under attack by anti-smoking campaigns. The exception to the small white smoking objects is the small brown ones, which happen to be called "More," a name very similar to the Africans who invaded and dominated Spain, known as the Moors.

The "Great Equalizer" (gun) being a phallus whose bullets imitate sperm cells, full of the potential to build and destroy life, is another shining example of the phallus-based symbolism embedded in the culture of white supremacy. One must ask, what is the gun equalizing? Dr. Welsing hypothesized it was used to counter the genetic potentials of the non-white penis and testicles. This theory has been supported time and time again by the shooting of unarmed non-white males, followed by the excuse that the assailant thought the victim "had a gun." This theory is supported further by the predominantly white male hunting culture, where white males arm themselves with guns and other gear and set out on a quest to hunt, kill, and display large bucks (male deer, a name given also to African males who were forced to breed while imprisoned on plantations), lions (kings of the jungle found in Africa), elephants for their tusks (another phallus-shaped item), or a number of other highly prized game.

This is very consistent with the behaviors displayed by white men as it pertained to the lynching of American African men. The souvenirs with the greatest value after the hunt were the castrated penis and testicles. One of the most feared occurrences—and the reason motivating many of these lynchings—was a non-white male having sex (consensual or not) with a white woman and doing something that no white man could ever do: assist her in producing a child of color. This addresses the underlying threat to white genetic survival which, according to *The Cress Theory of Color Confrontation*, led to the development of a highly refined system of white supremacy, under which those with the greatest genetic potential, African men, would be the most readily subjected to the horrors and hardships of racism. In turn, this neutralizes and renders them all but powerless to direct their genetic potential in ways that would support and best serve themselves and their own race.

In the story of Ausar and Auset, Auset set out to find Ausar's missing body parts, which had been cut up as a result of Ausar's lynching at the hands of Set and his violent mob of 72 confederates. She was successful in recovering every part except for his phallus (reproductive organs). According to some tales, it was eaten by a fish; in others, it was simply lost to eternity. As a result of this missing vital organ, Auset had to reconstruct his penis, restoring his reproductive potential in order that she may carry out her purpose of conceiving and birthing his successor, Heru, for the sake of restoring justice to the known universe.

Welsing's quest for the missing phallus manifested in her efforts to identify how Black males have been emasculated by the system of racism/white supremacy both by literal castration as well as through economic and social castration. She spoke often of how Black males and females use terms in reference to their relationship dynamic that often identified the male as less than a man. For example, in her chapter entitled "The Motherfucker and the Original Motherfucker," Welsing highlights how there are but five designations for humans in regard to gender and age: man, woman, boy, girl, and baby. She states,

> To begin with, Black males in particular, but also Black females, refer to the White male as “The Man.” Once this term “The Man” is thought or uttered, the brain computes that inasmuch as there are only five major categories of people (“man,” “woman,” “boy,” “girl,” and “baby”), if the White male is “The Man,” meaning logically “The only Man,” then any other male must be one of the four remaining people categories—“boy,” “girl,” “woman,” or “baby.”
>
> Historically, Black males have fought being referred to as “boy” by White males and females. Only recently has the use of this degrading appellation ceased to some extent, although there is a current television series called “Chico and The Man.” The title implies “the boy” and “The Man.” “The Man,” of course, is white and “Chico” is a non-White male.
>
> Because the use of the word “boy” in reference to Black males ceased, it only meant that Black males could then refer to themselves as any one of the remaining three categories of people: “baby,” “woman” or “girl.” It certainly did not imply that Black males would be referred to as equals of White males. This never could occur under the system of white supremacy domination.

When the use of the word “boy” was no longer the term of common reference for Black males by Whites, Black males began referring to themselves as “baby.” For until most recently, with the changes in dress and clothing styles, most Black males deeply resented any reference to themselves as “girl” or “woman.” But the recent style changes towards high-heeled shoes, curled hair, hair curlers, braids, earrings, bracelets, necklaces, pocketbooks, midriff tops, cinch waisted pants, etc., that many Black males have adopted now suggest that there is a developing tendency, widespread amongst Black males, to not mind (consciously or unconsciously) being mistaken for a “girl” or a “woman.”[4] Similar to the experiences of Ausar while being manipulated and assaulted by his Brother Set, the American African male has also experienced castration at the hands of Set (racism/white supremacy). This symbolic and literal emasculation has taken on economic, social, and political dimensions. The symbolically castrated American African male roams the world in a defeated state, compensating through various pop-culture informed displays of hypermasculinity that happen to negatively target other

American African men, women, and children. Dr. Welsing's search for the missing phallus was her attempt to reestablish the inherent power of American African men so that we may once again position ourselves as strong leaders and protectors of our families, homes, and communities. Welsing recognized that the system of racism/white supremacy had to make American African men its number-one target because they possess the greatest genetic potential to produce skin color.[5] She expressed the negative impact of the absentee father on the family unit, coining the term "survival units" to identify the home where there was only a mother to care for the children. Mass incarceration, drug use and abuse, chronic un- and underemployment, fractured identities, and mental illnesses of all kinds are the major white supremacy-sponsored ailments leading to the missing phallus syndrome.

Ruling in Ausar's Absence

Dr. Welsing, in her discussion of "survival units," elaborates on how the single Black female head of household is, in fact, ruling in the absence of Ausar. The major difference in this dismal reality is that the missing father (Ausar) is in many cases never to return. And in the case where he does come home, he is likely to have suffered unfathomable degrees of trauma and received little to no assistance processing and thereby alleviating the burden. This makes the returning father more of a liability than an asset. The fallout from the missing father is immense and has the potential to impact the family unit for generations to come.

In my work as a clinician and psychotherapist, mostly with children in foster care, I would constantly hear stories from children lamenting the abandonment of their mother, siblings, and themselves by their father. The children would tie their sense of value and worth to the value their father has placed on their family: in their eyes, there was none. Unfortunately, many women heading these "survival units" are not as equipped as Auset to journey to reclaim their divinity: by wedding themselves to a healthier and more empowered version of their identity. Racism/white supremacy ensures this. Instead, they are encouraged and rewarded for not developing themselves further by the provision of certain subsidies that require them to be "single," which increase with the number of children they have as a single person. Some have likened this situation to the breeding farms maintained throughout the United States once the importation of enslaved Africans was outlawed. Similarly, these breeding farms were designed to keep African women in baby production mode, with no sense of or hope for a solid and consistent family unit.

Dr. Welsing's remedy to this particular issue was simple: no sex until marriage and no marriage until the age of 30 for women and 35 for men. In the meantime, American Africans should go to college and improve upon their knowledge, resources, networks, and sense of self.

In her words:

> The more complex a social system becomes, the higher the level of emotional maturity and formal education needed to negotiate that system successfully. Often, the ultimate level of functioning reached by children is correlated with the level of emotional maturity achieved by the parent(s) prior to the birth of the child. In brief, emotionally immature and poorly educated parents raise children who are more likely to fail than children of emotionally mature and well-educated parents. Although income is an important factor, it is a less important factor than emotional maturity in successfully rearing a child—particularly a non-white child living under the conditions of white supremacy…[I]f present conditions persist, history will record that Black people failed to survive the 20th century AD.[6]

Travel in Search of Truth—Initiation

In order to master the great powers of *Ra* (Life Force and Vital principle), Auset first had to learn how to master Ra. She did this by finding his weakness, then manipulating him based upon it. Specifically, Auset observed the patterns of Ra in the form of the sun. Once she found his rhythm, she was able to create a snare for him, setting him up to be bitten by a snake. As a result of the bite, Ra fell deathly ill and called upon all of the Neteru possessing magic to see if anyone could identify the problem and present a cure. None but Auset knew the problem and, thus, only Auset could present the cure. The missing key to Ra's remedy was the pronunciation of one of his names, a secret which he kept guarded from all. Ra figured if Auset could bring him back from the gates of death, then she must be worthy of his respect as an equal. By revealing his name to Auset, Ra granted his power over to Auset.

Metaphorically, this story[7] represents Auset's initiation into a particular aspect of her spiritual powers. Her trial to master Ra simultaneously communicates the importance of mastering your own personal vitality (physical, mental, and emotional health), with the end result being empowerment. This is profound. Dr. Frances Cress Welsing, as Auset, identified the cycles and patterns of the system of racism/white supremacy. She too found its weakness and sought a plan to master it. She saw "Black Self-Respect" as the key to countering racism/white supremacy. In her view, once non-white (Black, Brown, Red, Yellow) people begin to respect themselves and openly show love for themselves and to themselves, racism/white supremacy would have to change its game which, currently, is dependent upon non-white people hating themselves and lacking in self-respect.

What Dr. Welsing has prescribed for years is a sort of initiation into a complete understanding of racism/white supremacy. She has consistently encouraged Black males and Black females to "master specific patterns of perception, logic, thought, speech, action and emotional response that would counter the white supremacy dynamic scientifically. We would codify such behaviors and practice them day and night. We would become single-minded in our activity…" (pp. 279–280). She calls for a level of self-discipline from victims of racism/white supremacy that closely resembles that required of any system of initiation that is worth the space that it takes up. As an initiate of several indigenous African spiritual traditions, as well as a Prince Hall Freemason descending from African Lodge #1 (later called African Lodge #459), I can personally attest to how the codification of behavior, single-mindedness, and the mastery of the various attributes listed by Dr. Welsing lead directly to a sense and experience of empowerment, an understanding of reality that is superior to that of a wayward mind, and the rendering of one less susceptible to the 24/7, 365 onslaught of attacks from the system of racism/white supremacy.

Conclusion

Dr. Frances Cress Welsing, the great queen mother and healer, has transitioned on to the realm of the Shepsu (Righteous Ancestors). She has been granted immortality and considered to be MaaKheru (True of Deed), meaning that she lived a life of integrity, consistently lived on purpose, and did far more good than she did harm while incarnated in the flesh. Her works live on through the thousands of people she touched directly and will continue on through the coming generations as each one teaches her wisdom to the next, until we eventually overcome the system of racism/white supremacy, replacing it with a system of justice. The most powerful lesson she taught and the most beneficial legacy that she has left to us is encoded in the hieroglyphic symbols found on the cover of her book and is embedded in the title of the same. May she continue to teach us from the Duat, and may her subconscious mind continue to reach ours, transmitting the knowledge and wisdom of our divine birthright as symbolically encoded by our Ancestors. Ashé, Ashé, Asheoooooooooo!

Endnotes

1 Sources include: *Metu Neter*, vol. 2 by Ra Un Nefer Amen; *Resurrecting Osiris* by Muata Ashby; and *Legends of the Egyptian Gods* by E. A. Wallis Budge

2 Water-gazing is a well-known and ancient method for gaining insight and has been used as an oracle for millennia. In Ancient Egyptian iconography, the Ibis bird has been correlated with the principle of deep insight and wisdom. This bird is often found to be standing perfectly still in a body of water, on one foot, gazing deeply into the waters. In modern times, there are "flotation chambers" wherein people experience virtual weightlessness by literally being enclosed in a chamber of salt water, upon which they float for an extended period of time in an attempt to reach calm and deeper states of consciousness.

3 Frances Cress Welsing, *The Isis Papers: The Keys to the Colors*, xi.

4 This was written in June 1976 and is more relevant today than it was then with the plethora of gender-ambiguous hip-hop artists and popular culture icons.

5 This is evidenced by both the "Obama Effect" wherein multitudes of white males began to purchase insane amounts of guns and ammunition immediately following the election of President Barack Obama and also by the "Tiger Woods Syndrome," which is when white males began disclosing sexual insecurities involving their white female partners and a paranoia that they were somehow having sex with Tiger Woods. This occurred after his "sex addict" scandal revealed that a large number of his partners were, in fact, white married women.

6 Frances Cress Welsing, *The Isis Papers,* 260, 262.

7 E.A. Wallis Budge, "The Legend of Ra and the Snake-Bite." *Legends of the Egyptian Gods: Hieroglyphic Texts and Translations* (USA: Dover Publications, 2012).

Let Her Name be Our Battle Cry (for Dr. Frances C. Welsing)

Laini Mataka

when UMOJA called, she said yes
and gathered herself around us like a force-field
impervious to mendacity & immune to enslavement
(no matter how diamond-studded the chains).

when KUJICHAGULIA called, she centered her mind,
balled up her fists & smashed the lies that
called us out of our sun-filled names
& negated our historical significance.

when UJIMA called, she rolled up her sleeves,
& displayed a half a century worth of examples
of how to be caretakers of our people, while taking responsibility
for the many errors we might make along the way.

when UJAMAA called, she often dug deeply into her own pockets,
& put her money where her mouth was. this she backed up with
pro-bono hours of sacred talks that were secretly known
to raise the dead.

when NIA called, she pioneered her way through white supremacy
& taking a machete to the redwhite&blue roots that ensnared our feet
she slashed away at the overhanging growths/that blocked out the sun
of our interrupted greatness.

when KUUMBA called, she used every aspect of her ase'
to eliminate our ignorance with technicolor glimpses
of what freedom could look like if we wld stop being afraid
of the people who are genetically afraid of us.

when IMANI called, she bequeathed her last breath to us,
so she cld take her place at the Round Table of the Jenoch
whose soul purpose is to arm us, encourage us, lead us and
join us in the fight to annihilate the negro and return control
of our higher selves to our blacker selves.
confused cries around me ask,
"where are we gonna find another Dr.Welsing?"
and i say, "why're u looking for another one, when we haven't
finished honoring this one?"
her body may be gone but her footprints
are still here and you can follow them if you dare.
don't stain her legacy with yr tears
unless you're prepared to spend the rest of yr years
tearing down white supremacy, brick by filthy brick
not just with yr mouth, but with yr actions.
not just in yr house, but everywhere you go.
not just one Thursday a month, but everyday, all day long.

don't let yr presence here be mistaken for a decoration,
but a clear indication, that you are signing yr name
on the dotted line of liberation.
don't just be mourners/be transformers.
wear that crown she fought so valiantly to regain for you,
use the insights she left in the ISIS PAPERS for you,
occupy the space she used her every breath to clear for you,
step into the armor of the theories she forged for you,
use the weapons her brilliance designed for you.
take yr declarations of love for her,
and carve out a reality where our children can be
wet-nursed by the truth,
a reality where we fine-tune our minds till our bodies can walk through
fire,
a reality where certainty replaces insecurity, study eclipses opinions
& WE, represents all the I's.

don't relegate our Queen Mother to being
just another face in this place,
or a February blast from our truncated afrikan past.
when you leave here today,take her with you.
sweep the white left-overs out of yr mind
and offer her a place to stay.
if we all claim a part of her essence,
she will never fade away.

Index

About the Contributors

Harry Allen is a Hip-Hop Activist and Media Assassin, who has written about race, politics, and culture for more than thirty years. As an expert covering hip-hop, he has been quoted in The Wall Street Journal, The New York Times, on National Public Radio, MTV, VH-1, CNN, the BBC, and other media channels. Many may know him for his longtime association with the seminal band Public Enemy, and his widely heard "cameo" on their classic record, "Don't Believe the Hype." Allen serves as an advisor to the Archives of African American Music and Culture (AAAMC) at Indiana University. From 2003 to 2015, Allen was the host/producer of his weekly WBAI-NY/99.5 FM radio show, NONFICTION. Harry Allen lives with his wife, Zakiya, near Washington D.C. Follow him on Twitter: @HarryAllen.

Dr. Marimba Ani was born and raised in Harlem, New York, and has been involved in the Afrikan Liberation Movement since her work as a field organizer for the Student Nonviolent Coordinating Committee in Mississippi. After traveling to Afrika, she began formal study of the nature of Afrikan Civilization under the tutelage of the renowned Afrikan historian, John Henrik Clarke, in the attempt to determine how culture formation could be used to achieve Afrikan liberation, reconstruction and sovereignty. The term *Maafa* was developed and presented in her 1980 manuscript, *Let the Circle be Unbroken: The Implications of African Spirituality in the Diaspora*; the word has subsequently been embraced by the Pan-Afrikan Community worldwide to refer to the systematic attempt to destroy and exploit Afrika and her children. Her book *Yurugu: An African-Centered Critique of European Thought and Behavior* was described by the late Dr. Asa Hilliard as one of the most important books written by an Afrikan author during the twentieth century. Ani holds a BA degree from the University of Chicago, and MA and PhD degrees from the New School for Social Research.

Anthony T. Browder is an author, publisher, cultural historian, artist, and an educational consultant. He is a graduate of Howard and has lectured extensively throughout the United States and five continents. Mr. Browder is the founder and director of IKG Cultural Resources and has devoted 35 years researching ancient Egyptian history, science, philosophy and culture. He has traveled to Egypt 56 times since 1980 and is currently director of the ASA Restoration Project, which is funding the excavation and restoration of two 25th dynasty tombs of Kushite noblemen on the west bank of Luxor, Egypt. Browder is the first African American to fund and coordinate an archeological dig in Egypt and has led 24 archeological missions to Egypt since 2009. He is the author of six publications (including the best sellers, *From the Browder File*, *Nile Valley Contributions to Civilization* and *Egypt on the Potomac*) and the co-author of four publications, including two written with his daughter, Atlantis Tye. Anthony conducts a monthly Saturday Academy called the Cultural Imperative Program for dozens of African American students in Northern California who are known collectively as, "The Browder Scholars." In 2019 the Cultural Imperative Program expanded to 13 sites throughout the U.S. and is changing the lives of young people in their formative stages of development. All of Mr. Browder's publications are currently used in classrooms around the world and he conducts annual study tours to Egypt for students and adults.

Chuck D aka Carlton Douglas Ridenhour is a Hip-Hop artist, author, and producer. As the leader of the seminal rap group Public Enemy, he helped create politically and socially conscious hip hop music in the mid-1980s. The Source ranked him at No. 12 on their list of the Top 50 Hip-Hop Lyricists of All Time. His major albums were Yo! Bum Rush the Show (1987), It Takes a Nation of Millions to Hold Us Back (1988), Fear of a Black Planet(1990), Apocalypse 91... The Enemy Strikes Black (1991), Greatest Misses (1992), and Muse Sick-n-Hour Mess Age (1994). For the album, Fear of a Black Planet which he dedicated to Dr. Frances Cress Welsing, Public Enemy's Bomb Squad production team sought to expand on the dense, sample-layered sound of the group's 1988 record It Takes a Nation of Millions to Hold Us Back. Having fulfilled their initial creative ambitions with that album, Public Enemy aspired to create what lead rapper Chuck D called "a deep, complex album". Ridenhour is politically active; he co-hosted Unfiltered on Air America Radio, testified before Congress in support of peer-to-peer MP3 sharing, and was involved in a 2004 rap political convention. He continues to be an activist, publisher, lecturer, and producer.

Patrick Delices is a Pan-African scholar and public intellectual who specializes in Black power movements and decolonial revolutionary studies. He has held academic posts at Hunter College in the Department of Africana and Puerto Rican/Latino Studies and at Columbia University, where he was a research fellow working under the late, Pulitzer Prize-winning historian Dr. Manning Marable. He also served as a research assistant to Dr. Leonard Jeffries Jr., former chairperson at the Department of Black Studies at the City College of New York. Currently, Delices is working on two books: a system analysis of the global impact of the Haitian Revolution and a biography of his father, Georges Chardin Delices, Haiti's greatest soccer legend.

Laini Mataka aka Wanda Robinson is a poet, teacher, activist and spoken word artist whose career began in 1971 with the album, *Black Ivory* (poetry to music) and followed by a second album, *Me and a Friend*. Afrika Bambaataa has mentioned her as being one the earlier artists now called rappers. As a spoken word artist she has shared the stage with Rashaan Roland Kirk, Gil-Scot Heron, Amiri Baraka, Sonia Sanchez, Haki Madhubuti, The Last Poets, Mutabaruka and prestigious others. Her first publication was a chap book, *Black Rhythms for Fancy Dancers*. Later works include *Never as Strangers*, *Restoring the Queen*, *Bein a Strong Black Woman Can Get U Killed* and *The Prince of Kokomo*. Ms. Mataka's work also appears in several anthologies including *Day of Absence* by Maulana Karenga and Haki Madhubuti; *In Search of Color Everywhere* by E. Ethelbert Miller; and *Body and Soul* by Rundu. She has received awards from numerous organizations and is an inductee into the International Literary Hall of Fame for Writers of Afrikan Descent at the Gwendolyn Brooks Center of the University of Chicago. She has taught creative writing in Baltimore and Washington D.C. (where she now resides) and has worked as a poetry therapist, a writing coach, a slam coach, and a memoir stimulator with senior citizens. She has just completed a new book of 500 quotes entitled: *Say*

Whaaat?, and a series of praise poems for Black men called: *I Can't Stop Loving You.*

Dr. Jeffery Menzise is a doctor of clinical psychology and a Research Associate Professor with Morgan State University's Institute for Urban Research. He is an internationally known educator, an author of six books, and the founder of Mind on the Matter Publishing and Consulting. Dr. Menzise's research interests include African spirituality, meditation, and the practical application of cultural principles.

Dr. Wade W. Nobles is Professor Emeritus in Africana Studies and Black Psychology at San Francisco State University, co-founding member and past president (1994–95) of the Association of Black Psychologists, and the founding Executive Director of the Institute for the Advanced Study of Black Family Life and Culture, where he spent more than 40 years researching, documenting, publishing, designing and implementing African centered service and training programs. He is the author of over one hundred (100) articles, chapters, research reports and books; the co-author of the seminal article in Black Psychology, Voodoo or IQ: An Introduction to African Psychology; the author of *African Psychology: Toward its Reclamation, Reascension and Revitalization; Seeking the Sakhu: Foundational Writings in African Psychology,* an anthology of over thirty years of African centered research and scholarship and his newest manuscript, *The Island of Memes: Haiti's Unfinished Revolution.*

Yaa Asantewaa Nzingha is an educator, lecturer. activist and actor living in Brooklyn, New York. She is a contributing author to *Should America Pay? Slavery and the Raging Debate on Reparations*. She is widely known for using her teaching and theatre skills to raise academics, self-esteem and consciousness in Black youth. In June 2018 the state of New York presented her with a proclamation acknowledging her years of Outstanding Educational Leadership. Presently, Yaa Asantewaa Nzingha spends much of her time working for the release of US held political prisoners. Many who have been "Behind the Wall" over 30-40 years.

Pilar Jan Penn graduated from Vanderbilt University Law School. As its first Skadden Fellow, Ms. Penn worked to enforce laws prohibiting discrimination against people with HIV/AIDS in Chicago and Atlanta. During this period of time she began to envision how her own practice might address the inequalities she saw and experienced personally. In 2005 she founded The People's Law Firm, Inc. in Atlanta, Georgia to serve marginalized communities and focused her practice on consumer protection, debt relief, and education. Ms. Penn's philosophy of lawyering helped her to understand and explain to others how economic restrictions and inequalities, rooted in racism and white supremacy, are suppressive and destructive of any plans we may have for a future. She believes pulling poor and marginalized communities out from under the burden of debt is important but teaching how to challenge unscrupulous lenders and collection agents by using the laws that are there to protect them, and knowing how the economic system is structured are essential tools for all the disfranchised. Ms. Penn is currently on sabbatical traveling in the Middle East, Asia and Africa, and working to improve the educational outcomes of girls and women in those regions. She is the author of *Roots of Self-Mastery: The Beginning of Practical Wisdom*, which encourages young people to develop good habits and strong characters.

Dr. José V. Pimienta-Bey is a tenured Associate Professor of African & African American Studies (AFR) and General Studies at Berea College in Kentucky. For the past 14 years he has taught courses within the AFR, History, General Studies, and Psychology programs. Pimienta-Bey's primary research interests include Moorish History, Black Psychology, Comparative Religious Studies, and African American Social and Political Thought. He is the author of *Othello's Children in the "New World": Moorish History and Identity in the African American Experience* (2002). In 2018, Pimienta-Bey was designated the "Robert Rosenthal Fellow" by the University of Chicago. The award is part of Chicago's "Platzman Memorial Fellowships" which are granted by the University of Chicago Library's "Special Collections."

Dr. Ife Williams holds the Ph.D. in Political Science from Clark-Atlanta University. She is an Africologist and President of African Heritage Studies Association as well as a three-time Fulbright award recipient Her research specializations include, CARICOM and the Caribbean

Pan African Network and the call for Reparations; African Descendants Caucus and the World Conference against Racism; and digital humanities mapping project on African resistance to enslavement. Educator and activist residing in Philadelphia, Pennsylvania.

Raymond A. Winbush is Research Professor and Director of the Institute for Urban Research at Morgan State University in Baltimore, Maryland. He is an American-African scholar/activist known for his systems-thinking approaches to understanding the impact of racism/ white supremacy on the global African community. His research and teaching have been instrumental in understanding developmental stages in Black males, and public policy's connection to compensatory justice. Winbush has lectured in Africa, the Caribbean Europe and throughout North and South America. He sits on the Editorial Board of the *Journal of Black Studies*. He holds a Ph.D in psychology from the University of Chicago and has taught at Oakwood, Fisk, Alabama A & M, Vanderbilt and Morgan State Universities. Winbush is the author of three books, *The Warrior Method: A Program for Rearing Healthy Black Boys, Should America Pay? Slavery and The Raging Debate on Reparations* and *Belinda's Petition: A Concise History of Reparations For The Transatlantic Slave Trade.*

Dr. Conrad Walter Worrill is an internationally acclaimed scholar, educator and activist. He was a full professor and former Director of the Jacob H. Carruthers Center for Inner City Studies, Northeastern Illinois University for forty years. Dr. Worrill retired from CCICS/NEIU, December 31, 2016. For over five decades, his activism has been defined by his leadership in organizations and activities that have been in the forefront of the struggle for racial and social justice, African centered education, African liberation, and self-determination for people of African descent. As National Chairman of the Black United Front, Special Consultant of Field Operations for the Million Man March, an Economic Development Commissioner for the Coalition of Blacks for Reparations in America, or a street organizer for Harold Washington's mayoral campaign, he has advanced causes such as educational restructuring, human rights, reparations, and political empowerment for the Black community.

Denise L. Wright attended Howard University where she obtained her Ph.D., in the discipline of Psychology. Taught and/or lectured at a number of universities, including Howard University, American University of Nigeria, Georgetown Medical School and others, with a focus on developing cultural competencies for clinicians in the medical and behavioral health fields. Has worked with a number of organizations, notably, Fisk University who sponsored the famous Race Relations Institute. Has traveled to West and South Africa for the past 20 years to conduct research with academic teams such as the Malawi Medical Laboratory Project, initiated by Howard University as well as working with other organizations providing education and presenting research in the areas of health (HIV/AIDS) and mental health. Her research focuses on public health, health disparities, the perception of wellness, as well as the implementation of cognitive, behavioral and nutritional strategies to reduce clinical presentations of depression and anxiety.

Dr. Jeremiah Wright is an historian of religions with a terminal degree from the Divinity School of the University of Chicago, a DMn from United Theological Seminary in Dayton, a M.A. and B.A. from Howard University and ten honorary degrees from schools and seminaries such as Colgate and Lincoln Universities. He has mentored a doctoral program in African Centered Religious Thought at McCormick Theological Seminary, co-mentored two Doctor of Ministry programs along with Drs. Jawanza Kunjufu, Cornel West and Molefi Asante at United Theological Seminary; and team taught two Master of Divinity programs at Drew University along with Drs. Charles Long and Iva Carruthers. With his area of concentration being Black Sacred Music in the West African Diaspora, Wright has lectured not only in the U.S., but also abroad at colleges and universities in Ghana, Togo, Benin, Bahia, Maranhao, Johannesburg, Durban, Kwa Zulu Natal, Pretoria (UNISA) and Cape Town, South Africa. The Africana Studies Department partnered with the History Department, the English Department and the Law School of Word University to present a week-long series of lectures given by Wright to celebrate his life-long academic, pastoral and preaching work in the fields of Black Liberation theology and African Centered Practical Theology. In addition, Wright also served as the Senior Pastor of Trinity United Church of Christ in Chicago for 36 years until his retirement.